digital PUBLISHING *to go*

ISBN 0-13-013536-4

90000

9 780130 135360

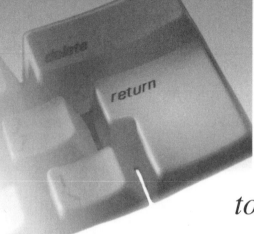

to go series

digital PUBLISHING *to go*

Jason I. Miletsky

Prentice Hall PTR, Upper Saddle River, NJ 07458
www.prenhall.com

Editorial/Production Supervision: *Joanne Anzalone*
Acquisitions Editor: *Tim Moore*
Editorial Assistant: *Julie Okulicz*
Buyer: *Maura Goldstraub*
Art Director: *Gail Cocker-Bogusz*
Interior Series Design: *Rosemarie Votta*
Cover Design: *Anthony Gemmellaro*
Cover Design Direction: *Jerry Votta*

The publisher offers discounts on this book when ordered in bulk quantities.
For more information, contact

    Corporate Sales Department,
    Prentice Hall PTR
    One Lake Street
    Upper Saddle River, NJ 07458
    Phone: 800-382-3419; FAX: 201-236-714
    E-mail (Internet): corpsales@prenhall.com

Printed in the United States of America

10 9 8 7 6 5 4 3 2 1

ISBN 0-13-013536-4

Prentice-Hall International (UK) Limited, London
Prentice-Hall of Australia Pty. Limited, Sydney
Prentice-Hall Canada Inc., Toronto
Prentice-Hall Hispanoamericana, S.A., Mexico
Prentice-Hall of India Private Limited, New Delhi
Prentice-Hall of Japan, Inc., Tokyo
Prentice-Hall (Singapore) Asia Pte. Ltd., Singapore
Editora Prentice-Hall do Brasil, Ltda., Rio de Janeiro

Dedicate to:
Lisa Bertman
Irving Miletsky
Mary Benrubi

CONTENTS

CHAPTER 2
GETTING THE PROJECT STARTED 35

CHAPTER 4
LAYOUT TECHNIQUES FOR EFFECTIVE PRINT DESIGN..............................71

CHAPTER 5
WORKING WITH ADOBE PHOTOSHOP..........123

CHAPTER 9
PRINTING—FINALLY, THE LAST STEP 251

ACKNOWLEDGMENTS

I would like to thank the people who supplied creative material, technical assistance or both to help develop this book. All of the following are experts in their field, and their contributions were invaluable:

John M. Leary (chapter 7)
4 Behnert Place
Cranford, NJ   07016
(908) 272-9367
atticart@aol.com

Bill Miranda (chapter 7)
PFS New Media
Wayne, NJ   07070
(973) 616-2700
www.pfsnewmedia.com

Mike Woodburn (chapter 7)
2237 Sherman Court
Antioch, CA   94509
(408) 297-6660
mike@kutha.com
www.kutha.com/illustration

Joel Dapper (chapter 8)
ElectroType
P.O. Box 426
Bergenfield, NJ   07621
Cranford, NJ   07016
(201) 439-1539

There were a lot of people, without whom this book would not have possible. So although mine is the name on the cover, I would to thank everyone else who contributed. If I missed anybody, please accept my apologies, and please don't think that you're ever forgotten.

As always, I'd like to thank my various editors Tim Moore, Jim Markham and Joanne Anzalone… not just for your help, but for not killing me for every missed deadline. I'd also like to thank my tech reviewer, Anthony Zaffiro.

Thanks to my parents for all of your help and support. I love you both.

Robbins Wolfe brochure and logo in Color Figure 12 is used by permission of Robbins Wolfe, Inc. All rights reserved.

Special thanks to everyone at PFS New Media, Dennis, Jil, Valerie, Mariana, and Bill, who picked up even more slack while I wrote this second book than they did when I wrote the first one.

Thanks to Colleen Meade and Joel Dapper for their help, advice and input on portions of this book.

I'd like to thank Chris and Ida—not because they've done anything particularly helpful in terms of this book, but just because I thought they might like seeing their names in print.

Lastly, I again want to thank Lisa. Everyday, I become more certain that you really are watching me. I still miss you.

INTRODUCTION

The art of print design is at both exhilarating and tedious, fascinating and gut-wrenching. It involves a combination of creativity, raw talent and technological savvy to pull it off well, and while the process can take a lot out of you, the rewards can be twice as great. There is nothing quite like standing at the press watching your own work being mass-produced for the world to see.

The trick to succeeding in print design lies beyond being creative and having a good imagination. There is a lot to know about computers, color, file formats, film and printers that all play a major roll in any print project coming to fruition. This book doesn't give you all the answers—in fact, each chapter could well deserve a book of its own. But what it will do is give you a beyond-the-basic look at the elements involved in the printing process, both technically and conceptually. Overviews of business practices as well as a brief tour of select programs will act as a springboard for launching you into the world of print design.

WHO SHOULD READ THIS BOOK

Simply said, this book has been written to have a little bit for everybody. Because it presents a segmented look at a number of topics, readers from beginners to advanced can find something in here that will be useful. Maybe you're a wiz at designing things, but don't know how to set up your files for the service bureau...or maybe you can create great Photoshop designs, but are clueless when it comes to developing quality page layouts in QuarkXPress. Even in these cases, the chapters in this book will not fill you in on everything that you need to know—but they will give you an overview, and enough of an introduction to know which print aspects you will need to study further. If there is not already a "To Go" book on the topic, don't worry—there will be!

For these reasons, I would not recommend that you read this book from cover to cover. Instead, jump around to the topics that you need to learn more about. Even better, keep this book nearby your computer as a reference for when you need it.

The only thing that you'll need to get something out of this book is the desire or need to have material printed, the money or equipment it will take to get yourself started, and a strong enough stomach to keep you sane when there is a lot at stake. If you have these qualities, then this book is for you!

HOW THIS BOOK HAS BEEN WRITTEN

Like the title says, this book is good to go. That means that any information that is deemed unnecessary, boring, or wasteful has been deleted. For example, the section about file types gives you what you need to know to decide which format you should use in your print design, but stops short at describing the history behind TIFF and the mathematics behind the LZW compression system. I know that you're more interested in getting started in designing your print projects as quickly as possible, so besides my witty interjections once in awhile (which, by the way, were far wittier before my editors censored me), most of the boring, fluffy stuff has been left out.

Throughout each chapter, you'll be confronted with an array of icons to help you better understand what you're reading.

 This icon gives a more detailed explanation of the topic.

 This tells you when there is a potential for a problem. You'll see very few of these—in my opinion, as long as you end up in your bed at the end of the day, there are few problems worth stressing about.

 This icon provides additional information of the topic.

Another thing that you may notice as you read is that most references, including screen shots, are taken off the Macintosh. When I give an example and include a keyboard command, the command configuration will be for Macintosh, and the equivalent Windows command will follow in parentheses.

QUESTIONS, COMMENTS AND OTHER GIBBERISH

I like to make myself accessible to everyone. If you have any questions or comments about this book, you can email me at jasonm@pfsnewmedia.com. I may take a bit longer responding to any negative comments, but I promise I will try to respond to everyone.

If you'd rather use U.S. Mail, you can drop me a line at the following address:

Prentice Hall
Attn: Jason Miletsky
One Lake Street
Upper Saddle River, NJ

Unfortunately, neither Prentice Hall nor I can act as a technical support system. For technical questions, please consult your users' guides for various programs and hardware.

If you send me mail, please be patient—I will make every effort I can to respond as quickly as possible, but please understand if that may sometimes take a little while.

On a more personal note, in my last book, *Web Photoshop 5 To Go*, I used this section to drop a subtle hint to the Today Show's Katie Couric. Since I haven't heard from her yet, I'd like to take this opportunity to let her know that I still have a crush on her, but she should hurry up… I won't be single forever!

PREPARATION AND GENERAL CONCEPTS YOU SHOULD KNOW

Throughout this book, I will refer at times to certain terms that may seem foreign to you. Even outside of this book, when you hang around the printer's place or your local service bureau (where all the cool kids go), you may hear terms that you are unfamiliar with. While it may be easy to just nod and pretend like you understand, your work will benefit greatly if you can speak the language.

This chapter will provide a comprehensive resource for many terms and phrases that are common to desktop publishing. It will also explore aspects of the process that don't necessarily fit into just one chapter, but have a more universal appeal.

A QUICK REVIEW OF THE PROCESS

There are many ways to reach fruition in a print project, depending, of course on the job specifications. *Projects*, as we'll discuss later, can be number of layout types, from books to newsletters, flyers, brochures, etc. This book will include many common aspects of a project, any one of which you may leave out depending on your particular situation (some are easier to leave out than others).

1. The Idea

You or your marketing department will do research into who your client's customers are, where to find them, and what type of message they're likely to respond to. This marketing research will be done through a number of methods, including surveys, focus groups, sample testing, previous sales records, analysis of competitive advertising, etc.

Once you understand who and where the audience is, you can develop the idea and present it to your client.

2. Obtaining the Photographs

You will gather all the necessary photography for your project. You'll do this through one or a combination of sources, including the purchase of stock photography, taking your own photographs, or hiring and directing a professional photo-rapher.

3. Writing the Copy

This is kind of a "floating" point, in that it doesn't necessarily have to be done at this particular time. Some people like to write copy at the very beginning of the project. Others, like myself, prefer to write the body of the text after everything else. In any case, at some point you will write the copy for your piece.

4. Retouching Photographs and Creating Photo-Realistic Graphics

After you have digitized and collected any necessary photographs for your piece, you will probably need to adjust their color, crop them, change their color mode to CMYK for printing, or make any other desired adjustments. If you've been a member of the graphics community for any length of time, you probably already know that Adobe Photoshop is going to be your source for this. You will also use Photoshop for the creation of any other graphics your piece might need.

5. Making the Illustrations and Line Art

Although most pieces will call for photographs more than they will for line art, many pieces you do may require you to provide some sort of illustration. You'll most likely use Adobe Illustrator for the creation of these files.

6. Laying Out Your Project

Once you have the individual elements collected and ready, you'll use a page layout program such as QuarkXPress or Adobe PageMaker to manage everything. Either of these programs will collect your photographs, illustrations, and copy and allow you to lay it out in practically any formation you wish.

7. Outputting the Film (for the Commercial Press)

If your project is a relatively small one (meaning it has a very low budget, or will only run in small quantities), you will probably skip this step. If your project is an ad that will run in a publication, or a piece that will need to be reproduced in large quantities, you'll be visiting the service bureau. The service bureau will separate the colors and (if desired) produce a matchprint for client sign-off and printer support.

8. Getting It Printed

In the final step (if you don't count doing tracking research to measure the success of the piece), you will output your design onto the printed page. For short-run work, you will most likely use a desktop printer or a digital press. For larger print runs, you'll take your project from the service bureau to the commercial press for final printing.

It may seem like a lot to swallow, but this book will explain each aspect in detail so that by the time you're ready to tackle your project, you will have the knowledge you need to make killer publications.

UNDERSTANDING POSTSCRIPT

If you're like a lot of designers, you've heard the term *PostScript* bounced around regularly at seminars, in books, or in backroom conversations at service bureaus where talks are often limited to PostScript and Star Trek. Well, for everyone out there who is unsure exactly what this term refers to, now's your chance to find out (by "term" I refer to PostScript, not Star Trek).

PostScript is, in basic terms, a programming language comprised of lines of code much like C, Pascal, and that funky code that will make the world blow up in the year 2000. (Personally, I'm not buying into this whole Y2K thing, but I guess it wouldn't hurt to buy some extra canned food just in case….) PostScript was created by Adobe years ago as a mathematical answer to early problems with desktop printing, which was plagued with slow and widely unuseable translations from computer to printer. With PostScript, images would print at the resolution of the output device without the danger of *bitmapping* or *pixelating*, the kind of thing you see in a low-resolution image in Photoshop (see Chapter 5). Because PostScript is based on mathematical formulas of path-defined shapes, anchor points, and percentages of color rather than pixels, PostScript elements can be resized without losing resolution.

As printer manufacturers (with Apple leading the charge and thus building the graphics foothold, which it still commands) began to install the PostScript page description language and fonts in their printers, the EPS (Encapsulated PostScript) graphics format, PostScript fonts, and the PostScript language became nearly universal.

The average designer does not think of PostScript as a programming language though, primarily since few of us know anybody who actually writes in it. Instead, we use PostScript programs such as Illustrator, PageMaker, and Quark to translate the code to Postscript printers in the background, which in turn translate that code into printed dots.

A FONT IS WORTH A THOUSAND WORDS

There are literally thousands of font styles for designers to choose from, and the type of font(s) you decide to work with can play a part in your concept, your Photoshop graphics, Illustrator images, and of course the general copy in your chosen page-layout program. If there's a style you need, chances are it already exists. Beyond the fonts that come preinstalled on your system, you can buy specific font faces or families for hundreds of dollars, or even thousands of fonts on a CD for under $10, depending on the styles you need.

There are three different types of fonts to be concerned with:

Bitmap Fonts

As you'll discover when you work with programs like Photoshop, bitmaps are comprised of a number of dots. The same is true for bitmap fonts, which are defined by square black dots. The larger the font size, the more dots are used to produce the image.

As was explained in the following section on PostScript fonts, each bitmap font comes in a number of preset sizes. However, unlike PostScript, there is no printer font for the pure bitmap font to use in resizing. So when you try to enlarge a Bitmap font beyond its specifications, there is no mathematical formula to keep the detail and resolution. The font in this case will look very pixelated and jaggedy, as shown in Figure 1–1.

PostScript Fonts

These fonts are the most commonly used, as they are recognized almost universally in every desktop and laser printer, output device, and WYSIWYG program (What You See Is What You Get), such as Quark and PageMaker. They are, however a bit confusing and could lead to errors because they come in two parts: the screen font and the printer font. Figure 1–2 shows samples of three PostScript fonts.

You need to have both the printer font and the screen font residing in the your system's Font folder. The screen font is a bitmap font (see Bitmap Fonts above), that displays the font on your monitor. The screen fonts usually come in a "suitcase," as shown in Figure 1–3. Inside the suitcase are individual files of the font at various sizes. As Figure 1–4 illustrates, double clicking on a file will show the font face and size in a sentence that uses every letter in the alphabet.

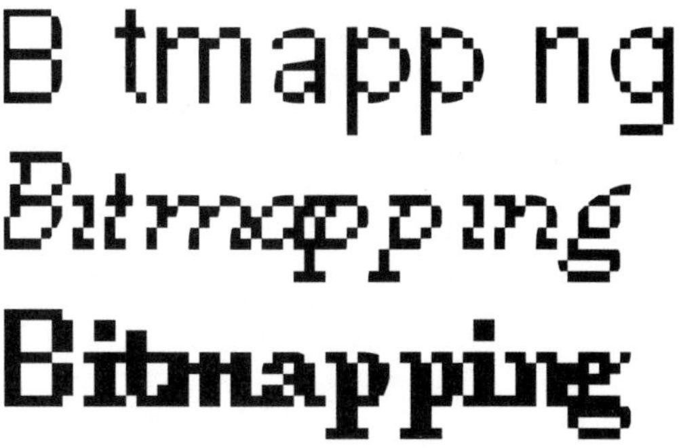

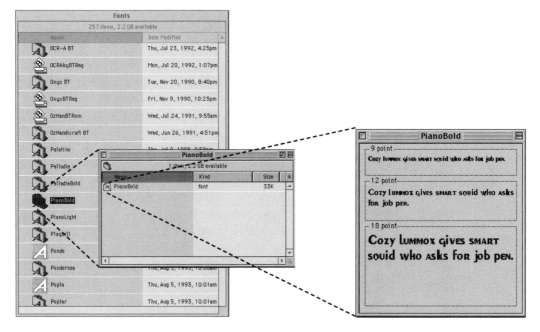

Figure 1–1 Bitmap fonts get jagged when they are increased beyond their designated size.

Figure 1–2 PostScript fonts look great at any size, as long as the screen and printer fonts are available.

Figure 1–3 PostScript screen fonts come in suitcases that contain the bitmap font..

Figure 1–4 Double click on the bitmap file in the suitcase to see how the font looks using every letter in the alphabet. The ridiculous phrase "Cozy lummox gives smart squid who asks for job pen" is used to display the characters.

The printer font is usually represented as an icon of a small laser printer. It resides in the Fonts folder, too, yet is separate from the screen font suitcase. It is necessary so that the printer can print the font smoothly. Each letter in the font is made up of outlines that the output device fills with dots. It will never be jagged or bitmapped—the higher the resolution of the output device, the higher the clarity in the font.

If you are delivering a project to a service bureau for output that uses PostScript fonts, make sure you include the printer font with it. If you don't, the printer will either rely on the bitmap screen font (ouch!) or substitute another font in its place, throwing your entire layout off.

To make the benefit of the PostScript printer font apply to the screen font, so that you can see sharp lettering at any size on your monitor, install ATM (Adobe Type Manager). ATM acts as a middleman between the printer and screen fonts. Newer versions of ATM also handle many of the tedious tasks of font management.

TrueType Fonts

Developed by Apple, and now the standard fonts in Windows machines, TrueType fonts are easier to use than PostScript because there is only one file to work with and their quality is just as good as that of PostScript fonts.

Even though Adobe (the creator of PostScript fonts) makes products like Photoshop, Illustrator, and PageMaker, all these programs can use the competing TrueType fonts. In theory, then, it shouldn't be too hard to work with TrueType fonts on a regular basis. The problem is that there are fewer TrueType styles available. Because PostScript fonts are easier to create, fontographers tend to make more of these and less of the TrueType fonts. The other drawback is that they will not look smooth beyond the available font size, and can pixelate at sizes that are unavailable. In addition, many high-end output devices, such as imagesetters, do odd things with TrueType fonts. Font designers can get around this by including reference font files with the TrueType font, usually at standard point sizes like 10, 12, 14, etc. TrueType uses the closest available reference file to the point size desired when scaling.

Adobe Type Manager

Chances are you already have this installed on your computer, either from Illustrator or some other source. If you don't have it, you're going to want to get it somehow. The Adobe Type Manager (ATM) is what allows the bitmap fonts to be viewed on screen with smooth letters at any size. Without it installed and turned on, the screen font has no way to reference the PostScript printer font, and will bitmap at sizes it does not have available. Newer versions of ATM also handle lots of font management tasks, freeing you from technical details so you can get back to designing.

IT'S NOT EASY BEING GREEN (IN A CMYK WORLD)

I vaguely remember lamenting as a kid that my box of 64 Crayola crayons just didn't have enough colors in it. Sure, it was great at first—there were plenty of colors, and that crayon sharpener in the back of the box was pretty cool. But then time goes on, and you realize that the crayon sharpener doesn't really work, and 64 colors really isn't enough to fill a whole coloring book. But it was simple, it was fun, and when you're a kid, that's all you really need to know.

COLOR IN NATURE

But when your print projects move from the coloring book to the computer screen the stakes are higher and more can go wrong than just the sharpener in the back of the box. Understanding color is a vital component in practically everything that you do when in comes to graphic design and printing. It is arguably the most difficult, and certainly one of the most inconsistent. But understanding color doesn't really begin with Crayola and it certainly doesn't start with computer graphics. It starts with the world around you and how your eyes work.

Although science texts can provide far greater detail about it, the basic truth is that color as you see it in nature exists only in your brain. When light from the sun or some other source reflects off the surface of an object, it is processed by *cones* in your retina. This light is a mix of all available colors in the spectrum (if you don't remember the spectrum lesson in fifth grade science, then check out the cover of Pink Floyd's *Dark Side of the Moon* album). These cones are responsible for filtering color into red, green, or blue light, depending on the chemicals in the object that the light is reflecting off of. When light filters into all cones at maximum intensity, you see white. When only the red and blue cones are needed to perceive an object, you see purple. Because color is so intangible, and is, in reality, only an illusion created in our minds, there is no guarantee that any one person is seeing exactly the same color as any other person. *Rods*, also part of the retina, are like cones but they respond more to light levels, bright and dark rather than color. Rods are used in night vision.

COLORS ON SCREEN: THE RGB COLOR MODEL

Computer monitors, TV screens, and other such devices work in conjunction with the cones in your eye. With the use of red, green, and blue phosphors that emit light, your eye sees pixels the same way that it sees other elements in nature. Purple color on a monitor is a mixture of red and blue light emanating from the screen.

You can surmise from this that almost every color you can see can be expressed with a mixture of red, green, and blue. This is what's being referred to when you hear the term *RGB color model*. As I said earlier, when all three colors are mixed together at full intensity, your eye sees it as white. In other words, the more primary color added, the brighter the resulting mix. Because of this, the RGB model is considered to be *additive*.

Most anything that you create that is meant for the monitor as a final destination is best done in RGB color. This includes graphics for web sites, video and CD-ROMs. How and why you would want to use the RGB color model for any specific project will be discussed in its respective chapter.

COLOR IN PRINT: THE CMYK COLOR MODEL

So far so good—it's an easy concept to handle that all color we see in our lives is really just the filtration and combination of red, green, and blue light reflected by any given object. It's also fairly simple to comprehend that the computer monitors we use emit red, green, and blue light to achieve the same effect.

Now life becomes a little more complicated. If paper could project light into your eye the same way that a monitor can, there would be no problem. But unfortunately, paper is able to do little more than reflect light into your eye. White paper, which is used most often when printing because it has the most versatility when it comes to color, reflects a full intensity of red, green, and blue light.

When a printer lays ink on a piece of white paper, that ink acts as a filter. Cyan (an aqua-like color), magenta, and yellow, the three primary printing ink colors, reduce the light and filter out the red, green, and blue aspects to form color combinations. The cyan ink, for example, filters out the red light, leaving the combination of green and blue light to pass through. Magenta filters out the green light, leaving the combination of green and blue. And the yellow acts as a filter for blue light, allowing both the red and green light to pass through.

Conversely, when primary ink colors are put together on paper, they can reproduce (to an extent), red, green, and blue. A mix of cyan and magenta will filter out the red and green light, leaving blue on the printed page. When all three colors are missing from the page, the page appears white, making this a *subtractive* color mode. Color Figure 1 shows the three primary colors in light and how each of the primary printing inks acts as a filter for them. When the maximum intensity of cyan, magenta, and yellow are mixed together, they produce black. Well, almost…

Because printed inks are just not as pure as light (really, what is as pure as light?), a full-intensity mix of cyan, magenta, and yellow actually produces more of a muddy brown than a black when they are put on paper. To compensate, a black component is added to the mix, so that the CMY color model is actually the CMYK color model, with the K standing for Black (if they abbreviated it with the letter B, it would be confused with the Blue from the RGB color model. I tell ya, those people who name things are just so damn smart…).

When people in the printing industry use the term *process color* or discuss four-color printing, they are referring to the CMYK color model and the use of these colors to produce images on a page.

Because the RGB color model deals in light and colors in nature, there are more colors in this model, or *gamut,* than in the CMYK model. Colors that are meant for print that cannot be reproduced using any mixture of CMYK are considered to be *out of gamut.* In general, the CMYK color model offers fewer colors than the vast array of colors that we can see in nature through the RGB combinations. Color Figure 2 shows the color range of both the RGB (dotted line) and CMYK color models, along with the areas of color that fall outside the CMYK area.

You'll want to use CMYK for any project that is meant for print. Depending upon the program you are working within at any given time, though, using CMYK or RGB each have different pros and cons, which we'll explore in the appropriate chapters. Color Figure 3 shows some examples of four-color printed pieces.

THE WORLD IN BLACK AND WHITE: UNDERSTANDING GRAYSCALE

So what's to understand? The truth is, not much. Grayscale images are images that lack any color and instead represent everything as black, white, or shades of gray. Its easy to work with, cheap to print and reproduce, and can be every bit as powerful as a color image, when used sparingly.

MANUFACTURED COLOR: SPOT AND SPECIFIC COLORS

Colors on a printed page are, as discussed earlier in this section, typically mixtures of cyan, magenta, yellow, and black. These mix together to fool your eye into seeing a wide array of colors and shades. Spot colors, though, are specific colors that are usually mixes manufactured by outside vendors to achieve colors that typically cannot be achieved with any combination of CMYK. For instance, you can add a spot color to a four-color piece for a logo that needs special attention, or, more often, you can add a spot color or colors to a grayscale image to create a two- or three-color piece, respectively.

The main reasons you would be inclined to use spot colors in your work are:

> To produce colors that are not possible to create with the CMYK mix. Fluorescent colors are a particular favorite of spot color users, since CMYK mixes cannot produce them. Specific colors for logos are also a popular reason for using spot colors, especially with companies that need to maintain a consistent image in the media and public eye.

Producing a two-color piece (usually black plus one spot color) can be significantly cheaper to print than a four-color piece. This is because the printer can use a smaller press with only two drums as opposed to a four-color press. As you'll learn in Chapter 9, printers can do process printing on a two-color press by re-feeding the paper through. I would recommend against this, though: it's still expensive, can take longer (the drums need to be cleaned after the initial use), and once the first two colors are placed, there is no way to adjust them, so a print check is almost useless.

Spot colors that are premixed are largely considered to be more vibrant than the same color mixed with CMYK.

Pantone is one of the most widely used manufacturers of color in the industry. Companies like Pantone, or TruMatch make a large number of premixed colors that your printer can insert into his press for your project. But beware, though, that adding a Pantone or other premixed color can oftentimes be more expensive. Especially when you add an additional color to a process piece.

Pantone colors are not the only thing that can act as an additional color, or increase the price of a process printing. Varnishing your piece to be fingerprint resistant (largely for dark or black pieces) or spot varnishing to bring reflection to a specific area can be considered an additional color, and can add significant dollars to your project. Check with your printer about this.

You can use any of the DTP programs mentioned in this book to choose a premixed color from Pantone or other manufacturers, or you can use a swatch book such as the one displayed in Color Figure 4. If you really want to get serious about color in your work, you'll want to be armed with one or more of these swatch books.

Problems and Other Things to Keep in Mind

It's a lot to take in, but understanding how color works will go a long way toward making your print projects easier. There are some points, though, that you should keep in the back of your head as you start on your journey through the wonderful world of color:

Color is an inexact science. There is really no way to guarantee the reproduction of color from one medium to another. But it is especially difficult when looking at an image on a monitor to know exactly how your printed piece will look. Don't forget even if you are working in the CMYK color space, you are seeing the CMYK mixture through the RGB phosphors of your screen. It's kind of like drinking a vanilla milkshake through a chocolate straw—it just won't taste like pure vanilla.

Use swatch books with a bit of caution. Make sure you know how old the book is. The pages and colors will fade over time, reducing the accuracy to what you'll see when your project comes off the printer.

Don't leave it up to the service bureau or print shop to make the final conversion to CMYK for you. As discussed earlier in this chapter, you'll need to convert your images into CMYK before getting them output and ready for print. If you neglect to do this, not only will it usually cost you, but you will be trusting a veritable stranger to making the conversion for you, which could lead to unwelcome results.

OTHER COLOR MODELS

There are other color models, and ways to perceive color beyond RGB and CMYK that you'll notice in programs such as Photoshop and Illustrator. These include CIE Lab, HSB, and others. While each has their place in the graphics world, you'll most often be working with RGB and/or CMYK.

TROUBLE WITH TRAPPING

If you have ever been to a printer to watch a project come off the press, you've see that the machines are simply monsters—large, loud, clunky Goliaths that apply ink to paper in an effort to reproduce the pages you designed on your computer (see Chapter 9 for more detail on the printing process). And after billions of dollars in technology and manufacturing, these Titanic-sized representatives of progress churn and burn and when the project is finally through—drum roll please—you have a printed piece with a half-point white edge around some of the colors that just wasn't supposed to be there.

When the press is rolling, each of the plates needs to be in *exact* position at all times to create perfect colors in your images. If a plate shifts ever so slightly, the press will be *out of register*, potentially causing you thousands of dollars to run the piece again (Figure 1–5). The truth is that they haven't built the press yet that can hold a plate so steady that the possibility of shift is not an issue. Thus, we endure painful color shifts and unwanted spaces between images.

Figure 1–5   When plates shift on the press, spaces between colors can appear.

The best answer to this is *trapping*. Trapping is the art of increasing the area of one color over another color in anticipation of plate shift. By doing this, any gaps created by slight plate shift at the printers is filled in by the excess color in your trap. In just a bit, we'll go into when there is a need to set traps, and how to go about doing it. How to set traps for each program is discussed at greater length in it's respective chapter.

A HEARTFELT PLEA

Before I continue, though, let me make a heartfelt plea: read this section, understand it, get to a point where you can speak intelligently about it. But do not, I repeat—not—set your own traps. Although the art and science of trapping has improved somewhat over the years, individual programs such as Quark and Illustrator still have somewhat archaic trapping methods. And it's never just as easy as pushing a button or moving a slider. You need to have a vast knowledge of color and the printing process and excess time on your hands to spend setting the traps (if you have to set more than just a few).

Setting traps is best left to professionals. More than likely, the service bureau you choose will be able to set traps for you. Yes, it may cost a bit more, but in the long run it could save you a tremendous amount of money by saving a print job that could otherwise have been doomed. These professionals will use more expensive dedicated programs like TrapWise. Programs like this can cost in the thousands of dollars, which is far too much for it to be a worthwhile purchase if your intent is to concentrate on design. So please, take my advice on this one. Let the dentist fill your cavity, let the mechanic fix your car, and let the service bureau set your traps.

WHEN AN IMAGE NEEDS TRAPPING, AND WHEN IT DOESN'T

Trapping will be a factor in your image or in portions of your image when:

◆ Your image has two or more spot colors that touch each other or overlap.

◆ There is small black copy that is not overprinted (overprinting is discussed later in this section).

◆ Your image has two or more process colors that touch or overlap and that do not share color values.

You won't need to worry about trapping in your image or in portions of your image when:

◆ Your image is a continuous-tone photograph such as one you might be working on in Photoshop.

◆ All spot colors in your image are separated away from each other, so that they don't touch or overlap.

Continuous tone photographic images don't need trapping.

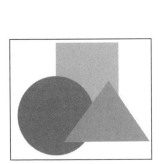

Overlapping objects with spot colors need trapping.

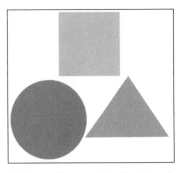

Objects with spot colors that do not overlap do not need trapping.

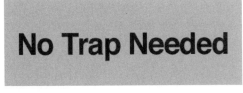

Large black text which overprints does not need trapping.

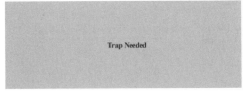

Small black text with serifs that does not overprint needs trapping.

Figure 1–6   Various instances when you do and do not need trapping.

◆ Your colors are overprinted rather than knocking each other out.

◆ All of the blacks are very thick.

◆ Your imported image is in EPS format.

Figure 1–6 and Color Figure 5, 6, and 7 show samples of images that do and others that do not need to be trapped.

If you are going to trap on your own, you should get a dedicated trapping program like TrapWise. If you don't have or don't intend to get such a program, but still want to do it yourself, you can set traps within the individual applications, like Illustrator and QuarkXPress.

If you plan on sending it to the service bureau for trapping, then leave the traps alone in the DTP programs. Adjusting them in any way will only confuse matters and detract from your chances of getting a well-printed piece.

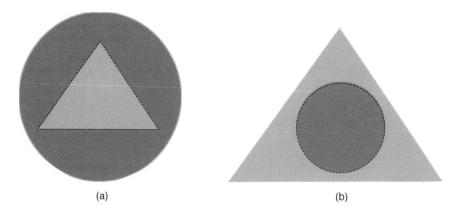

(a)   (b)

Figure 1–7   Spreading (left) and Choking (right).

TRAP TERMINOLOGY, ISSUES, AND SOLUTIONS

When two images are a potential threat for problems and a trap is necessary, the trap is created by the expansion of ink from one color to the other. In general, unless you specify otherwise in the software program, the lighter color is always the one that expands. This helps to reduce the gap between the colors, but does not make the trap very obvious, as would an expansion of the darker color.

Spreading and Choking

Figure 1–7 shows a sample of two images that are being trapped. In both examples, the triangle is filled with Pantone 2985c, which is a light blue. The circle is filled with Pantone 511c, which is a dark purple. In both instances, the dotted line shows where the trap is created. Figure 1–7 (a) is considered to be an instance of spreading because the expansion of ink from the lighter image is moving outward. Figure 1–7 (b) is an example of choking, as the lighter color is spreading inward on the darker color.

If possible, try and avoid using spot colors—they are potential hazard zones for gaps in printing because the change in color is so distinct and sharp. If it is within your budget and within the specifications of the project (you sometimes can't avoid using spot colors for work on logos or other corporate identity pieces) work in CMYK as much as possible.

Overlapping CMYK

If you change a spot color to CMYK, or are just working in CMYK to begin with, you probably won't need to trap. What you're going to have to check for is CMYK overlap, which is when the two adjacent CMYK colors share enough of at least one

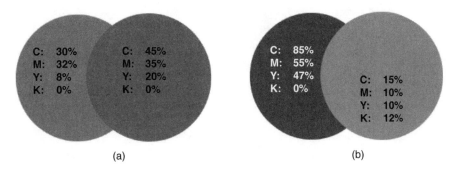

Figure 1–8   The two overlapping objects on the left (a) need trapping as spot colors, but not when converted to CMYK because there is a high enough percentage of magenta and cyan to compensate for any misregistration. The pair on the right (b) need trapping even in CMYK mode because there is no color that shares a high enough percentage value.

(preferably two) of the process colors (either the C, M, Y, or K) to kill the chance of a white gap occurring.

For example, Figure 1–8 and Color Figure 6 show two images, each with two spot colors that overlap. Because they overlap, they will need to be trapped. But it's a different story when they are converted to CMYK. In Figure 1–8 (a), the CMYK values show that there is at least 30 percent magenta and 30 percent cyan in each overlapping image. When this goes to print, any misregistration on the press will be compensated by a color that they both share.

Figure 1–8 (b) didn't fare quite as well, unfortunately. Notice that the CMYK values are very far apart, and neither shares at least 30 percent of any one (preferably two) component. In the event that the plates shift on press, the overlap could be pretty obvious, so you'll still need to apply a trap.

Overprinting

Overprinting is a tease. By using it you can virtually eliminate the need for having to set traps. *But* this benefit comes at a high price: your colors off the press will be largely unpredictable. That is obviously not a good trade-off.

When one color is placed over another, the color on the bottom is knocked out. In other words, it doesn't print at all, so that the color on top can have the spotlight. When you *overprint* your colors, though, they mix together, producing largely unpredictable colors and shades. Figure 1–9 and Color Figure 7 show the difference between an image that has been overprinted and one that hasn't.

Figure 1–9 shows two spot colors—one red, one blue, with the red square lying on top of the blue square. In Figure 1–9 (b), the red square knocks out the underlying blue one, so that the full-intensity red would print. However, notice that there is a stark difference between the two colors where they meet—a definite need for trapping here.

(a)   (b)

Figure 1–9   The two overlapping images on the left (a)show a color mix at the intersection, because they overprint. These do not need to be trapped. The overlapping images on the right (b) are not overprinted—there is no unexpected color mix but there is a need for a trap.

In Figure 1–9 (a), the colors are overprinted so that the area in which the red box overlaps the blue box will mix the two colors together, producing a shade of purple (the shade of purple will depend on the shade of red and blue in the original boxes). Because any shift in the plate will just fill with either the blue or red from the overprint, there is no need to trap. But the downside is that you probably don't want purple in your image—and even if you did, at the time of this writing most programs will not display the mixed color.

OVERPRINTING BLACK

There is one exception to the above description. The exception is when you are dealing with black. Quick quiz: black + any color = what? The answer is, of course, "black." When you overprint with black, you are removing any need to set traps. Most programs automatically overprint black for you, since it is almost always a benefit to overprint black (just make sure that you're using a good printing black—see Chapter 7 for more details). Small text, especially type that has sharp corners and curves (and those serif fonts are killers) is practically impossible to set traps for, so *overprinting them is your best bet.*

If you place small point-size type in any other color than black over another color, you're going to have to come to terms with either overprinting and not knowing exactly what color you'll get, or not overprinting and risking a plate shift and possible color gap.

Overprinting black holds true for line art as well as text. Even large fields of black are good candidates for overprinting. Talk to your printer first, though—overprinting large areas of black and large areas of other colors can cause an excessive amount of ink to be printed. Depending on the paper you choose to print on, too much ink can be damaging to your project, ripping through the paper or taking too long to dry. Too much ink may also cost you more. Ask your printer for pricing information regarding this.

ARMING YOURSELF FOR THE PREPRESS BATTLE

I'm going to be straight with you, because being less than honest up front will cost you unnecessary dollars. The two basic, universal truths about preparing and creating projects for print are:

It ain't easy.
It ain't cheap.

Sorry, but you may as well get used to that. There is a lot to know—from general information including color science, to software-specific items like reducing the red tint from a picture in Photoshop. And the equipment and costs of producing projects can get up there. There is no cutting corners or bargain hunting if your intent is to produce high-quality print work. The machinery you need will be expensive enough, and that's before you have to pay a deposit to a printer for a client that may take 30, 60, or even 90 days to pay you.

This is not said to dissuade you, of course, from jumping into the world of digital publishing. On the contrary: digital publishing can be a lucrative venture, earning you a fortune, especially if you discover that you're good at it! The amount of money you can earn will pay off your initial equipment investment many times over. But it's important, especially in the beginning phases, to prepare yourself as best you can to ensure success.

Because the actual printing process can be a great expense, you don't want to make any mistakes. The place to start is in the initial set-up. The better your equipment is, the better chance you'll have in producing an error-free project. You've already taken the first step in acquiring the information you need by picking up this book, and perhaps others that offer details about the specific software applications that I brush upon. Now get ready to break out the credit card and do a little shopping.

A little off the topic, but if you're about to go out and buy new equipment, do yourself a favor and use an American Express card. Computer equipment is expensive—and as of the time of this writing, Amex not only provides you with an extra guarantee on your new toys, but you'll also earn significant amounts of free travel miles if you belong to a club like OnePass. This could help cushion the blow of all the money you're about to spend.

Buying a Computer: Macintosh or PC?

This ongoing debate is one I may be better off avoiding entirely. If you're reading this, assume I resigned myself at the last minute to receiving tons of hate e-mail from platform loyalists who will disagree.

It's a simple fact that the only cult more steadfast in their beliefs than Heaven's Gate is the tight-knit Macintosh community. With unabashed dedication to Apple, most Mac users will swear until they're blue that Macs are simply better computers than PCs. As a Mac enthusiast I'm prone to agree on that point, although the Windows NT system is quickly closing the gap. (How's that for walking both sides of the fence?)

Being a Mac user has its drawbacks, no doubt about it. It's disheartening to walk into a computer store, pass endless rows of shiny new PC programs, and finally discover the lonely shelf in the back that has a few dusty Mac applications. We're also constantly hearing about Apple's imminent demise, although as of the writing of this book Apple has enjoyed its fifth straight quarter of growth and profitability. Also a few of us have felt slightly snubbed by Apple, which not only politely waited until I had bought three StarMax workstations before dismantling their license program, but also put a 90-day cap on free tech support.

I won't even mention how often Mac's tend to crash…we get used to that, eventually.

But the truth is that the Macintosh platform still rules the graphic design world. Colors tend to appear better on Macs, the keyboards are friendlier, and the filing system is typically easier. Macs can also handle many PC files and disks, while a PC doesn't usually want anything to do with a Mac disk, except reformat it. Not only that, but because Apple was the pioneer in licensing PostScript from Adobe, their computers quickly became the standard at design firms and, more importantly, service bureaus. Even today, most service bureaus are strictly Mac-based. Some will transfer PC files to Mac before outputting, but will often charge you for this and may encounter problems.

The bottom line is that as of this writing, Mac is still largely in control of the design community. They're growing, and the threat of them going under is becoming fainter. But their growth is not really cutting into the Windows NT market share, which is also gaining ground. If you are going to buy a workstation today, I'd say go buy a Mac. But keep your eye on NT, though. Next year could be a different story.

> Because of Mac's dominance in the graphic design community, most of the screen shots I'll be using in this book will be derived from a Macintosh, and much of the text will be leaning in that direction. If you're a Windows user, though, don't worry—you'll understand everything just as well, and any Macintosh keyboard command I give will be followed by the Windows command in parentheses. (Of course, this info was also in the Introduction, but who reads those?)

If you are going to buy a Macintosh, you're going to want to get a Power Mac with a G3 processor. I wasn't there to see it, but I've heard that the G3 beat the Pentium II processor (Windows) in a race at the 1998 MacWorld convention. The processor is what controls the speed of the computer, and will be largely responsible for how fast your projects get done. You'll be working with some pretty heavy files—you'll miss the speed if you don't buy it.

If you're a Windows enthusiast, the Pentium III will be out by the time this book hits shelves. This should provide you with incredible speed, but make sure that you buy software programs that were built with the Pentium III in mind. If you use a Pentium III but work on Photoshop built for the Pentium II, you'll not only be missing the advantage of the faster processor, but your program could ultimately run *slower*.

ONE SIMPLE RULE: GET MORE RAM!

Have you ever watched a dog eat? They have no idea when they're full. If given the chance, they'll just keep eating and eating until they explode. Well, think of your computer as a dog, and RAM as a big bag of Puppy Chow. Just keep feeding the RAM into your computer until you literally can't anymore—but don't worry, unlike your dog, the computer is unlikely to explode. (Your dog won't really explode either, but if he does, try and have a camera handy....)

RAM (Random Access Memory), measured in Megabytes, is the physical chip that allows your computer to increase the power to your system and your open applications. The keyword in the acronym is *memory*. The more you have of it, the more things you can do at one time.

Think of RAM as an electronic vat, whose mechanism works significantly faster than that of your hard drive. Out of jealousy, the computer takes up a bit of this vat just to run properly. Every time you open a new program, that program looks into the vat, and, if there is enough room, jumps in (well, it actually throws a copy of itself in). Some programs, like Photoshop, will get fatter with every command, taking up more and more room in the vat. The next program you open will measure the remaining room in the vat, and if there's enough space, it'll throw a copy of itself in, too.

This process will continue until finally a program is open that says, "uh, oh! Not enough room for me!" In this case, the program will take up the remaining portion of the vat and run the rest from its space on the hard drive. Then, alas, you're hit with a really frustrating message like, "Unable to perform last command due to insufficient memory." At that point, you'll have to start closing up some programs to free some of the vat (RAM), which has gotten crowded.

Keep in mind that a program that you unload from the bottom of the vat won't free up space at the top. You have to unload the top one first.

So what about that really fast processor I told you to get in the last section? Well, while your RAM is busy keeping all of your programs open, the processor is making them all run faster. What if you have a really fast processor, but not a lot of RAM? You'll definitely get that annoying "out of memory" warning, but at least the processor will make it come up faster.

How Much RAM Do You Need?

You really can't get enough RAM, so just keep loading it in until you either run out of room in your computer or you run out of money in your wallet. Remember, the more RAM you have, the more programs you can have open—and the more you can do in those programs. You're not doing accounting here—you're building large-scale print projects and you will be responsible for every detail in every photograph.

Figure it like this: your computer takes up about 6 Megs of RAM to operate. You need to work on a photograph—an 8.5" x 11" picture in need of some color correction. You open Photoshop, and poof! another 10 Megs of RAM is being used (at least). You open the picture up—8.5" x 11", CMYK (see color information earlier in this chapter), 300 ppi. The file size for this is 45 Megs. Even without doing anything to the picture, you've already used up 61 Megs of RAM. And you haven't done anything yet! Now consider this: most computers bought off the shelf come with only 32 Megs of RAM installed. A quick review of the math would reveal that you will have a LOT of trouble working with this file. The agonizing slowness of your work (remember, your programs will not have room in the RAM and be forced to run off the hard drive) will make you want to pull your nails out with a wrench.

Your best bet is to make sure that there is sufficient RAM installed on your computer when you first set about using it. RAM typically comes sold in chips of 8, 16, 32, 64, and 128 Megs. Tell your salesperson to stock the computer full of RAM—the most it will hold. If you can only afford a little to begin with you can always buy more later. Installing it is pretty easy, and the RAM chips usually come with straightforward instructions.

Don't waste money in the long run by trying to save a few dollars up front. Your computer will only hold a finite number of RAM chips in slots found inside the computer casing. Once those slots are filled, you're pretty much done. Don't waste a slot with a 32 Meg chip if you think you may add more RAM later—the new chip will have to take the place of a lower Meg chip, which is then rendered useless—a waste of money.

YOUR HARD DRIVE: THE OTHER MEMORY

RAM isn't the only kind of memory—it's short term, available when needed for opening programs. But where do you keep your files after you're done tweaking them? That's the other memory—the long-term storage area called your hard drive.

I remember a time, not too long ago, when I begged my parents to buy me a computer. It was an Apple IIe, a big, clunky thing that we tied to the roof of our car to get home. It had a hard drive capable of storing a whopping 256K of memory. Today's computers typically come installed with at least 2 Gigabytes of memory, if not 4, 8, or even 16. That means that on a computer with a 2 Gig hard drive, you can save up to 2 Gigabytes worth of files (minus, of course, the space used by the files that the computer needs to run and your applications).

Although all of that space can be used to save your files, don't do it. Try to leave at least 20 or 30 Megs available. Filling it up completely can cause horrible crashes to your computer. You also want to keep a good amount open for scratch space for when you're using RAM-hoarding Photoshop (see Chapter 5 for more info on this).

GETTING THE RIGHT MONITOR

Monitors come in a wide variety of sizes, ranging from 13" up to 21". If you're serious about getting into design and preparation for printing, then there really isn't a question. You need to have a 21" monitor. Yes, they're expensive, but they're worth it.

The most important reason that they're worth it is that they don't make Braille monitors. In other words, no expense is so great that you can neglect taking care of your eyesight. You're going to be working in front of your computer for long hours every day (and probably more than a few nights). A 21" monitor is the best way for you to protect your vision and not suffer through hours of staring at a computer.

Some doctors have given advice to help reduce the chances of damaging your eyesight from staring at a computer for long periods of time. Once every twenty minutes or so, turn away from your computer and look at a point in space that is far away—maybe look out a window or something. But get them focusing on something that is not shining bright lights right in your face.

I'm sure it's a no-brainer that you want to buy a color monitor. I'm not even sure if they still *sell* black-and-white monitors anymore, but if they do, don't bother. You're most likely going to need to do a lot of color correcting.

For the more professional rationale, a 21" monitor allows you to see more. You can view multiple pages in your layout program at once (almost life size), and maybe even more importantly, you can see more of your file at extreme resolutions in image-editing programs like Photoshop.

As Many Colors as Possible

Your monitor will be able to display 256 colors, thousands of colors, or, if there is a video card installed, millions of colors. Seeing images at millions of colors is going to be vital to the art of photo retouching, and to get as good an idea as possible of what the final printed piece may look like (don't, though, under any circumstance, *rely* on your monitor as an accurate representation of printed color).

You can check to see how many colors your monitor is capable of. For a Macintosh:

1. Open the Apple menu by clicking and holding the Apple icon in the upper left corner of your screen.

2. Choose Control Panels –> Monitors and Sound. The dialog box shown in Figure 1–10 will appear.

3. In the Colors portion of the dialog box, you'll see a short list of available color depths. If Millions of colors is not an option, try increasing the monitor resolution in the Resolution portion. If it's still not there, then you're going to need to purchase a video card.

To check how many colors you have on your Windows computer:

1. Push the Start button at the bottom left of your screen.

2. Choose Settings –> Control Panels –> Display.

3. Open the Settings tab, and in the Color Palette pull-down menu, look for True Color (24 bit). If it's not there, you'll need to purchase and install a video card.

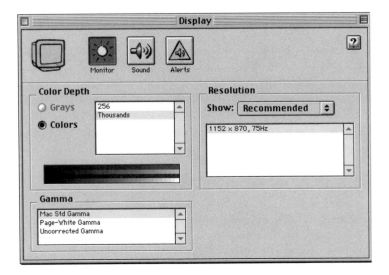

Figure 1–10   The Monitors and Sounds dialog box on a Macintosh.

QUICKER IMAGES AND AN EXTRA BONUS

When you resize an image, or make a radical change, the computer has to redraw your image. The monitor displays the redrawn image one pixel at a time—even with a fast processor, you're going to have to wait until the monitor is through. This can be agonizing, especially if you're anxious to see how your image will look after the change you just made.

Do yourself a favor and get a *graphics accelerator card installed* in your computer. You can install these yourself if necessary—they're pretty easy. The graphics accelerator cards typically run anywhere between $150 to $300 as of the writing of this book. By installing one, your graphics will redraw on your computer much faster, saving you a lot of time and aggravation.

But wait! There's more! If you're working on a Mac (and by now I think I've been pretty clear that you should be), your graphics accelerator card serves another purpose. You can use it to install a second monitor, as shown in Figure 1–10. With a dual monitor system, you can increase your work area significantly. For example, if you're working in Photoshop—a program replete with palettes and things "floating" around your work area—you can put all of your palettes on one monitor, which frees up your other monitor to display your entire image. Or, if you're working simultaneously with Photoshop and QuarkXPress, you can make each available in full view while you're working.

Personally, I like to work with two 21" monitors side by side. Now, financially *that* may be excessive. I know a lot of designers who work with a 21" monitor and have a throw-away 15" monitor as their second, simply to contain program palettes.

ADDING THE PERIPHERALS: SCSI AND THE SCSI CHAIN.

Okay, you've got a great computer with a kick-ass processor and more RAM than you know what to do with. You've got a huge 21" monitor to save your eyes and impress your friends. You even installed a really cool South Park screensaver, so you can see Kenny die every day. You're all set to start working, right? Well…not quite. There are a few more things you need, so don't put away that American Express card just yet.

Back-Up and File Transfer Devices

You're going to need a way to back up your files. (You'll be surprised how quickly 8 Gigs gets used up!) Not only do you want to conserve hard drive space, but you also want to protect your valuable files in the unhappy event of a major crash, which could potentially wipe out your computer. These don't occur often, but they *do* occur, and you should do what you can to protect your work.

Besides protecting your work, you're also going to need a way to transfer your files. Files that are destined for the commercial press are going to need to make it over to a service bureau sooner or later. Files that are meant for publication, like an ad in a magazine, are going to need to be sent to the publication in question. Floppy disks are too small (with a capacity of 1.5 Megs each, there's little that they can hold) to really be of any use to you or your service bureau. There are a number of different devices that you can use to accomplish these goals, however:

Zip Drives

The standard in the industry is the Zip Drive. These drives, which are increasingly appearing preinstalled into your computer as opposed to existing as a separate entity, use Zip cartridges to store information. Each cartridge can hold up to approximately 96 Megs of information (100 Megs minus some formatting room and that really annoying QuickTime self-promo that each disk holds). Practically every service bureau in the world has a Zip drive, so transferring back and forth on Zip cartridges is never a problem.

Zip cartridges can be costly, though, so use them sparingly. They come in packages of three, five, and ten, with ten being the only real value. A pack of ten Zip cartridges can cost anywhere between $100 to $150 depending on where you purchase them.

For as much emphasis as I'll put on color throughout this book, it doesn't matter when you are buying Zip cartridges. Don't get sucked into the trap of paying more for Zip cartridges that are colored red, green, blue, and yellow as opposed to the standard gray. There's no difference between them, except in the price. If you want color, go buy a box of Lucky Charms, but save the expense of the pretty Zips.

Zip cartridges don't come back! If you're sending files on a Zip cartridge to a publication or a service bureau, there's a good chance that you'll never see them again. Somehow it has become commonplace for people and companies to keep Zips they receive as their own. I've gotten into the habit of sending a note with each Zip that an invoice for $15 will be sent if the Zip isn't returned within 30 days. It may sound anal, but they can add up.

Jaz Drives

Zip's big brother is the Jaz Drive. Jaz drives, which use Jaz cartridges to accomplish what the Zip drive and cartridges do, can save up to 1 Gig worth of information per disk—a huge amount! These devices are a great help when it comes to backing up files—if your computer has a 4 Gig hard drive, you can back up a full 25 percent of it on one disk! But while these drives have also caught on in the industry, you're not as likely to find them at a service bureau as you would Zip drives. They're far more expensive than Zips, and a full Gig of information is likely to be far more than you need to transfer.

Tape Drives

Tape drives, like those made by Panasonic or Sony, can save a lot of information— 200 Megs, 300 Megs, and up—for a price that hovers around the same price as the 100 Meg Zip cartridge. So why aren't I hyping up the tape drives like I was the Zips? Because tape is tape—it's like trying to find your favorite song on a cassette. It takes a longer time than finding it on a CD, right? Besides that, if the tape breaks at the beginning, than that's all she wrote for all of the other songs, too. The Zip cartridge isn't like that—there's no tape, so there's a reduced chance that anything can go wrong and you'll lose your files.

If you really want to get a tape drive, I suggest you do so for your backup requirements. If you intend to use them for file transfers, find out from your service bureau if they accept files on tape.

CD-ROM Burners

A CD-ROM burner can be expensive—starting at around $450—but they are pretty cool toys. The benefit of writing files to CD is that they hold up to 650 Megs each, depending on how many CDs you purchase at once, each CD can cost you as little as a few dollars. They take a little more time to save files—you need a separate program to save a file to a CD instead of just dragging the files to the desktop icon like you would with a Zip cartridge. Because of this, you may want to consider using a CD burner for file back-ups and not for transferring files.

An extra benefit of a CD-Rom burner, though, is that it's a service you can resell. There's actually a fairly large market for burning files to CDs, so you may be able to offer this service and profit on the equipment investment.

Some of you might be wondering about transferring your files via the Internet. In most cases, this is not a possibility. Your files are likely to be upwards of 50 Megs or more—this is too large to transfer over a phone or cable line—at least given today's technology. But the Internet is still in its infancy, so maybe one day this will be the standard method of transferring. For now, though, you'll only want to use the Internet for transferring low-res files or the occasional font.

DESKTOP SCANNERS

You're also going to need a scanner for getting images into your computer. Although they're not the only way to go about this (you can hire a bureau to scan for you, or purchase stock image CDs), you will still want one around for when you are doing comp work or projects that may require a tad less detail.

Desktop scanners range in size and expense from free (bundled with a large software package) to just under $1,000. HP and Epson both make really excellent color desktop scanners, that are affordable and ultimately necessary. (See Chapter 5 for more information on scanning.)

All of the above-mentioned items are considered to be SCSI devices. Typically, you connect one of them to your computer, then connect another to the first one, a third to the second, and so on. This creates what's called a SCSI chain. For example, let's say that in addition to your computer and monitor, you also purchased an HP ScanJet, a Zip drive, and a Jaz Drive. You hook up the most important one to you, probably the Zip Drive, directly to the computer—creating the first link in the chain. The next most important item is the Jaz Drive, which connects directly to the Zip Drive (creating link number two). Lastly, the scanner brings up the end, creating the final link by connecting to the Jaz drive.

That doesn't have to be the exact order you put your chain in—choose whichever order you feel is best for your needs. The first in the line usually gets preferential treatment from both you and the computer. Also many SCSI devices come with only one SCSI port, which means they have to end the chain.

Each device in the SCSI chain has to have its own address, numbered 0-7. If two addresses are the same, you can have conflicts and serious malfunctions in your computer. To set the addresses, look on the back of the device. Somewhere you'll see a number. On the back of the Zip and Jaz drives, you'll only have a choice between two numbered addresses, usually 5 or 6. Set the addresses of all your SCSI devices so that no two devices share the same address.

Sometimes your computer won't be able to read a SCSI device. Nothing is worse than having to bring a project to the service bureau to meet your deadline, putting in your Zip cartridge, and finding out that the computer won't recognize it. To avoid this, download a program like SCSI Probe. This software packet helps you force your computer to locate the SCSI devices and recognize them.

The last item in a SCSI chain needs to be *terminated*, **otherwise the computer won't know that the chain is finished and could crash. Some devices have a switch for self-termination. Others need a separate physical terminator attached to do the job. Either way, make sure that you let your computer know when the chain has been ended.**

SCSI is not the only format for these type of items—it's just the most widely used. Other formats are available, such as IDE and the new kids on the block—USB and Firewire. Some of these can be far less costly than SCSI devices, but usually come with significant drawbacks, like working far slower, or an inability to link together.

Don't Forget the Printer!

Still money left in the bank? Good, because you'll still need just a little bit more. You'll need a desktop printer no matter what, but the type of projects you plan on doing will be a deciding factor in the quality and expense you need to endure.

If you plan on doing color work, you're going to need a color printer. You probably won't want to mass produce your project on one of these, but you will want to get one that prints in CMYK.

There are tons of printers on the market, and they vary widely in both performance and price. However, in recent months the competition between manufacturers has gotten so fierce that it's very possible to pick up a really good desktop color printer for a relatively low price (relative to what they used to cost and to what you'll be spending for the rest of the equipment).

There are a lot of magazines and web sites out there that will provide you with write ups and reviews of printers in different price ranges, including some of the following:

- ◆ www.sohoconsumer.com/1printer.htm
- ◆ www.zdnet.com/computershopper
- ◆ www.zdnet.com/pcmag

I personally have always had good luck with any printer made by Epson. The Stylus 800s that we use in our office to make comps run quickly and provide a higher than expected image quality for our drafts.

Regardless of which model you choose, though, there are a few things that you're going to want to keep in mind when purchasing a printer:

Does It Print in Color?

You need your printer to be in color. Make sure that it prints in the same CMYK process colors that a commercial printer uses.

How Many Color Slots Does It Have?

Most color printers use colors in cartridges put into slots under the hood. Make sure that your CMYK printer not only has an individual slot for each color (some have one slot, using one big cartridge partitioned off into CMYK components), but also, if possible, try to get one that allows for a double-sized cartridge of black. By finding this type of printer, you can add and replace individual colors to save expense and you can keep yourself from replacing the black too often, since that is the color that you will use most often.

Are Ink Cartridges Easy to Find?

If you're going to be printing a lot, you're going to want to keep a lot of ink cartridges on hand. But in the event of an emergency, or when you run low, you need to know that you can pick up some more at a moment's notice. Check your local Staples, Office Depot, or other local equipment store to see what type of ink cartridge they keep in stock.

Can the Printer Be Calibrated?

This is not a major issue since you're not going to trust a color desktop for color accuracy anyway (see the next section). But if your printer has the ability to be calibrated, it's a bonus. This is just one more step you can take in the battle for color consistency.

What Is the Resolution and Speed?

These two issues will largely determine the price of the desktop printer. The higher the resolution your printer can produce, the crisper and more accurate your proofs will be. In a similar manner, most printers advertise speed in pages per minute, with one figure for color pages, and one speed for black and white pages. Get the faster one and save yourself some time.

Does It Handle Your Desired Paper Size?

Most printers will work just fine with 8.5" x 11", with 8.5" begin the maximum width. If you're going to be working with pages that are significantly larger, you're going to either have to buy a standard desktop and view your images at a reduced size for draft purposes, or spend some extra dollars for a specialty printer.

I'm assuming in this section that your intentions will be that of the average design house and *not* of the average service bureau. There are far better printer you can get to do color correction work, such as IRIS printers, but these come with a minimum price tag of $10,000 and go up from there. They are also more difficult and expensive to maintain. Describing the specifications of what to look for in these devices is beyond the scope of this book.

WHAT NOT TO DO WITH YOUR PRINTER

Desktop printers have some significant limitations. Because of these limitations, there are certain things you will not want to do with you printer:

Don't rely on it as the basis for color correction. If you really need to check a color, send the project out to the service bureau and get an IRIS made.

On a similar note, don't have a client sign off for final acceptance of a project from a page off a desktop printer. The final piece off the press will look different—it will probably look better, but why take chances? Get a matchprint for final signoff.

Don't expect accurate readings for spot colors. While you should never trust colors on a desktop printer at all, this is especially true for spot colors. Your desktop printer does not have an extra slot for you to insert a Pantone premixed ink cartridge (which, as far as I know, they don't make anyway), so all your spot colors will print out in their CMYK equivalent.

Don't set your own traps expecting to get a good idea of them off your color printer, because you won't. At the same time, don't expect an accurate mix from over-printed colors, because that probably won't happen either.

Don't check your proofs on standard copy paper. Pay a little bit more at your office supply store, and get the high-quality film-coated paper instead. Depending on the printer you buy, images on film-quality paper can be surprisingly sharp.

The Real Reason to Fear Mice

When you're doing graphic design, you'll probably want to get used to using a pressure-sensitive tablet as opposed to a mouse. Although some graphic designers still swear by the mouse (Jerges Cortina, a designer in my office is annoyingly adamant in his love of the mouse), the truth is that for real comfort and detail in your design, you're going to want to invest in a tablet for your work.

A pressure-sensitive tablet is going to allow you to use an electronic pen to move your cursor. The pen is comfortable to hold and a more natural position for your hand to be in. Plus it allows you to use your fingers to control movement, as opposed to your wrist, which controls the mouse. This give you practically unlimited freedom in creating shadows, making selections, and creating intricate detail in most painting programs.

In my experience I've had a lot of luck with the Wacom brand of electronic tablets. They're fairly easy to install, offer a number of options to customize how the pen works, and usually come bundled with some pretty cool filters for Photoshop. As of the time of this writing, prices ranged from $200 for a tablet 4" x 5" to $450 for a tablet 12" x 12".

 If you're working on a Macintosh, beware that sometimes installing a Wacom tablet can cause certain extension conflicts. Although I hesitate to say that many others have had this problem, I've experienced many conflicts between the Wacom tablet and any Hewlett-Packard product, such as my scanner.

SOFTWARE YOU SHOULD HAVE

You're obviously going to need software to run your projects. The software that I would recommend are the programs that I am profiling in this book. These are Adobe Photoshop, Adobe Illustrator and QuarkXPress. These aren't, of course, the only software applications that you'll need, but these are the ones that you're likely to use most often. Other programs you should have include:

◆ Some type of virus protection software, such as SAM. You're likely to be getting a lot of files from clients. A bad virus brought in by an infected disk or file downloaded from the Web can cause havoc on your computer, ripping through files and destroying valuable programs. A virus protection program will not only check all disks before opening them, but it will destroy any viruses that do make it onto your computer and limit the damage that they do.

◆ A disk fix-it program, such as Norton Utilities. In case of a computer crash or file corruption, these types of programs can step in and fix it up (usually). In addition, if you accidentally throw out a file, these types of programs can usually recover it.

◆ Conflict Catcher. If you're on a Macintosh, you'll hear the term "conflict" a lot. Macs rely on a folder of extensions to make certain hardware and software applications run. Once in a while your computer will crash for some unknown reason. While there are a bevy of reasons why this could happen, one of the more common reasons is that two or more of the extensions are conflicting with each other. Over time you may find that you acquire *a lot* of extensions. Good luck figuring out which ones are conflicting on your own. Get a program like Cassidy & Green's Conflict Catcher, which will help you find the problem extensions.

LAST THOUGHTS ON THIS TOPIC

Although every need will be different. and some of you will undoubtedly need different types of hardware than others, that should cover the basics. Of couse, you'll need a keyboard, but that should come with the computer (I'm not a big fan of those glitzy, new-fangled keyboards that bend and stretch… the one that comes with the computer is fine). A few other things to keep in mind:

◆ Make sure that your computer comes with a CD-ROM drive. This should be a non-issue, because practically all computers do, but just double-check it, especially if you're buying a used computer.

◆ Get yourself a surge protector. One bolt of lightning in the wrong spot, and you'll own the most expensive paperweight in the world. Better yet, turn off your computers in a storm just to be safe.

 Make sure you surge protect your modem's phone line as well. Lightning surges on phone lines can wipe out a modem (or fax) also.

◆ You also may want to look into turning off the overhead lights and getting a few halogen lamps. Keep the dimmer turned low—the light from these is softer and will help your eyes, and the lack of bright glare will help you see the colors on your monitor more clearly

◆ I hate to sound like a parent, but you're going to be at your computer all day…buy comfortable furniture so that you don't kill your back when you get up after sitting for a long period of time.

ORGANIZING YOUR FILES

It might not be the fun part about creating print projects, but it's a highly necessary evil. And it's one that can cost you serious time and money if you don't do it right. Print projects usually have an inordinate amount of files, both on the computer and in hard copy.

Everyone has their own way of working and keeping organized. But if you're like me, staying organized is a real struggle. Especially when you're no longer working on just one project, but five, ten,…more? Who knows how many jobs you'll start doing once you get underway? But I can guarantee it's the same amount that you'll lose if you don't keep your files straight.

Of course, you'll develop your own way of staying organized. Here is the method that we employ at my office. After a few long years of trial and error (oh, there was a whole lot of error!) we finally came upon the method that worked for us.

OFF THE COMPUTER

Before we even get to the computer, there are steps you take in and around your office or workspace to help you out. Some of these steps may seem obvious, but they're worth putting some thought into. These are the steps that we take when working on a print job:

1. When the job comes in, we immediately build a file folder for it. The main file folder has the client name and a manila folder goes inside marked with the job type. All contracts, proposals, and paperwork associated with getting the job go into this file. These are *very* important documents and you'll want to know where they are if problems arise. The manila folder is to keep projects separate in the event that there is more than one at the same time from the same client.

   Any new documents that come in while the job is in progress go into their respective folder. The newest files get put at the front of the folder, as a means of keeping them in date order.

2. The client name, project type, deadline, and all other specs get written on a dry-erase board. This is to help keep a visual record of all jobs that are in progress so none get left behind.

3. Each designer has a special notebook in which they record the time spent working on any particular project. That way we have an internal means of knowing how many hours are spent on each project and what our profit margin is.

4. All verbal conversations with the client are briefed, bullet-pointed, dated, and put into the project folder. This is also true for any e-mail correspondence, which gets printed and placed in the folder as well. (Okay, so that last one was a computer issue under the Off the Computer title, but it happened to be appropriate.)

5. When the project is done it gets wiped off the board and the file folder gets moved into another file cabinet, which only houses archived material. By keeping good archives of files, any problems that arise can be well documented. Any time the client needs to rerun something or update a project, there is no down time.

ON THE COMPUTER

How you keep your files on the computer is just as important as how you keep your hard files around the office. We have developed the following standards at our office to help keep track of everything:

1. The only two folders that we keep on the desktops for easy access are called Transfer Folder and Accounts. The Transfer folder is a refuge for temporary files that need to be copied to the hard drive from a Zip cartridge or other external media. Once they've been copied to the Transfer Folder, we then sort out the files to their proper place on the computer.

   The Accounts folder is broken up into subfolders:

   ◆ Proposed
   ◆ In Progress
     • Client Name
     • Images
     • Text
     • Layouts
     • Fonts
   ◆ Completed
   ◆ Misc.

   As a project moves from being proposed to being worked on to being completed, the folder in which it rests changes. All files that sit in the Completed folder get archived on CD-ROMS and put on a shelf where they'll be safe. It's very important to never throw out any versions or drafts of a project, so that you can open them at a later date.

2. All files are saved with the dates that they were worked on. A photograph of a product that was worked on March 6, 1999 would be named "990306prodshot.tif." By doing this, the files are listed in the order they were manipulated or created, so I know that I am always working on the most updated version.

3. We back up every Friday. Nobody leaves the office Friday afternoon until all files are backed up on Zip cartridges. By doing this, we are confident that even in the event of a major crash, we will lose a minimal amount of work.

4. As I mentioned earlier, you'll want to save all e-mail and electronic correspondence. This can only help in the unhappy event that a dispute arises with the client, the printer, the service bureau, etc.

SUMMARY

There is a lot of information for you to know and tons of equipment for you to buy if you want to be taken seriously as a digital media publisher. Industry terms and definitions will help you maintain intelligent conversations with those you'll be working with and hiring out in an effort to produce a quality project. The equipment you arm yourself with is equally as important to help ensure that the project you create is the project you promised to your clients.

chapter 2

GETTING THE

PROJECT STARTED

Y ou have all this expensive equipment, and enough general knowledge of PostScript, CMYK, and halftones to get you through any cyber-geek, service bureau conversation. Now you need to put that to good use. You need customers. You need to know what they want, why they want it, and how to do it. Most importantly, you need to get them to agree that you're the person or company who is right for the job and make sure that you don't screw something up on the way to project completion.

The prepress work you will do incorporates far more than just your wizardry behind the computer. It involves understanding and catering to the proper market. You have to use your imagination to storyboard out the design and sell your client on it before you ever really get started. You're bound to be entrenched in preproduction work for a while before you ever start development.

This chapter will talk about how to work with your clients, get the deal, and protect yourself legally in the process. We'll also discuss the concerns and project variables that you'll have to take into account and explore methods of presentation for initial ideas to the client.

THE WORK ENVIRONMENT

Being a designer and selling yourself as an ad agency, design house, or publisher is all about image. That's what you're selling, an that's what you have to have. If you're a dentist, you need to have good teeth—who wants a dentist with rotting molars? If you're a psychiatrist, you most likely won't have many clients if you're insane. It's the same thing with selling an image—you have to play the part.

That doesn't necessarily mean that you should run out and buy a closet full of Armani suits. In fact, today's agencies gravitate toward the opposite. A large part of general industry has already moved past "casual dress Friday" to casual dress everyday. The graphic design industry typically takes that one step farther. The employees in my agency, for example, are encouraged to wear whatever makes them the most comfortable, with the exception of severely ripped jeans and sandals.

The concept is that creative people, more than anyone else, need to feel creative to allow their imagination to flourish. It's hard enough to tell someone that they have to be creative 9 to 5 (some agencies waive that and allow designers to come and go at any hours, as long as their projects get done), but it's practically impossible to expect an artist to be creative on demand when he's suffering in a three-piece suit. Clients today tend to expect designers to be as ultra-comfortable as they can be—if casual wear will help you develop a kick-ass project, then please, be casual.

If you intend on having clients to your facility for meetings, you'll benefit from having an office that reflects your particular design style. If you or your company has been set up to produce pieces that are moody, with a lot of shadows and depths, set up an office that is dark, maybe with smoky mirrors. Brighter types of designs can be harmonized with track lighting and large windows to allow plenty of light. If you don't already have a portfolio of work that you're proud of, make some designs and make posters out of them—your office walls are a good place to start showing off your talents.

Believe it or not, potential clients will judge you on how your office and your staff look. Remember that you're selling image, so you have to have one yourself.

THE INITIAL MEETING

The first meeting with a client will probably include a portfolio review so that the client can get comfortable with your design style. This is typically a crucial meeting in determining whether or not you or your agency is awarded the contract.

Over the years we have developed a method that tends to increase our odds of landing a project. I'll usually know before a meeting what the topic of conversation is going to be—print ads, brochures, or a full campaign development project. A little research will usually turn up the prospective client's old ads or brochures. When the meeting comes, I'll bring a standard portfolio but it will almost never get opened. Instead I'll show them low-res samples that my agency made of their already existing material—designed better than the original, of course. This tactic usually acts as the impetus for conversations and new ideas as to where we can take their project in the future.

BEING REALISTIC

While there are many variables that can account for the rise in popularity of the Internet, one of the primary reasons for its outstanding pace of growth is that a web site can, for the most part, be developed by one person. (Coincidentally, that's also the reason so many of them sre awful—that one person is usually the 15-year old cyber-geek nephew of a large corporate mogul who's too cheap to pay for a real web site. He's also more interested in publishing loud, disjointed graphics on the Web than playing ball with friends, where he belongs. That's just my opinion, of course). Web sites can also be done with little or no experience, too. Publishing programs like FrontPage and HoTMetaLPro make it so easy to put up a site that any schmo can do it, and any schmo usually does.

Digital publishing is different, though, and you can't expect that you can accomplish it by yourself, if in fact you can accomplish it at all. There are some real questions you have to ask yourself, and some important people you need to know before you begin.

ASK YOURSELF THE RIGHT QUESTIONS

For a long while, I was the eternal "yes" man. A client would ask me a question, like "can you design a 46" x 32" poster for me by tomorrow?" or "I need an 8-page full color brochure for my plumbing firm. Can you do it?" The answer would always be "yes." Those were miserable days, though, and from it I took one immutable lesson, that you can either accept now or find out the hard way: be discriminating.

There are a number of questions that you shuld ask yourself before accepting a project:

◆ **Do I have the proper equipment for the project?**

Designing an oversized poster or full-color photographic annual report is going to need a lot more powerful computer than designing one-color stationery and envelopes. If your equipment is not geared to deal with hi-res, hi-megabyte files quickly and efficiently, you'd best stay away from these type of projects.

◆ **Do I have the experience to design this project?**

If your client wants to do a highly specialized mailing that includes multiple folds and a customized die cut, can you handle it? Those type of projects demand measurements with pin-point accuracy, and an heightened attention to detail. There is plenty that can go wrong with this kind of exacting project, so if you do accept it, you will definitely want to consult with your printer and service bureau.

◆ **Do I have the desire to design this project?**

I understand that at the beginning you may need to accept any project that walks through the door. It may seem that way, anyway. But believe me—if you're even a little bit talented, the work will be there. So be discriminating. If you're not at all interested in the subject matter, and find it dry and dull, the production process can seem torturously slow. This can translate into sloppy work, and mistakes that can cost you real money before it's all over.

◆ **Is their enough money in it to make it all worthwhile?**

Let's face it—you're in this for the money. Digital publishing is not easy and it carries with it a certain value. Make sure that value is high enough to make it worth your time. I'll go into the issue of pricing later in this chapter.

KNOWING THE RIGHT PEOPLE

Digital publishing is a team sport and the better you get to know your players, the more your team will win.

The people you work with are going to change from project to project. Sometimes you'll be working with a photographer, other times you be working with a cartoonist instead. But no matter what the project is that you're working on, there are two players that you'll run into more often than anyone else:

◆ The service bureau

◆ The commercial printer (or print broker)

I would suggest that you get to know these people well. And treat them well. They are oftentimes your last line of defense in stopping a flawed project before it goes to press, and can be project-savers when it comes to keeping costs down. These guys are also going to be an invaluable resource to you throughout the life of your project, giving advice and answers to questions you'll have along the way.

Chapters 8 and 9 go into more detail as to what you need to know about both the service bureau and the printer. The following list is made up of questions that you need to ask regarding their business practices and technological abilities:

◆ What type of machinery do they use?

◆ What is their pricing policy?

◆ What is their turn-around time for various project types?

◆ Do they do their work in-house or do they farm it out?

◆ Will they extend credit to you?

◆ Do they have a standard service contract that details who is responsible should a problem arise?

◆ Do the printer and the service bureau know each other and if they don't, are they willing to collaborate with each other to solve problems?

Don't Underestimate the Power of Beer

Invite your printer or service bureau contact out one night for a beer, a game of pool, anything. I'm not kidding. These are the guys who can ultimately save you hundreds, maybe even thousands of dollars at the end of the day. I'm not suggesting you be shallow and only forge friendships where money is concerned, but if you do strike up such a friendship, it can be a real benefit. I can't tell you how many times, when I first started out, the service bureau would call to tell me that I didn't have enough cyan in my black field and that he was going to fix it for me. And they never ever charged me for it. That's the power of a few nights of drinking beer and hanging out.

PRICING

Go ahead, lie to yourself. Bill Clinton didn't really commit an impeachable offense, O.J. is innocent, and your work as a digital publisher is about art, not money. All very noble and optimistic beliefs. And all, of course, false.

Producing a printed piece is going to to cost you hard and soft dollars. Hard dollars are measured by the money spent in phone calls and travel to your client, payments to the service bureau, printer, photographer, etc., which are needed to get the job done. Soft dollars are the more ambiguous expenses like your time, the value of your talent, wear and tear on your equipment, etc. To succeed in the world of digital publishing, you're going to have to make sure that not only are all of these costs covered, but that your profit margin is high enough to make your time investment a good one.

There are a lot of factors that go into determining a price, including the following:

◆ **Type of Job**

What type of project is it? A job to design a business card is going to be a lot less expensive than a job to design an 8-page full-color brochure. Try to at least determine the general category of job before developing a price.

◆ **Usage**

Depending on who your client is and what their knowledge and experience is in advertising, this will probably be the point of greatest contention and confusion. Here's a quick math quiz: your client asks for a price on designing an 8.5" x 11" full-color flyer, for internal use only, to alert employees of a new product that the company is developing. Your design price for this piece is, say, $2,000. Before you're through with the design, though, your client calls and says not to send it to print. They're going to use the design as a full-page print ad for a large industry publication instead. The publication has a circulation of 50,000 readers. What happens to the $2,000 design fee in this instance?

If your client were going to answer, he'd probably say "nothing, the design fee stays the same." After all, the same amount of work is going into the project, regardless of where it ends up. This is not the case, though. What is being left out of that rationale is the *potential benefit differential* between the two media. The benefit of an internal flyer is going to be limited, at best, and most likely not going to be a direct factor in generating income. The flyer is, in fact, a direct loss to your client as the only benefit in generated sales would be indirect.

The magazine ad, however, carries with it a very large benefit. It introduces the message to potential clients and is likely to be directly responsible for increasing corporate sales. This benefit is worth far more than $2,000 and the project should be priced accordingly. That same design price could potentially be increased to $8,000, $10,000 and upward, depending upon the circulation of the publication.

This will be a point of contention at some point in your negotiations. That's practically guaranteed. But the difference in price is so great that you're going to want to make sure it's clear up front. If it becomes an issue, you can sell the universal rights, allowing the client to use the work for any purpose at any time, but of course the price for this should be higher to reflect this added benefit.

◆ **Deadlines**

How long do you have to complete a project? Do you have a month before you have to deliver the finished project, or is this a rush job due next Tuesday after the upcoming three-day weekend? Make sure you understand the deadline when deriving a price. Rush jobs can typically incur an increase of 50 percent to 100 percent depending on the type of job and how much of a rush there is.

◆ **Creative Freedom or Mac Monkey?**

Oftentimes a client will hand you over all of the necessary files, tell you exactly how it's supposed to look, and basically just direct the whole thing. All you're really needed for is your expertise in layout and preparation for the printer. These jobs are typically easy, if not somewhat tedious and your price will most likely not create your retirement fund. The client can find a Mac Monkey (a person to just robotically assemble a job on the computer) anywhere.

If you are going to be using your creative powers, though, that's a different story. Creativity is tough to measure from one design house to another. Besides that, the extent of your services has increased from simple layout assembly to the imaginative development of a corporate theme, style, or design. Don't sell that short by undercharging for creativity—your imagination will influence potential clients and their purchasing decisions.

◆ **Experience and Reliability**

Basically, the more you have, the more you're worth. If the extent of your design experience is your father's business card, your younger brother's fake ID, and the menu down at Joey's Pizza Place, then good luck using your portfolio as leverage when negotiating a price for brochure work at Nabisco. If you're just starting out, do a few quality jobs at cost to bulk up your portfolio. Give any big-name com pany a great deal just to get them into your portfolio—this kind of experience will pay off huge dividends in the long run.

◆ **Vendor Prices**

As we said earlier, you can't go it alone. Don't just guess at the prices that your vendors will charge you. Speak with each one of them (the service bureau, printer, illustrator, etc.) at length about the project and have them submit their prices to you in writing. Keep up a constant communication with these guys as you start making decisions about the project on things like paper quality, Pantone colors, and other variables, so that there are no surprises when you get an invoice. These prices are, typically, passed on to your client, plus a traditional 15–20 percent upcharge. The upcharge is to cover the cost of your time arranging the project with the vendors, delivery of all files, and acting as an overseer once it's on press.

How you charge is strictly up to you and your company. Conventional ways of pricing work include:

◆ **Retainer Work**

This type of payment structure usually implies either a long-term project or a number of different projects to be developed over time. You'll promise your client that you will complete a certain amount of work or hours of work (usually on a monthly basis), and your client agrees to pay you $x at regular intervals. Typically you'll have to have a good track record of high-quality work and good reliability to get a retainer account. These accounts are optimal, as you can plan your finances out well in advance.

◆ *Project Basis*

Prices are quoted for the project that will be created. Individual prices and contracts are developed for each project. Once a price is agreed upon, that is the amount that you'll receive—whether the project takes an hour to complete or a month.

◆ **Hourly Work**

Quote your client an hourly rate for the work that you'll be doing. Make sure that you keep careful records of the time that you spend working on a project.

Our agency uses a combination of these payment structures. For regular clients who have a steady stream of projects for us and have proven themselves to be reliable when it comes to paying invoices, we set up a retainer. Otherwise, we set up a project price, with hourly charges for any changes made along the way (that have been signed off on by the client—see more about this in the section on contracts later in this chapter).

For more information on pricing standards in the industry, call the Graphic Artists Guild at 212-463-7730 and order their handbook entitled *Pricing and Ethical Guidelines*. This is an invaluable resource, especially for the new designer who is just breaking into the field. Experienced designers can benefit from it too, as it provides important information on contracts and standard business practices.

Once the price has been established and the project is well under way, watch out for anything that could potentially affect the cost or price along the way. Fortunately, or unfortunately, digital publishing is not an exact science and variables are apt to change along the way. Following are some of the issues likely to change (pronounced: increase) the agreed-upon price of a project while it is in production:

◆ Additional pages

◆ Better paper quality desired

◆ Additional photography or illustration

◆ Extra folds

◆ Additional spot colors or varnishes

◆ Bleeds

◆ Special die-cuts

◆ Sudden time constraints

◆ Last-minute changes

Any one of these can radically change the cost of a project, and you should make your client aware of this as soon as it happens to avoid ugly disagreements later.

WRITING AND SIGNING THE CONTRACT

This step is of immense importance. Don't start any project for any client until you have a signed contract filed away somewhere. This is for your own protection, and could, if problems arise, save you thousands of dollars down the road. *The Handbook to Pricing and Ehical Guidelines* by the Graphic Artists' Guild (212-463-7730) shows a couple of sample contracts that you can use as prototypes for forging your own agreement between you and the client.

Although the contracts provided in the Appendix are standard contracts that are commonly used, you'll most likely want to customize portions of it for the specific project that you're working on. Some of the elements of the contract that you'll want to be sure to put in include:

◆ **Scope of Project**

Write in detail exactly what services you will provide to your client, including type of job, intended use, and how you will deliver it upon completion.

◆ **Rights**

This is not a point that you're going to want to leave out. Establishing who retains the rights to the project, including copy, photographs, illustrations, and overall copyrights, will most likely save you a zillion headaches later in life when your client asks for his files back or wants to use certain images in other types of media. Depending on what you can work out, it's possible to establish two different prices. One price is for you "leasing" the design out to the client, where you or your company retain all rights to the material. This method often allows you to charge a percentage of creative fees every time the project is reprinted. You can also offer a higher price if your client gets to retain all rights to the project upon completion.

Be careful what you give away. If you're using stock photography, you can't hand over exclusive copyrights for those images—well, you can, but good luck getting out of hot water when your client angrily calls you wanting to know what his copyrighted brochure image is doing on another company's billboard.

◆ **Dates and Timeline**

Make sure that you include all of the pertinent dates for when the proposals were submitted and agreed upon. You'll also be wise to establish a timeline for when different phases of the project will be completed, so that there is no ambiguity. Include a clause that you will not be responsible for any missed deadlines due to the client being inaccessible or not sending you necessary information in a timely fashion.

◆ **Price and Payment Policy**

Make clear the costs, whether hourly or on a project basis, so that there are no questions. Most clients hate nothing more than being surprised with excess charges that were not spelled out up front. And you don't want the aggravation of a billing confrontation without written confirmation as a back-up. Also include how payment is to happen. Standards change based on the length of the project and your relationship with your particular client, but many companies (including mine) typically arrange payment in thirds: a 33 percent deposit with the signed contract, 33 percent due upon delivery of the final project, and the balance due net 30 days from delivery. If the project is especially long, or billed hourly, then you may want to incorporate a "bill in progress" policy, where you send an invoice every two weeks or so.

◆ **Changes**

Include in your contract a clause stating that you will need client approval (in signature form) at certain phases of the creative process. The project should only progress once a signature has been given. If any changes are made to approved portions of the project after sign-off, those changes may be subject to additional fees over and above the project fee, usually billed at a separate hourly rate. Trust me when I tell you that this will save you a lot of time and aggravation in the long run.

If you can afford one, I would recommend having an attorney review your contracts before submitting them. There are a lot of things that can go wrong with a print project, and having a contract with gaping holes in it is about as helpful in court as not having one at all.

SPECIFICATIONS OF YOUR PROJECT: PREPRODUCTION

There is a lot to consider before you hire the photographer, write your copy, or lay your printed piece out. The more and better preproduction that you do, the better your chances for success will be.

Some of the issues that you will have to decide upon will largely be determined by the budget for the project. You can't very well do a 26-page full-color catalog for a client whose budget is only $3,000. Other preproduction issues may not even be up to you—the client may not give you full creative freedom and instead insist that the project take on certain aspects, such as prewritten copy, a certain color background, page dimensions, etc. Or another company altogether could handle an aspect of the job and you'll be expected to work with them in development.

The responses to each variable are going to change for each project. This section will go into more detail about each of the following areas that you will likely have to take into consideration:

◆ Who is the audience?

◆ What is the best way to reach that audience?

◆ What type of project will you create?

◆ How many colors will you use?

◆ What paper type will you choose to print on?

◆ What materials, if any, will be provided by the client?

◆ How much will the job cost you, and how much can you charge your client?

THE AUDIENCE

Knowing the audience that you're trying to reach may not be as easy as it sounds. And it's more important than you may think. Who the audience is, what they respond to, and where they can be found will form the foundation and rationale for what you ultimately create.

Figure 2–1 and Color Figure 8 show two ads that my agency created for Da Vinci Coachworks, a large limousine manufacturer. This print ad minicampaign was meant to be two pronged: The same message designed in two very different ways to reach two essential target audiences.

"History, Art & Elegance"
Target Audience One: The Corporate Market

The first ad was designed to reach a corporate audience—executives who would be interested in purchasing a limousine either for themselves or for their company. The *demographics* of this audience was refined, highly educated males over 45 years old with a well-above-average income. This audience was generally well traveled and had an interest in art and literature, among other things.

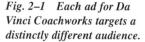

Fig. 2–1   Each ad for Da Vinci Coachworks targets a distinctly different audience.

The collage of Da Vinci's work was carefully selected and assembled to tell a story with images—the horse drawing behind the vehicle indicates the power; the gears and machinery represent the technology in the vehicle; and the figure sketches indicate the precision in the body. Of course, the master himself looks over the piece, inferring his approval of the vehicle as an object of art as powerful and as beautifully constructed as his own. This ad, a two-page spread placed in the *Robb Report*, was designed to be sophisticated and elegant, in accordance with the qualities that audience is drawn to.

"Hi Tech Elegance"
Target Audience Two: The Livery Market

The second ad is more colorful and direct, featuring a young, attractive couple blended into the background of New York City at night. This ad was designed to reach a less corporate market and penetrate the consciousness of the livery owners, who purchase limousines to rent for weddings, proms, etc. The ad was meant to reflect an atmosphere that this audience of livery owners could relate to—happy clients out on a perfect night on the town.

This ad was another two-page spread, but instead of appearing in a magazine for millionaires like the *Robb Report*, it mostly ran in limousine and transportation industry publications. The limousine is exactly the same way in both ads to add consistency. (See more about consistency later in this section.)

There are many ways to find out who the audience is for the piece you'll be creating. Often times, as was the case with Da Vinci in the above example, the clients themselves know from experience who their audience is and who they want to reach. Past records of marketing efforts and sales will usually reveal much of what you need to know about the target audience. In the case of a new company, new product launch, or new focus on existing materials and lines, you'll probably be working with a market research team or employing some research tactics of your own.

MARKET RESEARCH

You or you firm may or may not provide this service. If you don't currently, you'd be wise to stay away from tackling it on your own. You're setting yourself up to be a digital publishing firm and the intricacies of demographics and psychographics are completely separate. And although it's important for you to properly interpret the market research results before designing your piece, you may not want to accept the responsibility for describing the market landscape without proper training.

Although you will likely not be involved in conducting surveys or focus groups as a dedicated market research company might, there are ways you can go about doing some important research on your own before developing a design:

◆ **Collect preexisting demographics**

Your client may already have a demographic report from previous research that could give you some clue as to the audience. Let's say that they don't have such a report, though, but want you to develop an ad for their new line of widgets that will run in *BusinessWeek*. Even before you know what a widget is (if you've ever taken a college economics course, then you're aware that you will *never* know what a widget is), you can get an idea of who the target consumer is. Call *BusinessWeek* and ask for their media kit. Among other useful information, this media kit will provide a demographic profile of their readership, including the following (reprinted with permission from *BusinessWeek* from their 1999 demographic survey):

Demographics:

Male/Female Ratio	86% / 14%
Median Age	47.7 years
Graduated College +	86%
Median Household Income	$112,000
Median Personal Income	$ 89,000

Purchase Involvement:

Computer Hardware	64%
Computer Software	59%

Lifestyle:

Own Car/Cellular Phone	60%
Participated in Sports inPast 12 Months	79%

Obviously, by advertising in this magazine, the client's product is meant for an upscale, intellectual male market, and not for twelve-year-old girls. Interpreting these figures will, as discussed later in this chapter, provide guidelines as to how to design the piece.

◆ Check Out the Competitors' Material

Does your client have any direct competitors? Chances are, they do. Ask your client who their competitors are and which ones are the most likely to be tapping into your client's desired market. From there it's a simple task to call and request a brochure and any other marketing material they may have. Look at the design of this material. It should give you a roadmap to follow as to who their audience is and how they chose to go about attracting them. If material from three different competitors each has the same type of style, chances are they know exactly who the market is and what they respond to.

This is a little bit sneaky, but it works. If you really want to find out about a competing market strategy, ask their Marketing Director. Say that you're a college student, doing a term paper for a marketing class, and that you want to use their company as a case study. If you don't have a young-sounding voice, get someone else to call. More often then not, the Marketing Director won't reveal any trade secrets but they will divulge a good amount in the interest of higher r education.

ANALYZING MARKET RESEARCH

Demographics is the statistical composition and profile of a group of people in a given market. *Psychographics* is the analysis of what that particular audience positively responds to. Are those really annoying TV commercials that have a bunch of teenagers screeming into a camera while doing some stupid skateboarding stunt meant to appeal to a market of 65-year-old women? No, they're meant to grab the attention

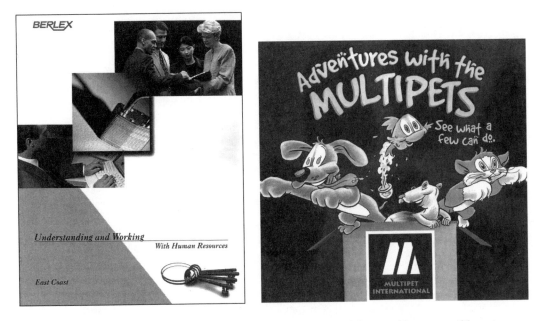

Fig. 2–2 **Each piece targets a different market through its use of imagery and layout.**

of teenagers (although I don't think they do—the GenX market has proven particularly difficult to penetrate through advertising and the screaming-into-the-camera thing is just a silly insult to their intelligence). You get my point though. Whether successful or not, different types of designs and ideas are expected to capture different markets.

Much of how you interpret the demographics of an audience will rely on common sense, experience, and any research that you do. Look through magazines and brochures. Read through books dedicated to the topic. The more you understand your audience, the more likely you are to capture their attention.

Figure 2–2 and Color Figure 9 show two different pieces that my agency designed. The first was an internal brochure for Berlex Labs' HR department. The brochure was designed to reflect Berlex's corporate nature. The fields of green (their corporate color) and white allow for a healthy dose of empty space and for subtle and corporate sophistication, while the photographic imagery implies that this brochure is meant for the active employee and his place in the work environment. The second brochure is aimed at a completely different market. It was designed for Multipet International, a toy manufacturer. Because their audience is wholesale toy buyers, the brochure was created with the color, noise and excitement that is indicative of that industry.

Keep in mind some of the following points about your target audience when developing your work:

- Age

- Gender

- Education

- Annual income

- Employment status and rank

- Marital status

- Race

- Religion

- Likes/interests

- Publications read

Of course, that's only a short list of some of the demographics you'll want to consider when designing. Further research on your part will reveal others.

TYPE OF DESIGN

Oftentimes your client will make the choice of project type very easy for you by telling you in advance what they want. Other times they'll just tell you what its use will be, such as a mailing or a tradeshow promo piece. Sometimes they'll just say that they want marketing material and leave it completely up to you.

It's important to know all of your options when deciding what type of piece you want to create. Even if the client tells you what they want, by knowing more you might be able to suggest something that could work better for their needs (and maybe even earn you some more money).

Talk to your printer for a complete understanding of your options for print, what it possible, what is impossible, and what you can expect in terms of pricing for each project type. It's likely that your client's budgetary constraints may significantly narrow the field of options you have. Remember printing is not a cheap art form.

Brochures

Brochures can come in all sorts of shapes and sizes. Their main focus is usually to provide general information about a company or a product in the interest of arousing consumer interest.

- **Standard One Fold:** These brochures are folded once, usually down the middle. The fold of one sheet of paper creates four panels, or pages. Take an 8.5" x 11" piece of paper, for example, and fold it in half once. The booklet you create has become a 5.5" x 8.5" brochure, with the cover and back printed on one side and the entire inside information printed on the other side.

There is no set size for these brochures—if you can fold a page in half, you can make one. 11" x 17" folded to 8.5" x 11" panels is the standard size and larger sizes could potentially increase the price from the printer and the service bureau, so check with them for prices before creating your piece.

Brochures like this typically get bound in the center with staples. Because of this, you have to create pages for your brochure in multiples of four. One piece of paper folded creates four "pages." Two pieces folded and bound create eight pages and so on.

If you plan on creating a brochure with more than four pages, read Chapter 8 to learn more about setting up your pages in printer's spreads.

Although you can always print any piece in any number of colors and on practically any paper stock, these are usually printed four-color and on a nice, heavy stock. Images are usually expected to be clear with crisp detail and color. If you're working on a piece like this you're going to want to get any photographs professionally scanned.

◆ **Tri-Fold:** These grossly overused brochures are typically 8.5" x 11" folded twice to create six useable panels—three panels on each side. More panels can be added by printing on longer paper and adding more folds, but this will add to the expense, so check with your printer first.

Depending on its intended use, tri-fold brochures range in quality and color, with two-or even one-color brochures not uncommon.

◆ **Pocket Folders:** These handy brochures are more like brochure and paperwork containers. Typically 18" x 12" folded in half to 9" x 12" with one or two pockets glued on the inside. Figure 2–3 shows a sample pocket folder. Because they are meant to carry smaller brochures, samples and other paperwork in the pockets, these are usually printed on very stiff card-stock paper. Depending on how they are designed, these pocket folders can look elegant even if only printed in one or two colors.

Depending on the purpose, there can sometimes be a call for specialized folds or configurations or various pocket sizes. You may want to look into a catalog by a company called Presskits that we use often for odd pockets and sizes. You can call them at (800) 472-3497.

Newsletters

Newsletters are usually the same as the standard brochure described above, but typically not printed on as nice a paper. They are also commonly printed in just one or two colors, as they are usually meant to provide snippets of semi-up-to-date information,

*Fig 2–3   Pocket folder brochures are
attractive and functional.*

and then tossed away. Color and image quality are not, typically, considered super-important. You may be able to get away with digitizing images through your desktop scanner.

Flyers

Flyers can be used for any number of purposes, ranging from a mass mailing to sales sheets placed in a pocket folder. Although flyers are usually 8.5" x 11" with no folds, there is really no standard as far as number of colors or paper quality. Specifications will rely largely on a combination of intended use and budget.

Catalogs

Catalogs are usually meant to provide an entire stock of items to consumers for easy ordering. Photographs are almost always used for presentation purposes, especially when consumer products are being advertised. Jewelry, clothing, watches all require crisp color to display the product accurately. Industrial catalogs are often less spectac-ular, providing fewer photographs. In their place are long lists of product ID numbers and specifications. These are typically printed in only one or two colors.

Regardless of how many colors are used, though, catalogs are most often printed on thin, cheap paper, as they become outdated and need to be reprinted often.

Oversized Work

Posters, banners, backdrops for trade show booths—all have become more popular as printers have improved and come down steadily in price. The hard part about creating oversized work is that the file sizes are usually quite large—depending on the size of the piece, an image in Photoshop can be 200 Megs or even 300 Megs. Higher? Sorry, 300 Megs is as large as I've gone. The good part about running an oversized piece is that you don't have to worry about making plates—the "press" is actually just a really large desktop printer. Well, kind of. They usually use ink cartridges, like your desktop printer does, instead of rollers, so there is no need for plates to be made. There is more about oversized printers in Chapter 9.

Annual Reports

These are probably some of the nicest pieces you'll ever create. These reports, the substance of a corporation and their shot at impressing stockholders and potential investors, are usually printed only on high-quality paper stock. Attention to detail is of great importance, and images have to be perfect.

Advertisements

The only one on the list that you probably won't have to send directly to the printing press, print ads range in size and shape depending on the publication. Specifications as to line screen and how the film should be produced are set by the publication. The number of colors in the ad (assuming the publication prints in color) is dependent upon how much money your client wants to pay: more color, more money. Each publication has different requirements as to whether they want you to provide film or a disk—if you're to provide film, then speak with your service bureau about the specs before beginning the project.

Try to place the ad yourself, if possible. If you establish yourself as an advertising agency, you'll typically be privy to a 15 percent discount in the ad rate. Some firms, like my own, waive the design fee for creating ads for certain publications for the right to keep the difference in the ad rate. Others work out their own deals.

PAPER STYLE

There is a wide variety of paper stocks for you to choose from. Your printer will have samples of each different paper type for you to feel. These samples will help you make your decisions as to which you want to print on—you may want to have your client help in the decision-making process so that they are satisfied with the paper quality.

Paper is measured in one of two ways: pounds (or points), and either coated (shiny) or uncoated. Thinner paper is measured by weight, i.e. pounds, and typically starts at 60#, which is very thin, and goes up to 120#, which is considerably thicker. For even thicker needs, you can choose a card stock, measured in points. The most popular of these would be thin card stock starting at 8 pt, thicker at 10 pt, and even thicker at 12 pt. Be careful when choosing paper types and weights, though—heavy stocks, especially card stocks, are quite a bit more expensive, plus they have a greater chance of cracking at the folds if you use solid colors. However, card stock is a lot nicer and more impressive. Lighter paper, like 60#, is much cheaper, has a reduced chance of cracking at the fold, but is not as impressive and may not hold inks as well. Consult with your printer as to which paper type would be best for your particular job.

OTHER STYLES

Of course there are more types of printed pieces you can create, including full-blown magazines and books. But unless you work for a publisher, you probably won't be asked to produce either one of these. There are so many aspects and variables that go into developing both of these that describing them in detail would be far too involved and is beyond the scope of this book.

CONSISTENCY

Consistency has to take a front seat in your head when you create your design. It's a universal truth in advertising that repetition in design, tag lines, theme, or other aspects of a marketing effort can be the key to ensuring that your message becomes ingrained in your audience's subconscious. Remember, the main point of anything that you create is to generate interest in a product or company. Consumers are more apt to buy from or listen to an entity that they are familiar with, and they are more apt to become familiar with an entity through repetition of its logo or message.

Consistency also paints a picture in the consumer's mind that the advertiser is an organized company and that they provide quality services or products. If your clients web site is blue and red with loud animations all over the place but their brochure is a soft white with an elegant marble border, what is a consumer to think? They certainly won't associate the two designs as the same company, so the chances of logo recognition are reduced. And if they do recognize them as the same company, they'll probably think that the company is quite disorganized.

Color Figure 10 shows the marketing pieces for my own agency, PFS New Media. Displayed in the Figure are our pocket folder brochure, eight-page brochure, odd-sized tri-fold brochure, two magazine print ads, CD-ROM, and web site screen shots. As you can see, the Statue of David is our running theme—he appears somewhere in every promotional piece that we run for ourselves. Similarly, the font used in all pieces is the same and the logo is prominently displayed in all. The idea is that should someone see our print ad and decide to visit our web site, they will be instantly hit with a familiar image—in fact, the graphic appearing on the homepage of our web site is simply a revamped version of the print ad. Should they receive our brochure or CD-ROM for review, they'll again be seeing the Statue of David, which will, after time, begin to spark an association of high art with PFS New Media. When those two thoughts become synonymous, the chance of gaining new accounts is increased.

Notice, though, that consistency does not in most cases mean completely copying a design from one place and putting it somewhere else. The David on the cover of our eight-page brochure is lying in a pool of blood—a sharp contrast to the David in the print ad, whose head is exploding with ideas. Different imagery can be used while still maintaining the consistency in theme.

Ask your client which aspects of any existing marketing material they would like to keep consistent in the projects that you'll be doing. They may even have photographs or other elements digitally saved for you to use in trying to keep the design consistent between pieces.

If your client does not currently have any marketing material or any type of theme established, then be careful in your pricing—you could be short-changing yourself. Designs you create that will be repeated from one marketing piece to another are a form of *branding* and creating a corporate identity. Typically the price for creating a corporate identity can be significantly higher than the price for creating a printed piece.

THE INITIAL CONCEPT

There is no set way to go about developing your idea—every designer has his or her own way of going about it. But they nearly all agree that an initial draft is always necessary.

Some designers insist that the drawing board is the best place to start when it comes to laying out a first draft. A pencil sketch is designed on standard paper, as seen in Figure 2–4, to design the basic layout and assemble ideas visually.

Other designers, like myself, use the computer to create initial drafts of a piece. I find this to be especially helpful when developing a print piece that will have a lot of graphics. Layouts are easy enough to put down on paper, but there are so many filters and combinations of commands in Photoshop and Illustrator that pencil and paper would only limit your imagination.

However you decide to design your initial draft, you're going to eventually need to show something to your client for approval. There are a number of ways you can show an initial design to your client:

Fig. 2–4   Pencil sketches are a good way to start building ideas.

◆ **Desktop Printer Output**

These are good for smaller clients or for work that isn't going to involve a tremendous amount of color reproduction or detail. The argument can be made that it's only a first draft, after all, so even detailed color work could be initially displayed on a desktop printer. For your own use, I would agree with that. But you're going to want to impress your client from the outset—especially when trying to sell them on your ideas for the project. Desktop printer output won't impress anyone.

◆ **Fiery Prints**

Fiery prints are usually done at the service bureau and can usually be expected to take about an hour to a day to print, depending on the file size of your document. They're not terribly expensive (about $15–$25 for an 11" x 17"), but they're not terribly accurate when it comes to color, either. These are best used when quality in layout, and not color, is the primary concern.

◆ **IRIS Prints**

Your service bureau should also be able to provide you with IRIS prints, which typically run between $30–$40 for an 11" x 17" print. These are printed on a glossy type of film material, so beware—if your client's project is going to be printed on a matte paper stock, the gloss will give them a false impression of what the finished product will look like. The best part about these is that if the IRIS output device is well calibrated and maintained, the IRIS can range anywhere between 92–95 percent true to color. The service bureau that I use for my IRIS prints (Pro Set Color), provides me with such high quality work that I often use these in place of the more expensive Matchprints (see Chapter 8) for color check off the press.

◆ **The Internet**

With the new growth of communication and information, your client does not have to be within driving distance for you to work well together. Overnight delivery companies are reliable enough to deliver any of the aforementioned draft methods to your client and the Internet is so widely available that they no longer even have to wait for overnight shipments.

Reduce a copy of your Photoshop file to low-res (72 ppi) and save it as a JPEG as well as the standard TIF or EPS that you'll print with (Import Illustrator files to Photoshop then save them as JPEGs). If you need to show an entire layout, choose Save As EPS from QuarkXPress and open the EPS file in Photoshop. Then save it as a JPEG. If you know even a little HTML and can post files on a server, you can create a mini-web site comprised of your client's drafts. Otherwise you can e-mail the files to your client.

SUMMARY

There are many important issues to address before you get to the really fun part of watching your ideas come to life on the computer or on paper. Prepress work is more than just preparing images and setting up files for the printer. It's also about understanding who you are marketing toward, the vehicle you will use to reach that market, and ensuring that you're properly compensated and protected in the work you are going to be doing. If you follow the advice offered in this chapter, as well as handle any of the unique situations you may run across in your experience, you will be well equipped for your journey in the creation and development of print projects.

chapter 3

QUARKXPRESS AND PRINT LAYOUT

QuarkXPress will play a major part in your design process. In Chapter 4, I'll explain the conceptual issues of effective layout design. While I do that, I'll also be explaining how to go about achieving many of these techniques using QuarkXPress. XPress is today's leader in page layout software. I say "today's" because unlike Adobe Photoshop and Adobe Illustrator, which go largely unchallenged in their field (yes, there *are* others, but none that challenge their title as "standards" in the industry), Quark has competing programs like Adobe PageMaker poised to take over as leader. Until that happens, though, Quark is still the program to know, and, as much as I love Adobe in general, future versions of this book will still feature XPress. I just like it better.

If you're already experienced in creating printed pieces, you may be wondering why the layout/QuarkXPress chapter is falling before the chapters dealing with photography and illustrations. QuarkXPress is, after all, the final design step, after you have all of your other elements ready to go. This is the Mecca where your ideas come together and the threshold beyond which your creativity becomes reality. (You can quote that last line, if you'd like.)

However, in nearly all cases, you're going to have to have a good sense of how you expect your page will lay out before you even think about the photography or the illustrations. If you don't, you'll really be shooting from the hip when you try to develop any type of graphics. So for that reason, this chapter is up in front, even if you won't implement many of these techniques until much later in the design process. We'll be revisiting XPress later though, in Chapter 8, when we discuss getting your project ready for the service bureau.

One of the truly fascinating things about Quark is that it is simultaneously simple and complex at the same time. You can sit at a computer, open the program for the first time, and learn enough to get you through a small project in less than an hour. In fact, I'm about to teach you everything you need to know to lay out a simple project in the span of just a few pages. But that's just the bare essentials. It's the bells and whistles that make Quark such a powerful program, the mechanics that make it essential for quality printing, and the flexibility that make it a great creative tool.

But realistically, if you need to lay out a project on a deadline and do not have the time to invest in really digging deep into its capabilities, you can learn just enough to complete your project on time and with good results.

This chapter is not a comprehensive explanation of how to use QuarkXPress. Beyond a few brief paragraphs provided later that explain how to import graphics and place text, the XPress descriptions largely relate to how you can put the conceptual aspects of this chapter into use.

QUARK-ABILITIES

So what makes Quark such a great tool? Everyone knows that it's used for laying out ads, pages, and booklets, but what are the features that make Quark so powerful?

◆ **Customized Page Setup:** Setting up files for print takes more than just having a good eye for color and content. It also takes the rigors of setting up the pages properly. Quark allows you to choose a page size from 1" x 1" up to 48" x 48", as well as set up margins practically any place. Quark will display pages and margins in an organized fashion for quick and easy reference.

◆ **Easy Placement of Content:** Quark allows you to easily establish areas for text and imagery, as well as measuring columns and gutters. Textboxes can be linked together, so that copy can continue from one area to the next, even across different pages.

◆ **Easy Viewing:** The zoom viewing allows you to see any page up close or from far away, and the thumbnail page layout allows you to easily jump from one page to the next—a great help for large projects.

◆ **Automation:** Another big help for creators of large projects is that Quark provides extensive automation. Pages can be automatically created as needed, as can columns for text. Even better is that with Master Pages, each new page that is created can duplicate specified attributes and even place page numbers in order for you.

◆ **Importing the Pieces:** What good is having a table to make the jigsaw puzzle on if you can't use the pieces that you want? Quark allows you to import all of your text and graphics onto each page from other programs such as Word, Photoshop, and Illustrator. Text elements can take on predetermined values from the Quark *Style Sheets* and be made to wrap around graphics for a less blocky look. Images can be skewed, stretched, and rotated, and, depending on the file type, adjusted for contrast, brightness, color, and other effects (though in most cases you're better off returning to Photoshop for these adjustments).

◆ **Ease is the Word:** Who needs Microsoft Word when you have QuarkXPress? Although not as full-bodied as specialized word processors, Quark is my personal choice for a text editor. You don't need to rely on importing copy from another program—you can type the whole thing in Quark to begin with. Quark has all the controls for quick copy manipulation, including font size and type, style, kerning and spacing. It will automatically wrap text around any image that stands in its way, and remain within the confines of its designated area. With style sheets, you can save important attributes to be created automatically.

◆ **Quark-Specific Design:** Any image or box can be decorated with borders and underlines, as well as with flat and gradated colors. Boxes can take on multiple shapes, including the standard square, the clichéd western-saloon-door inward-indented corner box, ovals, and circles.

◆ **Printer Spec Setup:** Quark will help you tackle all of the rigors that can make working with a printer such a chore, such as allowing for bleed, setting crop marks and registration, and even formatting into printer spreads (more details on this are given later in this chapter).

◆ **Collection of Document Data:** One of the most aggravating phone calls you can receive is from the printer, informing you that one of the pictures in your print piece is missing from the Zip cartridge you just dropped off. (What do you mean, that's never happened to you? I can't really be the only one....) With Quark's Collect for Output feature, all of the elements in your file, with the exception of fonts, will be collected and placed in a nice, neat folder with a written report of its contents.

That's a basic description of what QuarkXPress can do, and why it plays a vital role in the creation of print material. But those basics have been almost universal in Quark for years now.

VERSION 4.0 UPGRADES

Although both hailed and criticized throughout its life, Quark 3.3 had become a powerful force in the design world, overtaking PageMaker as the industry standard. In 1998, Quark released its first major upgrade in years with version 4.0. Although expectations were high, the new version was controversial, with its proponents giving it Star

Wars-like reviews, and its detractors panning it like _____ (fill in your least favorite Kevin Costner movie).

Note ✱ Since I like Quark, I won't go into detail about how the initial releases were so buggy that practically everyone uninstalled it from their system. Quark has, by the time this book is published, long since fixed a majority of the problems.

There were *a lot* of changes in the new version of Quark. Regrettably there was a lot that was left out, too, such as a layers palette, and instant HTML conversion for web development. But you can't miss what you never had, so I'll concentrate instead on the upgrades and changes that I like the most and have had the most effect on my work.

◆ **An Illustrator Facelift:** Although highly qualified for all types of work, Adobe Illustrator is used by many designers in large for one feature: the ability to place text along a path. Now you can do that directly in Quark, plus much more! With the inclusion of the pen tool, designers can now make Bézier paths, boxes, (in any shape!) and lines.

◆ **Easily Manipulated Boxes:** If you're still working with version 3.3, you'll never know how useful this feature is until you upgrade to 4.0. Now you can instantly convert text boxes into picture boxes and vice versa, and even turn lines into boxes. Just as exciting is that you no longer have to choose the Item tool to import text or graphics into boxes—you can do this with either the Item OR the Move tool.

◆ **Upgraded Runarounds:** The ability to make text run around images and other objects has always been a popular one with designers, and in 4.0 it gets even better! You can use the previously described Bezier paths to create custom runarounds and even set your text to run around both sides of an image or object—a difficult effect to set up in earlier Quark versions.

◆ **Resizing Objects in Groups:** This upgrade is my personal favorite. The new QuarkXPress lets you group text and images together and resize them all at once. This is a major improvement from the previous version, in which you had to resize each item separately.

◆ **Enhanced Style Sheets:** Style sheets are a large part of what makes Quark such a powerful and time-saving program. With Quark 4.0, you can now apply style sheets to individual characters, words, and sentences. A full description of style sheets is provided later in this chapter.

◆ **Better Management of Clipping Paths:** The benefits of saving files in the TIFF format have traditionally been negated by the jagged edges that would appear when you imported them into Quark. Well, maybe *negated* is an overexaggeration—there are workarounds—but the new version uses hi-res image information to render perfect cuts with PostScript clipping paths.

◆ **The Color Revolution:** The new Quark has traded in the EfiColor color management system for the more reliable ICC-based cms for more color consistency. Also, two- and three-color projects can enjoy the multi-ink color feature, which allows you to mix spot colors.

Once again, this is not a complete list of the new upgrades by far. For a full description, look for the upcoming QuarkXPress To Go book in this series.

A FEW USEFUL TECHNICAL ISSUES IN QUARKXPRESS

The remainder of this chapter deals with working with text, imported images, or both. For convenience, I have provided a few brief paragraphs to quickly explain how to go about placing images and text into your XPress document.

BEGINNING A NEW DOCUMENT

The first place you'll start in XPress is with a new file. Each new file will start you with a canvas upon which you will place your print elements. To open a new document in XPress:

1. Launch the program and select File –> New –> Document to access the dialog box shown in Figure 3–1.

2. Choose US Letter from the Size pull-down menu, so that 8.5" and 11" appear in the Width and Height text boxes, respectively. If you need a different canvas size, either select from one of the other presets or type in the dimensions manually.

3. Choose Portrait (vertical page) or Landscape (horizontal page) orientation.

4. If they're not already, set all of the Margin Guides (Top, Bottom, Left, Right) to read .5, measured in inches. You can set the margins at any value you'd like, although most desktop printers will only print to .5" from the edge of the page.

5. If you're working on a very small project, such as a one- or two-page flyer, then leave the Facing Pages checkbox (in the Margin Guides info section) off. This option will set up your files to be arranged in twos, with right- and left-hand pages in the order that it would be assembled. The left pages (*verso*) will always be even numbered, and face the right pages (*recto*), which will be odd numbered. Turn it on if you'll be creating a catalog or other publication with a lot of pages.

6. Leave the Automatic Text Box unchecked—this will place a text box on each new page, which is great if you're writing a book, but annoying if you're creating an ad or a brochure.

7. Click OK.

The 8.5" x 11" square in the center of the screen in your canvas is called the Document Page. This is where you will lay out your print piece. The white space around it is called the Pasteboard. If you do not see the full Document Page on the Pasteboard right now (if you can't see four distinct sides and corners of your Document Page with Pasteboard around it), click View –> Size to Fit, or click Command (Ctrl in Windows) + 0 to do this from the keyboard. Figure 3–2 shows what the page looks like.

The blue (color by default) lines around your image are the guides that show your margins. These were set to .5" in Step 4. Typically, if you are going to be printing from a desktop printer, that's about as close to the edge as you're going to get—everything on your page beyond that gets cut off. This is because your desktop printer would be very unhappy if it got ink on its rollers, so it protects itself by leaving a healthy margin. Chapter 8 tells how you can increase the room you have to print by reducing the margin to .25".

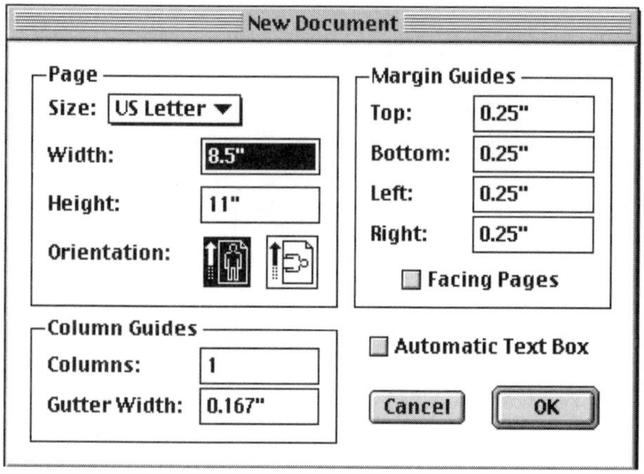

New Document

Page
Size: [US Letter ▼]
Width: [8.5"]
Height: [11"]
Orientation: [portrait] [landscape]

Margin Guides
Top: [0.25"]
Bottom: [0.25"]
Left: [0.25"]
Right: [0.25"]
☐ **Facing Pages**

Column Guides
Columns: [1]
Gutter Width: [0.167"]

☐ **Automatic Text Box**

[Cancel]   [OK]

Fig. 3–1   The New Document dialog box.

Fig: 3–2   A new XPress document.

SAVING QUARKXPRESS FILES

On Windows, Quark uses the .qxd file extension. Saving files is a rather simple process, but there are a few areas that can really make a difference to the final result of your document.

To save a file in XPress:

1. Choose File –> Save As to access the dialog bix shown in Figure 3–3.

2. Just as you might in any other program, find the place on your computer where you want your document to reside and give it a name.

3. The first curveball of saving in QuarkXPress is under the Type pull-down menu. You have two choices: Document and Template. Saving as a document does just that—it saves your page permanently in your desired location. The next time you open that file and make changes to it, though, you will be allowed to save over it, thus destroying the original document in place of the new document. Choosing Template from the Type pull-down has a different effect. A Template can't be changed. The next time you open your page, Quark will open a copy of the original and the title will come up as Document One instead of its original name. The original document, then, is preserved.

4. The second curveball is the choice in Version. You can choose to save your file either for Version 3.3 or 4.0. Earlier in this chapter, I provided a list of some of the upgrades in Version 4.0. If you have used these features in your layout and then save your file with 3.3 selected as your desired version, those features will be lost. For example, let's say that your page used text on a path as part of the layout and you saved the file as Version 3.3. The next time you open your document, your copy will appear in a boring rectangular text box. The bottom line is that unless you're positive that you won't be using any Version 4 features and that you'll need to open the document in 3.3 at some point, just save all your documents as Version 4.0.

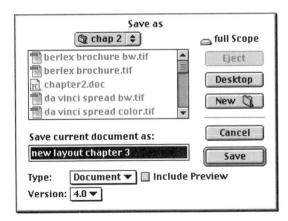

Fig: 3–3   The Save As dialog box.

You won't be able to open your XPress document in Photoshop or Illustrator, since neither reads the Quark format. However, if you do need the entire layout of a page from your XPress document, you can choose File –> Save as EPS. This will save the active page as an EPS, which can be opened in either Photoshop or Illustrator.

PLACING IMAGES

You can place images from any source into your layout, preferably in either the EPS or TIF formats.

1. Choose the Rectangular Picture Box from the Tools palette (as indicated in Figure 3–4).

2. Click anywhere on your pasteboard and, holding the mouse button down, drag diagonally away from the point at which you clicked. As you drag, you'll see that you are creating a bounding box such as the one shown in Figure 3–5. The handle bars on each side and at each corner allow you to manipulate the box should you want to make it bigger or smaller. The big X in the center tells you that this is meant to be a Picture box and that an image of some sort should be placed here.

3. Notice that even though you had the Picture Box tool selected, XPress changed your active tool to either the Item Tool or the Content Tool. With the box still selected (you can tell it's selected by the black border and appearance of the handlebars), choose File –> Get Picture. If you're brand new to QuarkXPress, this won't matter to you, but with Version 4.0 and higher you can now choose Get Picture with *either* the Item or Content tool. That alone is worth the price of admission.

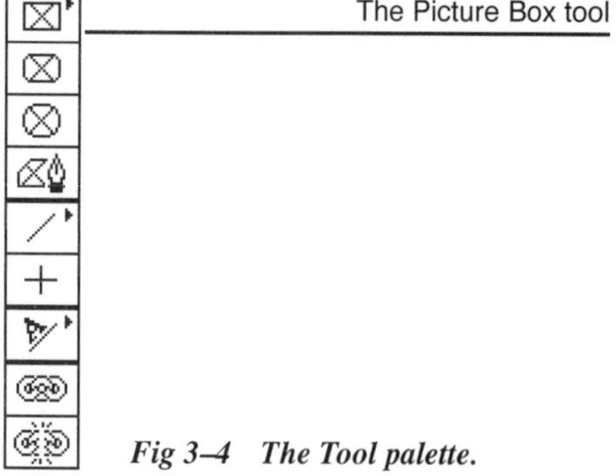

The Text Box tool
_____

The Picture Box tool
_____

Fig 3–4   The Tool palette.

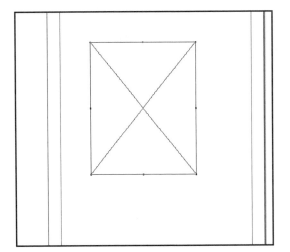

Fig. 3–5 The picture box is displayed with a large X in the center of it.

4. In the navigation window that appears, locate the image you want to import. TIFF and EPS formatted images will be the most common. Click OK when you've found your desired image.

5. Your image appears in the Picture box, where the X used to be.

The image is always put in the top left corner of the picture box, so that it is kissing the top and left side of the box. If your image is smaller than the area in your Picture box, make your box smaller by dragging the appropriate handle bars inward. If your image is larger that the box, make the box larger by dragging the appropriate handle bars outward.

ADDING TEXT

You can place text in QuarkXPress by either importing a completed file from another source (such as Microsoft Word) or by using XPress as a text editor and typing directly into your layout.

1. Activate the Text Box tool shown in Figure 3–4.

2. Create a Text Box the same way you created the picture box. Do this in the area in which you want to place your text. You'll notice that there is *not* an X in this one like there was in the Picture Box.

3. If you're going to be using copy that was prewritten in another program, like Word, choose File –> Get Text and find the desired file from within the navigator. If you're going to type original copy directly into your document, activate the Content Tool from the toolbar.

If you're going to be importing text, make sure that the file format is either .doc or .txt. Quark doesn't like ASCII formatted copy.

4. Click in the Text Box that you just created. You'll see a type cursor in the upper left corner where you can start typing. If you've imported text, you can use this tool to edit or make revisions.

If you see a very tiny square with an X in it at the bottom right corner of your text box, it means that your Text Box was not big enough to contain all of your copy. Drag the box larger with the handle bars to make the box bigger or select all your text and reduce the font size. If your text is larger than the page, add additional pages and/or additional text boxes, and "link" them together with the Link Tool.

GENERAL LAYOUT ISSUES

Beyond the how-to's of QuarkXPress, there are a number of important issues you'll have to keep in the forefront of your mind while developing your layouts.

UNDERSTANDING THE DIFFERENCE BETWEEN READER'S SPREADS AND PRINTER'S SPREADS

There are basically two types of binding when it comes to putting a booklet together:

Perfect Binding

Look at the binding of this book. The pages are glued to the binding in groups of folded pages called signatures. Each signature is printed and glued separately. This is called *perfect binding*.

Saddle Stitch

Find a smaller publication—a catalog, a brochure, an annual report. If you look along the edge, you'll notice that it is most likely bound with staples. This is called a *saddle stitch* from the days when it was actually sewn stogether. Saddle-stitch binding is the type that can cause you major headaches when it comes time to lay out your project and prepare your files for print.

Unless you are working for a major publisher of books or magazines, you probably won't be doing too much in terms of perfect binding, which usually requires a significant number of pages before it can be considered cost-effective. You'll have less to worry about as far as layout goes, however, as each signature will simply be printed, cut, and corrated as individuals.

If you're an independent designer or if you work for an agency, you're more likely to be producing work that has fewer pages, such as catalogs and annual reports. For items like these, layouts will be significantly more difficult.

Open your smaller publication again; the one with the saddle stitch. As you'd expect, the pages are numbered in a sequential order—page one, page two, page three, etc. But look deeper than that and you'll notice some fairly interesting qualities about your publication:

◆ With the exception of any fold-outs, the number of pages in the publication will be divisible by 4. For the sake of an example, let's assume that each page of your publication is 8.5" x 11". If you open the book to the middle spread (the center of the book, where the staple binding can be seen) you'll see that the pages aren't really 8.5" x 11"—they're 11" x 17", folded once, right in the middle. That creates four panels, each 8.5" x 11". If each 11" x 17" spread *yields* four 8.5" x 11" panels, then the entire publication must be divisible by four.

◆ Let's assume that the publication is 24 pages (six 11" x 17" spreads, folded into 24 8.5" x 11" panels). Carefully take the staples out of the binding. With all the spreads now independant of each other, find the panel for page one. Lay it flat and you'll see that page one, the first page, is on the same spread as page 24, the last page. Turn it over, and you'll see that page 2 is on the same spread as page 23. You'll see this same thing on every spread that was in the publication.

So what does all this mean to you? Well, if you're working on a 24-page book that is to be saddle stitched, you will most likely want to lay it out in reader's spreads—the same order that you would read the publication. You'll do this for your own benefit as well as to present it to the client. However, although you'll need to do this to understand the logistics and order of the piece, you can't deliver it to a printer like this. Instead, you'll have to tear it apart and re-lay the project out in printer's spreads. This will ensure that when your project is printed and bound, it will make sense to the reader.

Make sure you measure everything out exactly! If you don't spend time measuring everything before you change your layout to printer's spreads, you run the risk of having all of the overlapping images being visibly off. Even a sixteenth of an inch can be detrimental, sufficient to cause your client to insist that you redo the project—at your expense!

TRI-FOLD MEASUREMENTS

Tri-fold brochures are all too common for my tastes. But they're a necessary evil in print design. At some point in your design career, you'll probably have to create a few.

The important thing to keep in mind when designing a tri-fold brochure is the measurements of the panel. Let's say that you are going to be creating your tri-fold from an 11" x 8.5" page. If you measured it exactly, each panel would be 11" / 3 = 3.667". But if you create it this way, you'll be running into problems—you need to compensate for the small area that will be wasted in the actual fold. Since the back panel will fold into the piece and the cover will fold over both the center and back panel, compensate for the fold by making the back panel a little smaller.

In short, check with your printer to be absolutely sure what they recommend (since they know their folding machine), but if you're looking at the front, the cover and the middle panels should each be approximately 3.83" and the back panel should be approximately 3.667". Keep in mind that these measurements are approximates, and depending on the topic of the piece you are working on, the back panel could be significantly shorter.

"LIVE SPACE" IN A MAGAZINE AD

When you are working with magazines and other such publications, read the specs carefully. Don't make the mistake of designing an ad with bleeds for an 8.5" x 11" magazine page the same way you might for a saddle-stitched eight-page brochure. When designing for a perfect-bound magazine, you need to design for the *live area*, or the area of the page that the reader will actually see. Don't forget that you will likely lose up to .25" of your image as it falls in the binding of the publication.

That's enough for a brief introduction to QuarkXPress. As later topics discuss various techniques and concepts, I'll show how to implement them using the tools of Quark.

SUMMARY

No matter how great your concepts, ideas, or client relationships may be, you will be hardpressed to accomplish much in printing without a clear understanding of a page layout program. While there are others on the market, QuarkXPress is currently the best one of the bunch. With this tool in-hand, you will be able to accomplish a variety of exciting layout styles and projects. This knowledge, combined with the next chapter's conceptual guidelines, are the keys to true printing success.

chapter 4

LAYOUT TECHNIQUES FOR EFFECTIVE PRINT DESIGN

GENERAL CONCEPTS AND QUARKXPRESS

Any person will immediately notice what their profession trains them to notice. Talk to a dentist, even socially, and he'll be noticing your teeth as you speak. Discussions with psychiatrists can always be fun, since they're most likely analyzing your every word. It's just human nature. As a designer of print material, be prepared to never read a magazine or brochure the same way again. Rather than just enjoying them for what they are, your mind will instantly recognize fonts, layout issues, even how images are used in relation to the rest of the page. But what you'll notice most are the ads and brochures that really, really are awful. You will see every mistake, every poor layout, and every weak attempt to send a message.

This chapter won't turn you into the next Andy Warhol. It won't even make you creative if you aren't already. But what it will do is detail layout issues for ads, brochures, and designs that work and why they work. Most importantly, you'll discover enough techniques to keep other designers from using your work as the example of bad taste.

"Rules" of good design change for different types of print material. The techniques for developing print ads in certain cases may not work if you're designing brochures or catalogs. At the same time, the rules for designing a corporate brochure for an architectural firm might be wildly different than creating a brochure for a video game company. And then you have to consider the reason why I hated art classes while growing up: quality in art is ambiguous. Who's to say what the "rules" are to good design? What appeals to me may not appeal to you, so who's to say who is right?

The answer is that those philosophies are fine for the starving-artist, stand-up-for-principal anarchist in you. But this is the real world, and for better or for worse, quality in art is defined by the client and how much money your work will make for them—and for yourself.

Follow the tips in this chapter as general guidelines, not rules carved in stone. Mix and match them with your own creativity. You should then be able to create print projects that succeed every time.

GENERAL LAYOUT ISSUES

The place to start is where the most of the common mistakes are made, and often where you have the most room to make a great impression.

WHAT YOUR READER SEES

Because of conditioning that we all got during our early school years, we are used to seeing a printed page in a certain way. Typically an English-language reader views a page from the upper left to the lower right. Consider the examples of advertisements in Figure 4–1. Figure 4–1 (a) is well laid out, allowing the reader's eye to start where it would naturally fall on the page, and from there providing a path to follow through until the contact information at the bottom. Figure 4–1 (b) is not as successful—the main message is at the bottom, typically the last place a reader's eye will fall. There is no clear path for the reader's eye to follow. It even appears to have been laid out upside down.

(a)   (b)

Fig. 4–1   The ad on the left properly leads the reader's eye, while the ad on the right is poorly laid out, providing no path for the reader's eye to follow.

Fig. 4–2   These ads for Da Vinci Coachworks are each two-page spreads. Notice how the tag line and the product are on the right-hand side, where the reader's eye will likely first fall.

This rule changes a bit, however, if your ad or project is more that just one page. When a reader sees the inside of a brochure, or an ad that is a two-page spread, the eye will usually see the information on the right-hand page first. Check out the two ads for Da Vinci Coachworks that we discussed back in Chapter 2 and shown again in Figure 4–2. Both are two-page spreads that have appeared in magazines. This type of ad is best laid out along different rules than one-page designs. In both, the tag line and the limousines were placed deliberately on the right side of the ad because the reader's eye is more likely to fall there first. The ad on the left show the path the reader's eye follows. Look for yourself the next time you are flipping through a magazine. The majority of you will find your eyes focusing on the right side of the spreads first.

Unfortunatley, since they are not reproduced full size, your eye probably went to the upper-left first instead.

MAKING THE MESSAGE PROMINENT

When you design a printed page, one of two things will be dominant: the message or the design. Your first thought might be that either option is effective. However, making the design of your page very noticeable probably indicates that it was either done poorly or incorporates such fantastic artwork that the message is lost. Creating print pieces is not a cheap venture, and your client is not paying you to draw attention to the design, whether it's good or bad. They'll be paying you to assemble a page that will prominently display their message.

That's not to say that you can't be cute, clever, or creative in your work—if you're not, then you probably won't be hired again. But it does mean that there are some basic techniques you can follow and mistakes you can avoid to help bring the message of the piece into the spotlight.

HEADLINES

The word headline naturally conjures images of the *New York Post* screaming today's latest news to the world. But a headline isn't limited to newspapers. Many of the pieces that you print will have headlines in them to give the reader a short and sweet idea of the topic they are about to read about. Headlines can accomplish this if they are worked into your piece properly and in such a way as to be effective. Issues like size, proportion, and placement are all important matters that can be the difference between successful headlines and project-killers.

The Importance of Size and Proportion

Take a quick look at the headline in Figure 4–3 (a). The main message is obvious. It holds the most value to the reader not only because of its placement in the area where the reader's eye is most likely to fall, but also because it is the largest copy on the page. By being proportionally larger than anything else on the page, the reader has little doubt as to the message that's being relayed. In contrast, the same headline in Figure 4–3 (b) loses its message because the main headline is no larger than any other text on the page. The reader in this case has no direct clue which idea is the most important or what the message is without having to search for it.

Promotions Announced at XYZ Corp.

John Doe Looks Forward to New Responsibilities

Text Goes Here. Blah Blah blah. Text Goes Here. Blah Blah blah.
Text Goes Here. Blah Blah blah. Text Goes Here. Blah Blah blah.
Text Goes Here. Blah Blah blah. Text Goes Here. Blah Blah blah.
Text Goes Here. Blah Blah blah. Text Goes Here. Blah Blah blah.
Text Goes Here. Blah Blah blah. Text Goes Here.

(a)

Fig. 4–3   The top headline screams to the reader because of its size relative to the rest of the page. The headline in the bottom example doesn't work because it's no larger than the subhead and therefore loses its emphasis.

Promotions Announced at XYZ Corp.

John Doe Looks Forward to New Responsibilities

Text Goes Here. Blah Blah blah. Text Goes Here. Blah Blah blah.
Text Goes Here. Blah Blah blah. Text Goes Here. Blah Blah blah.
Text Goes Here. Blah Blah blah. Text Goes Here. Blah Blah blah.
Text Goes Here. Blah Blah blah. Text Goes Here. Blah Blah blah.
Text Goes Here. Blah Blah blah. Text Goes Here.

(b)

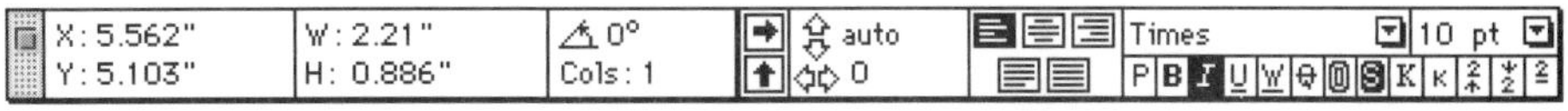

| X: 5.562"
Y: 5.103" | W: 2.21"
H: 0.886" | ◿ 0°
Cols: 1 | ➡ ⇕ auto
⬆ ◇ 0 | ▤▤▤ Times ▾ 10 pt ▾
▤▤ P B I U W ⊖ ⊚ S K κ ⨦ ⨦ ² |

Fig. 4–4   The Measurements palette.

WORKING IN XPRESS: FONT SIZES

To set the font size in QuarkXPress:

◆ Choose a pre-set font size from the Style –> Font or the pull-down menu in the Measurements toolbar (shown in Figure 4–4).

◆ Highlight the current size (default is usually 12 point) and type in your desired font size.

To change the size of type that is already set on the page:

◆ Highlight the desired text in your document and change the font size with either of the two methods described above.

◆ Click on the textbox to activate it. With either the Move tool or the Item tool, click and hold on one of the corner handle bars of the textbox. Hold the Command + Option + Shift (Ctrl + Alt + Shift in Windows) keys and drag inward or outward. Your type will change size proportionally.

Release the Option key (Alt in Windows) to resize your text without constraining the proportions.

Length

Headlines are meant to provide a short, concise overview of what the message is. As an overview, be careful to keep them short and to the point—the idea is to hook the audience and make them want to investigate further. Long headlines, like the one in Figure 4–5 (a) are counterproductive. The sheer length of this headline will cause the reader to work harder than they'll want to just to find out what the piece is trying to say. The brief and to-the-point headline in Figure 4–5 (b) is far more effective.

In short, try to keep your headlines to a maximum of two lines—the quicker you can make your point the better off your piece will be.

(a)   (b)

Fig. 4–5   The headline on the left is too long—the reader needs to work too hard to extract the message. The headline on the right, though, is more effective, as it is concise and to the point.

Headline as Graphic

Because headlines are meant to be short, there is no reason why you can't have a little fun with them and make them "pop" off the page. While you would never want to use Photoshop to lay out the entire body of your text, there are plenty of instances when Photoshop can be put to work for your project's headlines. Figure 4–6 shows a flat headline placed in QuarkXPress, and its improved counterparts with the headline manipulated in Photoshop. You can see the obvious difference and how the latter samples create more excitement for the reader.

IMAGERY

Imagine reading this book without the benefit of the figures. You not only would be largely bored but you may also have trouble visualizing many of the points that you're reading about (While I'm proud of this book, I'll be the first to admit I'm no Stephen King. There is no surprise ending here.) How you treat your images and have them interact with the copy will play a major role in how your message and aesthetic content are displayed.

Tips and methods for actually curing photographs will be detailed in the next chapter. The following information deals only with how images relate to the overall page.

Super Bug–Zap!

New Super Bug-Zap Kills Insects Fast!

Text Goes Here. Blah Blah blah. Text Goes Here. Blah Blah blah. Text Goes Here. Blah Blah blah. Text Goes Here. Blah Blah Blah blah. Text Goes Here. Blah Blah blah. Text Goes Here. Blah Blah blah. Text Goes Here. Blah Blah Blah blah. Text Goes

Here. Blah Blah blah. Text Goes Here. Text Goes Here. Blah Blah blah. Text Goes Here. Blah Blah blah. Text Goes Here. Blah Blah blah. Text Goes Here. Blah Blah Blah blah. Text Goes Here. Blah Blah blah. Text Goes Here. Blah Blah blah. Text

Goes Here. Blah Blah blah. Text Goes Here. Blah Blah blah. Text Goes Here. Blah Blah blah. Text Goes Here. Blah Blah blah. Text Goes Here. Blah Blah. Text Goes Here. Goes Here. Blah Blah blah. Text Goes Here. Blah Blah blah. Text Goes Here. Blah

(a)

New Super Bug-Zap Kills Insects Fast!

Text Goes Here. Blah Blah blah. Text Goes Here. Blah Blah blah. Text Goes Here. Blah Blah blah. Text Goes Here. Blah Blah Blah blah. Text Goes Here. Blah Blah blah. Text Goes Here. Blah Blah blah. Text Goes Here. Blah Blah Blah blah. Text Goes

Here. Blah Blah blah. Text Goes Here. Text Goes Here. Blah Blah blah. Text Goes Here. Blah Blah blah. Text Goes Here. Blah Blah blah. Text Goes Here. Blah Blah Blah blah. Text Goes Here. Blah Blah blah. Text Goes Here. Blah Blah blah. Text

Goes Here. Blah Blah blah. Text Goes Here. Blah Blah blah. Text Goes Here. Blah Blah blah. Text Goes Here. Blah Blah blah. Text Goes Here. Blah Blah. Text Goes Here. Goes Here. Blah Blah blah. Text Goes Here. Blah Blah blah. Text Goes Here. Blah

(c)

Super Bug-Zap!

New Super Bug-Zap Kills Insects Fast!

Text Goes Here. Blah Blah blah. Text Goes Here. Blah Blah blah. Text Goes Here. Blah Blah blah. Text Goes Here. Blah Blah Blah blah. Text Goes Here. Blah Blah blah. Text Goes Here. Blah Blah blah. Text Goes Here. Blah Blah Blah blah. Text Goes

Here. Blah Blah blah. Text Goes Here. Text Goes Here. Blah Blah blah. Text Goes Here. Blah Blah blah. Text Goes Here. Blah Blah blah. Text Goes Here. Blah Blah Blah blah. Text Goes Here. Blah Blah blah. Text Goes Here. Blah Blah blah. Text

Goes Here. Blah Blah blah. Text Goes Here. Blah Blah blah. Text Goes Here. Blah Blah blah. Text Goes Here. Blah Blah blah. Text Goes Here. Blah Blah. Text Goes Here. Goes Here. Blah Blah blah. Text Goes Here. Blah Blah blah. Text Goes Here. Blah

(b)

Fig 4–6   Headline (a) is typeset in QuarkXPress. You can see that it's flat and unappealing. But (b) and (c) are set in Photoshop and imported as graphics. These add more "pop" to the overall layout.

File Formats

When you create images in Photoshop, save them as either Encapsulated PostScript (EPS) or Tagged Image File Format (TIFF) files. Quark will accept either format. I recommend that you use TIFFs as often as possible, with the LZW compression turned on. The compression will significantly reduce the file size without causing any harm to your file. In addition, any white in your TIFF file will be read as transparent when placed into QuarkXPress, which can be a huge benefit when you want more flexibility than you may get from a blocky photograph.

EPS files from Photoshop will let you save clipping paths, which will also extract the background from an image when you import it into Quark. However, clipping paths are somewhat annoying to make and can take some time to perfect when trying to create a clipping path around tight curves. EPSs are also usually pretty large in terms of file size.

If you're going to be bringing an Illustrator file directly into QuarkXPress, you need to save it as Illustrator EPS for use in your XPress layout.

Image Size

The size of your image is much like the size of your headline—the bigger it is, the more prominence and attention it will demand. You'll want to make the most important picture the biggest to help send your message to your readers. Figure 4–7 (a) shows a

(a)   (b)

Fig 4–7   The main image in (a) is larger then the others and adds to the message. The images are all equal size in (b) making it tougher to extract the message.

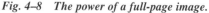

Fig. 4–8   The power of a full-page image.

layout in which the main picture, which deals directly with the central message, is the largest. The layout in Figure 4–7 (b) shows how the meaning behind the imagery can get lost if the size of the graphics is no larger than any other graphic.

One of the most effective means of sending a message is by using a full-page picture, and placing your text over it. As Figure 4–8 demonstrates, there is practically nothing more powerful than a full-size graphic jumping off a page.

(a)   (b)

Fig. 4–9   The bounding box around the image in (a) does nothing for the overall look of the layout. When the box is lost, as it is in the layout in (b), the result can be a much more effective piece.

THE SHAPE OF THE IMAGE

Images don't have to be placed in rectangular boxes. In fact, while that works sometimes, shedding the confines of a rectangular box can sometimes really add to the overall aesthetics of your layout.

Figure 4–9 shows how you can potentially improve a piece by extracting the confines of a bounding box, or by at least changing the shape to one other than a rectangle.

Don't do this too often—you don't want to make it look obvious that you're shedding the box. That will just draw more attention to the layout and less to the message, which you want to avoid.

Working in XPress: Removing the Rectangles

To remove the box from an image:

1. Create your image with a white background in Photoshop and save it as a TIFF file.
2. In Quark make a picture box and choose File –> Get Picture.

3. Navigate through your system and locate the desired graphic.

4. Open the Color palette by choosing View –> Show Colors.

5. With the picture box still selected, choose None from the Color palette.

or

1. Create a path around an image in Photoshop and save it as an EPS with a clipping path.

2. Import the image into a Picture Box in XPress and select None from the Color palette.

or

1. Create an illustration in Illustrator and save it as an Illustrator EPS.

2. Import the image into a Picture box in XPress.

3. Choose None from the Color palette.

To create a nonrectangular shape for a box:

1. Choose any of the predetermined shape tools, the Freehand Picture Box tool, or the Bézier Picture Box tool from the Tools palette.

2. Create your customized picture box.

3. Import your graphic.

DIRECTION OF YOUR IMAGE

Which direction your image faces may play a subconscious role in how your reader sees your layout. Look at the layout in Figure 4–10 (a). Notice that because the person in the picture is facing away from the rest of the layout, the reader's eye is drawn away from the page and away from the main message.

This is fixed by simply flipping the picture around and having the person face the other direction—*toward* the page, as shown in the layout in Figure 4–10 (b). A reader's eye, while tending to follow a fairly obvious trail from the upper left to the lower right of a page, can be distracted and take a detour because of the power of a graphic facing the wrong direction.

Working in XPress: Flipping Images

To flip an image in XPress:

1. Select your image by clicking on it.

2. Make either the Item tool or the Content tool active in the Tools palette.

3. Choose Style –> Flip Horizontal or Flip Vertical.

(a)

Fig. 4–10 The subject in (a) is facing in the opposite direction of the page, pulling the reader's eye out and away from the primary message. The subject in (b) has been flipped to face the ad. The reader is no longer tempted to look away, but rather continues to focus on the message.

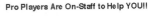

(b)

Fortunately, the example in Figure 4–10 was a simple one, which didn't require any additional work when flipped. The example in Figure 4–11 is a different story, however. When that image is flipped, the words in the picture are backwards. Be careful not to flip images in XPress that could look backward. If this happens, you'll want to do your flipping in Photoshop, where you can use the Rubber Stamp and other tools to fix the problem (More on this in Chapter 5).

MORE THAN WORDS CAN SAY: THE FONT FACTOR

There are literally thousands of font styles on the market and thousands more created every year. The array of styles that are available can be a dizzying barrage destined to make you wonder why so many had to be created in the first place. The answer is a simple one: The font style that you choose can play as much of a part in your design and overall project success as your images and copy.

Figure 4–12 shows a couple of different print pieces, each directed to a different audience. In each project design, the font works specifically to relay the message not only in the words they spell out, but in the way they each look.

Fig. 4–11   Flipping pictures haphazardly can have horrendous results. In cases like this, where words would appear backward, do your flipping in Photoshop, where you can make necessary corrections.

(a)

Fig 4–12   Different fonts help a piece appeal to different audiences.

(b)

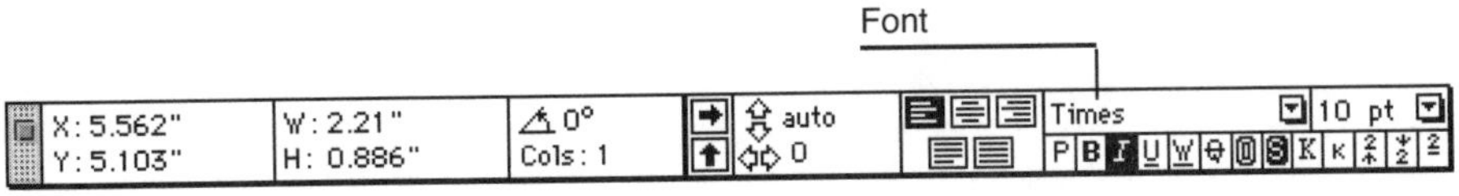

Fig. 4–13   The Measurements palette.

◆ The brochure cover in Figure 4–12 (a) is hoping to gain a child's attention for the toy it's promoting. The font (XPSchooner) used is whimsical and fun, and is likely to attract a child's eye from the shape and positioning of the letters.

u The image in Figure 4–12 (b) is a poster aimed at factory and warehouse employees. One of the fonts utilized here is a sans serif lettering (Frutiger), clear and bold to catch the attention of an audience that may only have a moment to look at the piece, as well as for a bilingual reader who may use English as a second language.

The shape and style of the fonts chosen help send the message as powerfully as the words they form.

Working in XPress: Font

To set a font:

◆ Choose a font from the Type menu or the font pull-down menu in the Measurements pallet, as indicated in Figure 4–13.

or

◆ Highlight the font name that already appears and type in the name of your desired font (provided that your desired font is installed in your system).

To change the font of existing type:

◆ Highlight the copy on the page whose face you want to change. Make your change using either of the methods described above.

BEER BEFORE LIQUOR, NEVER SICKER — THE TROUBLE WITH MIXING FONTS

One of the detriments of having so many fonts on the market is that when they're in the hands of overzealous designers, there can be an explosion of bad taste. As Figure 4–14 demonstrates, when too many fonts are added to the mix, the results can be too cluttered or busy and attention can be drawn to the different styles, detracting from the underlying message.

As a general rule, try to avoid using more than three fonts on any page or spread and only one font for the body text. This will help keep the focus on the message and off the design problems.

Fig 4–14   Too many fonts make the page almost unreadable.

USING LOGOS

Undoubtedly the most important part of any printed piece you'll work on, the client company's logo unquestionably needs to be placed in a prominent location on your page. The logo is the mark that will hopefully stay in the forefront of your audience's mind and represents every product or service your client's company provides.

Where on the page the logo appears will likely determine whether the logo is effectively placed for recognition, hidden in the fray, or so obtrusive as to be an annoyance. Figure 4–15 shows three different print pieces. Figure 4–15 (a) has the logo of the company the same size as all of the other images and has so many of these images that the logo becomes lost. Figure 4–15 (b) has the logo so big and prominent on the page that it detracts from the message of the piece. Only Figure 4–15 (b) uses the logo wisely, placing it at the bottom of the page at the end of the path that the reader's eye will follow. There is enough white space (*white space* is detailed later in this chapter) to keep the logo isolated and easily viewed, yet it doesn't take away from the message that the rest of the piece is delivering. It is also important to keep the logo, especially if it doesn't contain the company's name, close to the company name and address.

Fig. 4–15 The ad in (b) most effectively displays the most important factor—the company's logo.

ORGANIZING THE MESSAGE

There is, of course, plenty more to know than what's been covered so far. Headlines, images, and fonts are just elements of your piece—how you organize these elements is vital as well. A bold, well written headline in a beautiful font will prove a wasted effort if the rest of your work is disorganized. On that point, it's important to note that there could be more at stake when it comes to the issue of organizing your page—while a poor or misplaced headline could keep your audience from missing your message, a poorly organized page could have a far more devastating effect. Just like a disorganized web site, a disorganized ad or brochure sends a message that the company itself is disorganized and lacks a necessary attention to detail.

There are steps you can take to help the organization of your page, including breaking up the copy and message with the use of subheads and bullet points, understanding layout balance, wrapping text around various elements, and, maybe most importantly, using white space wisely.

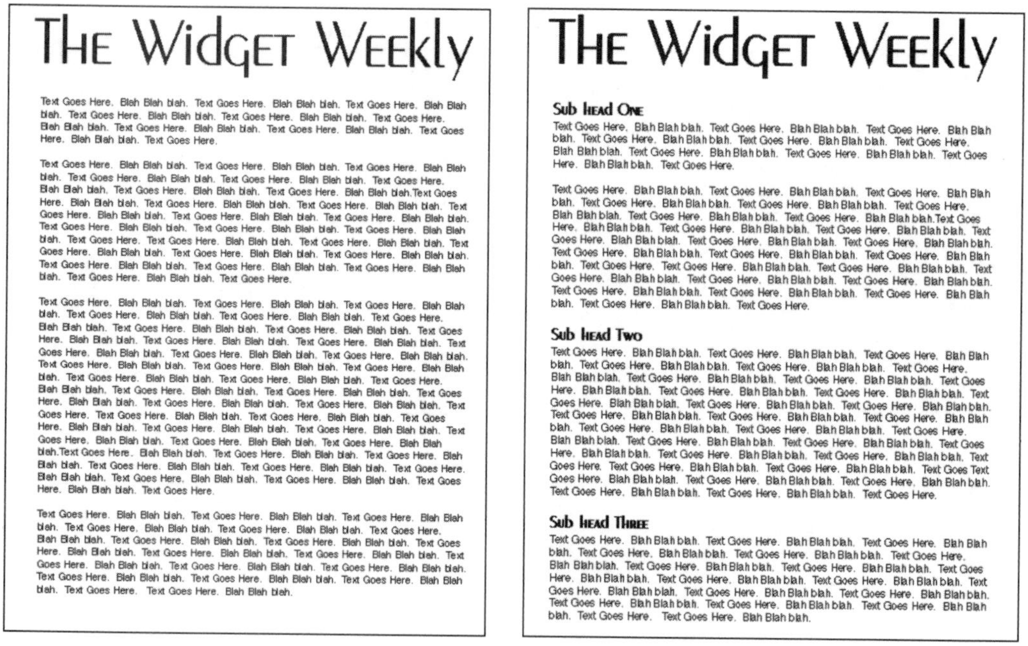

(a) (b)

Fig. 4–16 Subheads help break up the monotony of text and make the page more visually appealing.

USING SUBHEADS

Figure 4–16 (a) shows the page of a newsletter that has a good, prominent headline, but the body copy has been placed as one solid text block. The only thing that breaks the copy up at all in a few instances are paragraph breaks. You can see that there is so much text on the page bunched together that it ceases to look like copy at all. Instead it looks like one large gray block.

Subheads, inserted conservatively throughout the blocks of your copy, can help break up the text and make your page more readable and visually appealing. The layout in Figure 4–16 (b) shows the same newsletter with subheads. You can see how the entire page benefits from being broken up.

SIZING AND SPACING SUBHEADS EFFECTIVELY

In order for your subheads to be effective, you need to create them in such a way that they're serving an obvious purpose. Often this can be accomplished by separating them from the body text and the headlines with a different color, font, size, or other distinguishing factor.

Text Goes Here. Blah Blah blah. Text Goes Here. Blah Blah blah. Text Goes Here. Blah Blah blah. Text Goes Here. Blah Blah blah. Text Goes Here. Blah Blah blah. Text Goes Here. Blah Blah blah. Text Goes Here. Blah Blah blah.

Subhead One

Text Goes Here. Blah Blah blah. Text Goes Here. Blah Blah blah. Text Goes Here. Blah Blah blah. Text Goes Here. Blah Blah blah. Text Goes Here. Blah Blah blah. Text Goes

blah. Text Goes Here. Blah Blah blah. Text Goes Here. Blah Blah blah. Text Goes Here. Blah Blah blah. Text Goes Here. Blah Blah blah. Text Goes Here. Blah Blah blah.

Subhead One

Text Goes Here. Blah Blah blah. Text Goes Here. Blah Blah blah. Text Goes Here. Blah Blah blah. Text Goes Here. Blah Blah blah. Text Goes Here. Blah Blah blah. Text Goes

Fig. 4–17 Playing close attention to spacing helps differentiate the subhead from the body copy.

In addition, pay close attention to the placement of your subheads from the underlying copy. As Figure 4–17 proves, keeping the space above and below the subhead consistent can make your subhead seem more like an overemphasized portion of your text and less like the topic of a new section. The subhead in the bottom layout of Figure 4–17 is more effective because it has unequal space around it. There is extra space preceding it to separate it from the end of one paragraph and associate it as the topic of the next.

Placement on the Page

For aesthetic reasons, you're going to want to watch the placement of your subheads on your page. Two very common errors that can detract from your design and layout are displayed in the examples on Figure 4–18. The first problem is that one of the subheads starts at the very bottom of the page, followed by only a couple of lines of text. It gets lost here, and can easily be overlooked by the reader.

The second problem with Figure 4–18 is one of pure design only and there may be many cases in which it can't be fixed at all. The subheads, because of various lengths of the underlying copy, appear at odd locations on the page, breaking up the flow more than may be necessary.

The example in Figure 4–18 (b) solves both of these problems. By paying attention to the small details and making adjustments to the line spacing of the copy, as well as adding a few other discrete elements, I was able to move the subheads so that they line up next to one another and contribute to the overall harmony of the page.

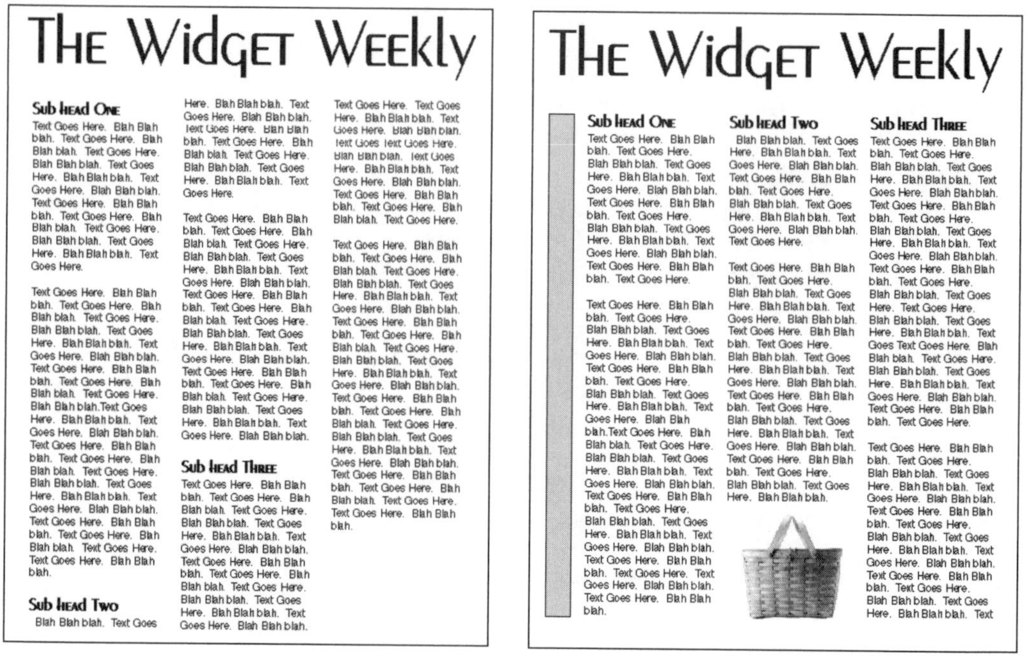

(a)

(b)

Fig. 4–18   A little planning and tweaking can turn the layout in (a) into the layout (b), where the look is helped by the even placement of all subheads.

BALANCING THE PAGE

Keeping your page in balance is a key factor in keeping it organized. Figure 4–19 (a) shows a page in which all of the images and heavy text fall on the left-hand side. The page looks uneven, though, because the right-hand side of the page looks so devoid of anything meaningful. This lopsided layout results in a disorganized feel to the piece.

A better layout is shown in Figure 4–19 (b). It keeps the page well balanced by better allocating the graphics and other elements. The readers eye is no longer distracted by the uneven placement of important pieces of the layout, but rather can follow a natural path.

UTILIZING COLUMNS

Columns can help break up your copy to be more legible. Use columns when your text is small and your layout is wide to avoid problems of your readers losing track of the line they're on. Large blocks of text, such as were seen in the layout in Figure 4–16, are difficult on the reader's eyes and tiresome to read. Creating columns will help your reader focus more on the text and help their ability to understand your message. Figure

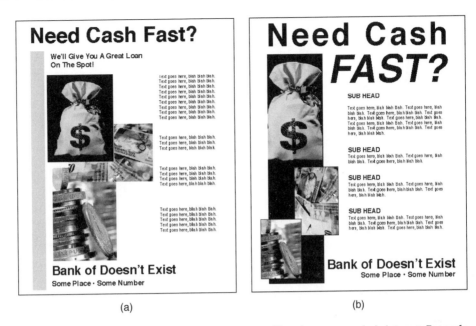

(a)   (b)

Fig. 4–19   Balancing a page is an important part of keeping your reader's interest. Properly allocating elements, or smartly using white space can help keep a page in balance.

4–18 shows the drastic improvement in the overall look of Figure 4–16 when the text blocks are broken up into columns.

Be careful that you don't get too out of control creating columns. On an 8.5" x 11" page that uses (primarily) a 12-point font, four columns will typically be as many as you'll want to have. More than four can create columns that are too narrow to be comfortable for the reader. In addition, don't draw too much attention to the layout by creating columns that are of unequal width, as illustrated in Figure 4–20. You don't need your reader to marvel at your ability to create columns—you just need to make sure that they read the copy more easily.

You can also avoid problems with columns by properly adjusting the *gutter* width. The gutter is the space in between columns. You'll usually be able to judge for yourself if the gutter width is too small or too large just by looking at it, but for general reference:

◆ Increase gutter widths as your font size increases.

◆ Decrease gutter widths as your font size decreases.

◆ Increase the gutter width (slightly) as you create more columns. Too many columns will be annoying enough without the proper spacing between them.

◆ Don't make the gutter widths too wide as it looks like your text columns don't connect to each other.

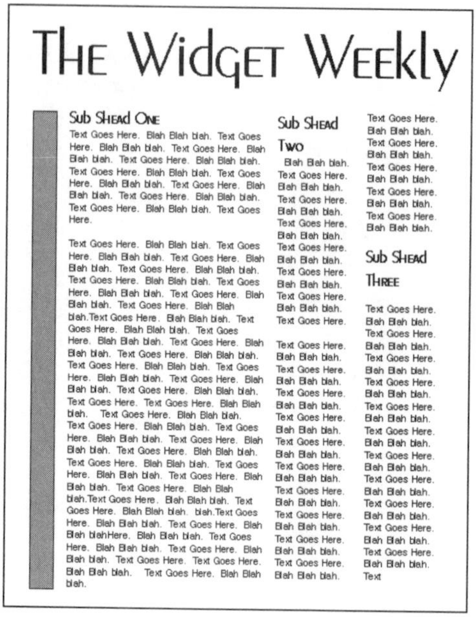

Fig. 4–20   *Unequal column widths often draw attention to the layout and away from the message.*

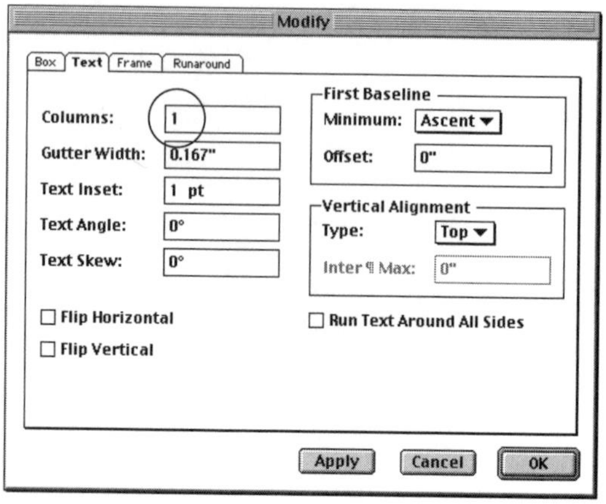

Fig. 4–21   *Use the commands under the Text tab in the Modify dialog box to create columns.*

Working in XPress: Creating Columns

To break a text box into columns:

1. Create a text box on your page. Make it large enough that you can break it up into columns cleanly.

2. With the text box selected, choose Item –> Modify. In the dialog box shown in Figure 4–21, push the Text tab.

3. Enter the amount of desired columns in the Columns value box. Set the width of the gutter space in the Gutter Width value box.

4. Click OK when through.

FASTER THAN A SPEEDING BULLET

Sure, that one was a goofy title, but it's as true in print design as it is the classic Superman comics. The truth is most people who are looking at your print ad or brochure probably won't be reading them. It's an ugly truth, but one you may as well face as quickly as possible. People have, over the years, become desensitized to the copy in most print pieces. This is due to the millions of marketing geniuses that take pride in writing such catchy phrases as "We've built a solid reputation in the industry," " We really care about our customers," or the ever-popular "We stand for quality service." (Like a company would ever write "We're incompetent, and we're proud of it.")

It's because of this desensitization to overworked and usually false copywriting that images and headlines will play such a large part in your print projects. The copy will usually be lost completely. But if you break the main parts of your copy off and organize them into a bullet-pointed list, there's a fairly good chance that your audience will glance over your ad or brochure and extract at least the main points that you're trying to get across. Consider the ads in Figure 4–22. Each is trying to get across the same information but one does it with straight copy and the other with bullet points. Ask yourself honestly what the likelihood is that you would actually read through these ads should you be flipping through a newspaper. If the answer is that you probably wouldn't, look at both ads quickly and see for yourself that a quick glance at the bullet points leaves you with at least the general idea of what the ad is trying to say.

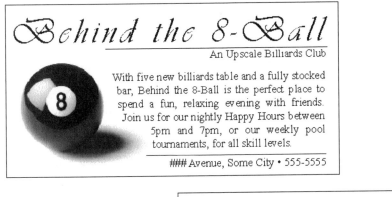

Fig. 4–22   Bullet points help deliver a message to a desensitized audience.

You may be asking at this point, what value print work has if nobody is going to read the content anyway. Well, the first answer is that if somebody is skimming through and sees a bullet point that catches their attention, then they are likely to go back and read the piece in full. But the more important reason is to leave an indelible impression of the corporate logo in the reader's mind. The more a person sees the logo, especially if it is associated with a good design, the more trust they will gain in the company and the more apt they are to take advantage of that company's products or services.

THE IMPORTANCE OF WHITE SPACE

"Minimalist" artists, in my opinion, are by and large nothing more than very talented con artists. A huge white canvas with a blue dot in the corner causes people to stare in wonder as to its deeply emotional meaning while the artist is in his million-dollar loft laughing his ass off.

But while a blue dot on an otherwise blank canvas may be nothing but overpriced crap, there is something to be said about the power of white space. *White space* is simply an area or areas on your piece in which there is no type or image—the page is left blank. Don't get confused, however, with the use of the word *white*. If the background of your piece is entirely black, then areas in which no type or images appear is still called white space, not black space. If you're printing on light blue paper, portions left empty are still called white space, not light blue space.

White space can draw attention to an area or relieve tension from crowded areas. Check out the brochure page in Figure 4–23 (a). It is very crowded and cramped—not only is it tough to find the message, but it's tough to just look at.

The other examples show the same page designed differently, with each new version taking advantage of white space to relieve the stress of the original.

◆ Figure 4–23 (b) has kept the basic layout the same but has added white space around many of the elements. This gives the headlines, body copy, and images some breathing room, and a chance for the reader's eye to focus more clearly on the topic at hand.

◆ Figure 4–23 (c) adds a significant amount of white space along the left-hand side of the page. This helps streamline the information and is more pleasing to the eye.

◆ The layout in Figure 4–23 (d) does the same but leaves a horizontal stretch of white space along the bottom of the page.

◆ Figure 4–23 (e) uses white space to bring attention to each subhead that appears in the body copy.

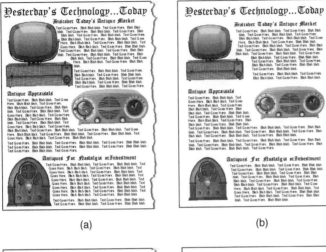

(a)   (b)   (c)

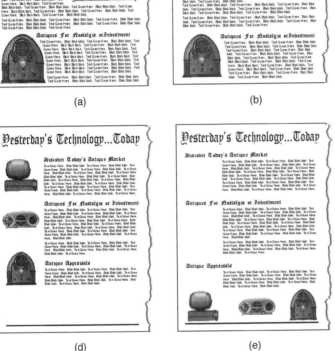

(d)   (e)

Fig. 4–23 White space is an important factor in keeping your layouts legible.

Working in XPress: Margins and Space

To set the margins for space around the perimeter of your page:

1. Start a new document by choosing File –> New. The dialog box is shown in Figure 4–24.

2. In the upper-right-hand corner, insert the desired margin measurement values.

3. Click OK. The blue outline around the edge of your canvas indicates the margins.

Unfortunately, it isn't easy to reset the margins of an existing document in Quark. This is why you need to plan your margins before you start.

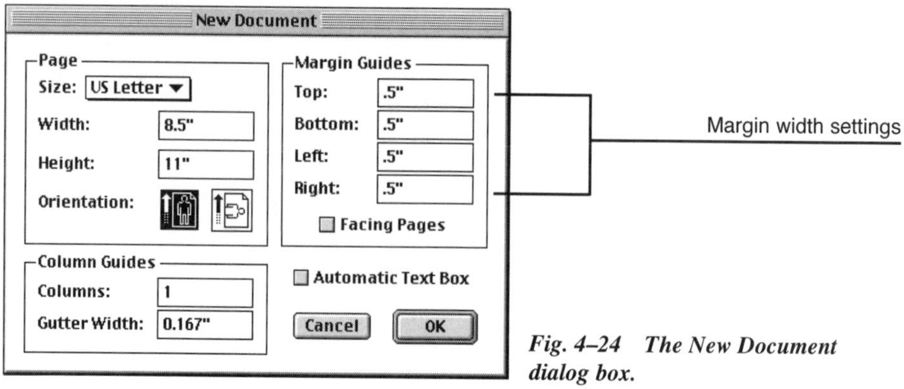

Fig. 4–24   The New Document dialog box.

To set a space holder for white space within a document:

1. Create a picture or textbox in the area that you want to preserve as white space.

2. Choose Item –> Content –> None to turn the box into nothing more than a place-holder. This will help indicate to you the areas of your page that you wish to keep empty and devoid of content as you work.

This box does not lock off your chosen area from all other content. Text or images can still appear in this area if you put text or picture boxes over it. Make sure that the space holder is always on top by selecting it and choosing Item –> Bring to Front.

AVOIDING PROBLEMS CAUSED BY WHITE SPACE

One of the primary points that was just made was that white space can bring attention and emphasis to certain areas of your document. That being said, make sure that the emphasis you bring is *desired* emphasis. White space that occurs in unwanted areas or that appears to be forced and unnatural can ruin your piece entirely. These problems most often occur in the following instances, as pointed out in Figure 4–25:

◆ At the bottom of a page when a column ends early.

◆ When there are uneven amounts of white space between elements, such as sub-heads and body copy.

◆ Gutter widths in text columns are too wide.

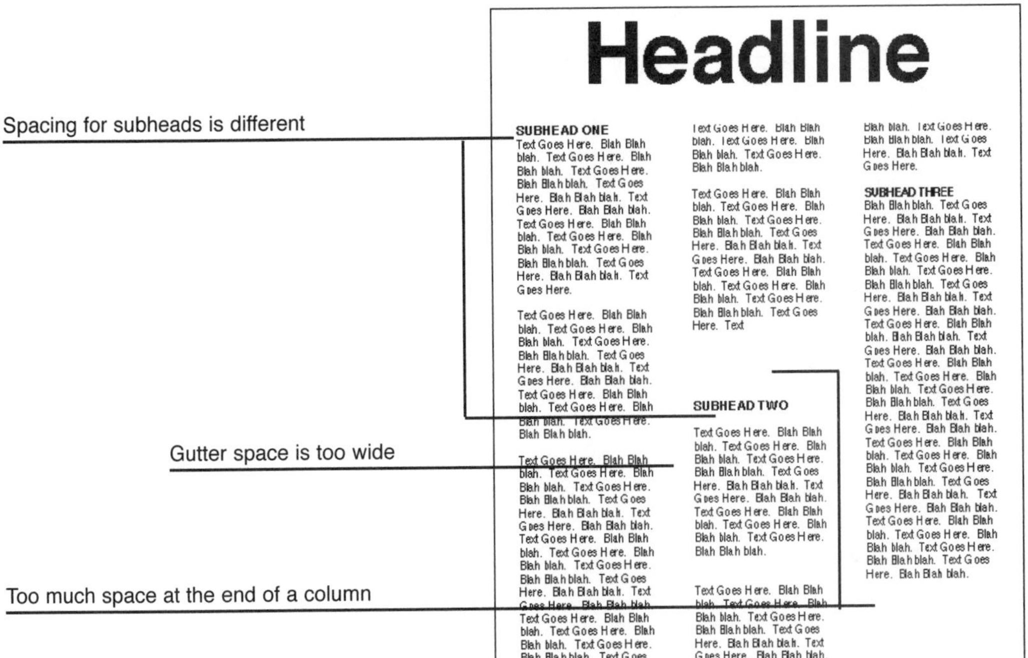

Headline

Spacing for subheads is different

SUBHEAD ONE
Text Goes Here. Blah Blah blah. Text Goes Here. Blah Blah blah. Text Goes Here. Blah Blah blah. Text Goes Here. Blah Blah blah. Text Goes Here. Blah Blah blah. Text Goes Here. Blah Blah blah. Text Goes Here. Blah Blah blah. Text Goes Here. Blah Blah blah. Text Goes Here.

Text Goes Here. Blah Blah blah. Text Goes Here. Blah Blah blah. Text Goes Here. Blah Blah blah. Text Goes Here. Blah Blah blah. Text Goes Here. Blah Blah blah.

Gutter space is too wide

Text Goes Here. Blah Blah blah. Text Goes Here. Blah Blah blah. Text Goes Here. Blah Blah blah. Text Goes Here. Blah Blah blah. Text Goes Here. Blah Blah blah. Text Goes Here. Blah Blah blah. Text Goes Here. Blah Blah blah. Text Goes Here. Blah Blah blah.

Too much space at the end of a column

Text Goes Here. Blah Blah blah. Text Goes Here. Blah Blah blah. Text Goes Here. Blah Blah blah. Text Goes Here. Blah Blah blah.

Text Goes Here. Blah Blah blah. Text Goes Here. Blah Blah blah. Text Goes Here. Blah Blah blah.

Text Goes Here. Blah Blah blah. Text Goes Here. Blah Blah blah. Text Goes Here. Blah Blah blah.

SUBHEAD THREE
Blah Blah blah. Text Goes Here. Blah Blah blah. Text Goes Here. Blah Blah blah. Text Goes Here. Blah Blah blah. Text Goes Here. Blah Blah blah. Text Goes Here. Blah Blah blah. Text Goes Here. Blah Blah blah. Text Goes Here. Blah Blah blah. Text Goes Here. Blah Blah blah. Text Goes Here. Blah Blah blah. Text Goes Here. Blah Blah blah. Text Goes Here. Blah Blah blah. Text Goes Here. Blah Blah blah. Text Goes Here. Blah Blah blah.

SUBHEAD TWO
Text Goes Here. Blah Blah blah. Text Goes Here. Blah Blah blah. Text Goes Here. Blah Blah blah. Text Goes Here. Blah Blah blah. Text Goes Here. Blah Blah blah. Text Goes Here. Blah Blah blah.

Text Goes Here. Blah Blah blah. Text Goes Here. Blah Blah blah. Text Goes Here. Blah Blah blah. Text Goes Here. Blah Blah blah.

Fig 4–25   In some cases, unintentional white space can cause problems.

Working in XPress: Guides and Rulers

To set nonprinting guides for measuring assistance:

1. Make the rulers visible by choosing View –> Show Rulers.

2. Choose View –> Show Guides. This will show you the outlines of all of your text boxes, picture boxes, margins, etc.

3. Set a horizontal guide by dragging down from the horizontal ruler (top of screen) and placing your guide near a box. Notice how the vertical location of the guide is displayed in the Measurements palette.

4. Set a vertical guide by dragging to the right from the vertical ruler (left of screen) and placing your guide near a box. Again notice the Measurements palette and the dotted line in the ruler.

5. Avoid white space inconsistencies between separate elements by choosing View –> Snap to Guides.

To change the units of measure on the rulers:

1. Choose Edit –> Preferences –> Document.
2. In the Horizontal Measure and Vertical Measure pull-down menus, select your desired unit of measure.
3. Click OK.

Keeping a good balance of white space and taking care that all the white space is deliberate, necessary, and appealing, can make all the difference in organizing your project.

KEEPING CONSISTENT

I simply can't stress this point enough. The single most important advantage I can sell to a prospective client considering my agency is the assurance that their work will be kept consistent—not only from one medium to another, but throughout each individual piece as well.

The importance of keeping consistent is part of the psychology of advertising and part of understanding how the human mind works. Now, before I get a slew of angry e-mails asking what an economics major would know about psychology, let me admit right here that I am no Dr. Joyce Brothers. Some of what I will be claiming in this section is instinct and some is general textbook knowledge. But all of it is more or less accepted as true, and it's an important lesson to learn if you want to succeed in creating quality print material.

Deliberate images are everywhere. Individuals and companies are in constant competition with each other to attract and keep the consumer's attention in an effort to increase business and/or exposure. Technology's increasing role in this barrage of information has both helped and hurt individual or corporate efforts to convey a message. The ease in which information can be delivered has helped tremendously and allowed smaller, less experienced, and less financially affluent entities to reach a broader market. However, so much information is now available that the average consumer's attention span has rapidly deteriorated from oversaturation.

Advertisers can go about penetrating the consumer psyche in many ways. Shock value, which can stir controversy and hopefully garner media exposure, gains attention by presenting a message so far outside our everyday comfort zone that it may offend a certain segment of the audience. Take, for example, the outlandish campaign for Outpost.com, currently running on television at the time of this writing. With the goal of driving traffic to the site, the Outpost.com commercials show the president of the company sitting comfortably in an armchair, discussing with the viewer that he intends to publicize the existence of the site. In one spot, they do this by catapulting live hamsters at a wall, trying in vein to get them through a small hole (at the end, one lucky hamster actually makes it). In another spot, they publicize the site by releasing a pack of hungry wolves on a school marching band. The entire campaign generated a lot of noise—some people were offended (I laughed, privately, while insisting to my more liberal friends that I was very sad for the hamsters), awards were won, but at the end of the day, traffic to the site increased tremendously. It's the value of shock.

Even more ads try to shock their audiences with sex, vulgarity and innuendo. But while there will always be the odd example of a jarring concept that succeeds in its efforts (these are usually the ones than can mix a clever concept with a shocking vehicle), by and large these efforts are starting to show signs of fading. The bottom line is that it has become increasingly difficult to shock the general populate any longer (after the stained blue dress, what more is left to shock us?). Other avenues that advertisers have taken to grab our attention include extreme humor, endorsements by movie stars and athletic stars, and creating a sense of urgency (such as with a one-day sale). But regardless of which vehicle is used in any given piece or campaign, the consistency factor remains a vital component.

Consistency not only gives an audience the impression that the advertising company is organized, but also helps to ingrain the logo, tagline, and corporate image into the reader's mind. The more deep-seated it becomes, the greater the chances that increased recognizability will turn into increased sales. A reader who sees a company's web banner ad may not notice it with more than a passing glance, but should they come across the same company's print ad in a magazine, they may stop for a second look. The consistency between the two ads can cause a spark of subconscious recognition that will inevitably lead to increased sales.

This section will discuss how to maintain consistency within a printed piece, as well as how to continue the consistency through other media vehicles as well.

CONSISTENCY WITHIN A PRINTED PIECE

There are a number of different steps you can take to ensure consistency in your printed piece. Consistency through image types, fonts, and general layout issues will help make your printed piece successful.

Image Type Consistency

While there will always be exceptions to this rule, you'll typically want to stay away from mixing image types too often. The type of image you use can say just as much as the image itself. Image types can come in many forms. Illustrations can be mechanical, detailed and serious, or cartoonish and campy. Photographs can be hard-edged and claustrophobic, or stand-alone for wraparound text. These are just a few types of images; of course there are others. Figure 4–26 illustrates how these work together on a page to create an effect. Figure 4–26 (a) uses the cartoonish illustration to promote a fun, happy message. Figure 4–26 (c) shows a page with a more corporate appeal through the hard-edged photography.

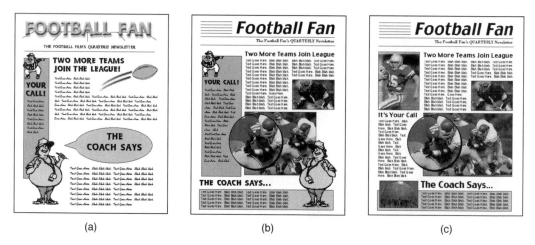

(a)   (b)   (c)

Fig. 4–26   Consistency in image types can project a certain mood about your piece.

Each of these examples works as individual pieces for their particular markets. However, if you mix the various image types together into one piece, such as shown in of Figure 4–26 (b), you can see that the result is a mish-mosh of confusion, with the reader left wondering what, if any, point there is to this piece.

As I said earlier, there are always going to be occasions when you can break this rule. An illustrated logo, for example, can still work well with an otherwise photographic piece. But generally speaking, you should in most cases avoid having too even a mixture of different image types, and instead strive for consistency throughout each piece with a consistent image type.

Font Consistency

Fonts are fun to play with, no question. As I explained earlier in this chapter, fonts come in literally thousands of shapes and sizes. I won't rehash the point here, save to say that besides being careful not to use too many fonts in a piece, you should make sure that the fonts you do use are consistent throughout. For example, don't write one subhead in Helvetica and another in Courier. As shown in Figure 4–27, it will make your project look disjointed and disorganized. Fonts can be used to convey themes, ideas, and emotions just as much as the words they write, but they can become distracting if used incorrectly.

Working in XPress: Style Sheets

Creating consistency with type can be a difficult process, especially for long pieces such as books, newsletters, or even brochures. You can make your life vastly easier by taking advantage of QuarkXPress's style sheets. Style sheets allow you to collect all the attributes that you may set for a portion of text and save them under one name. An example of this would be a style sheet called "subhead," which would change text to

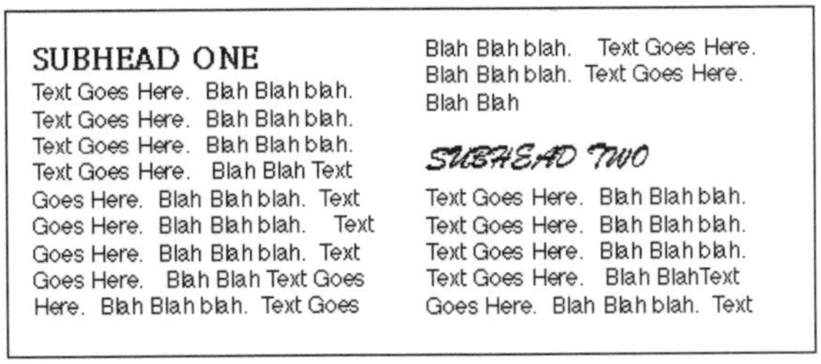

SUBHEAD ONE
Text Goes Here. Blah Blah blah.
Text Goes Here. Blah Blah blah.
Text Goes Here. Blah Blah blah.
Text Goes Here. Blah Blah Text
Goes Here. Blah Blah blah. Text
Goes Here. Blah Blah blah.   Text
Goes Here. Blah Blah blah. Text
Goes Here. Blah Blah Text Goes
Here. Blah Blah blah. Text Goes

Blah Blah blah.   Text Goes Here.
Blah Blah blah. Text Goes Here.
Blah Blah

SUBHEAD TWO
Text Goes Here. Blah Blah blah.
Text Goes Here. Blah Blah blah.
Text Goes Here. Blah Blah blah.
Text Goes Here.   Blah Blah Text
Goes Here. Blah Blah blah. Text

Fig. 4–27   When fonts, such as these subheads, are not consistent, it will detract from the piece.

Times, italics, bold, 14 point with an extra 14 pts. space preceding it. Every time the "subhead" style is applied to a paragraph, the words in that paragraph would receive that treatment. Although it may be a bit of a pain at the beginning to create the style sheets, it will save you immeasurable amounts of time over the long haul. Imagine having to set each subhead individually with those specs every time you needed to? If your project is more than a page long, it could take you hours.

In addition, suppose that when you are through with the piece, you present the final draft to your client, who then says that he's had a change of heart, and can you un-bold all the subheads? If you had used style sheets, you only have to make this change once and the effect will be universal.

In earlier versions of QuarkXPress, you could only create style sheets for paragraphs. With Version 4, you can create style sheets for individual characters as well. This can be useful when you only want one letter or word in a particular area to be different, such as the product name to be universally bold throughout a long brochure or catalog.

To create a paragraph style sheet in XPress:

1. Create a new text box and write a paragraph.
2. Format the paragraph the way you want it with desired font sizes, bold, underlines, etc.
3. Place the cursor anywhere in the paragraph.
4. Choose Edit –> Style Sheets to access the dialog box shown in Figure 4–28.
5. Choose Paragraph from the New pull-down menu to access the Edit Paragraph Style Sheet dialog box shown in Figure 4–29.
6. The formatting that you had set in your paragraph will be already entered in the Description box. Enter a name for your Style Sheet.
7. Click Ok, and then click Save from the original dialog box.

To set a style on an existing or new paragraph:

Place your cursor in the desired paragraph.

1. Choose View –> Show Style Sheets.
2. Click on the desired style to change the formats of the paragraph.

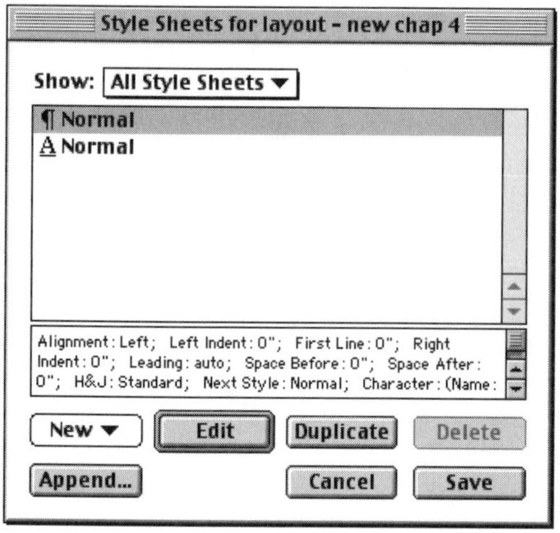

Fig. 4–28   The Style Sheets dialog box.

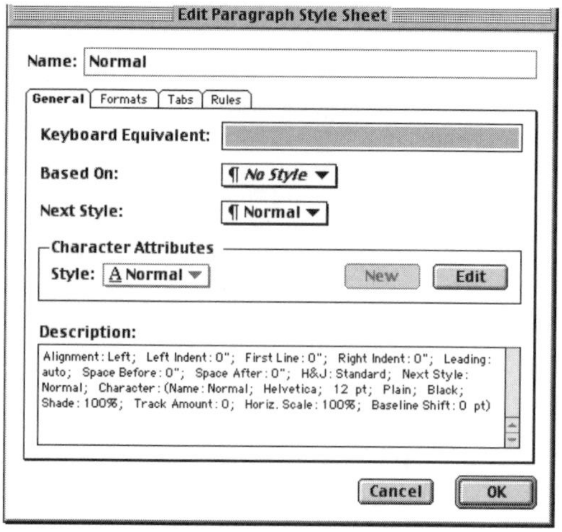

Fig. 4–29   The Edit Paragraph Style Sheet dialog box.

Two-Page Spreads

The trick to maintaining consistency over two page-spreads, such as in the inside pages of a brochure, is to forget that there are two pages. If you don't do this, you could end up with two single pages that would each look fine on their own, but which work against each other when put together in the same spread, as demonstrated in Figure 4–30. You can avoid these problems by treating the spread as one complete page rather than just two singles put together. The exception here is the point discussed earlier in this chapter: because your spread will likely be folded in the middle, the reader's eye will usually fall on the right side upon opening it, rather than fall on the upper left as it would in a single-page piece.

Working in XPress: Adding Pages

To add an additional page for a spread:

1. Make sure the document is set up for spreads by choosing File –> Document setup and clicking on the Facing Pages checkbox.

2. Choose View –> Document Layout to access the dialog box shown in Figure 4–31.

3. Drag the Blank Single Page to the main body of the dialog box and place it where you would like it—either to the left or right or top or bottom of the existing page, marked "1." The new page will be marked "2."

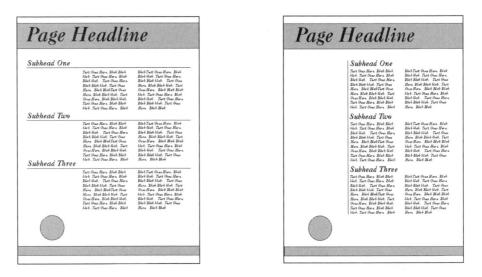

Fig. 4–30   *Separately, each page is attractive and works well. But when put together as a spread, the layout types clash. Spreads should be treated and designed as one page.*

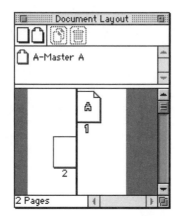

Fig. 4–31   The Document Layout palette.

Before you design a two-page spread in which the graphic elements overlap the fold, make sure you read Chapter 3. It's important to understand the concept of printer's spreads vs. reader's spreads and how to separate your pages so that they lay out properly off the press.

Consistency Throughout Other Media

Since this book is primarily about preparing your files for print work, it may strike you as odd that I'm including this small section on dealing with other media outlets. But that's because this book is not really about digital prepress as much as it's about making money, and there is plenty of money in maintaining the consistency of your piece through various media.

Some of the other media outlets you can prepare for include the Web, CD-ROM, and video. Figure 4–32 shows how the same theme can be transferred from one medium to another, in this case between print and Web. Try to keep the following tips in mind to leave yourself the option of offering your clients other media:

◆ Develop a design that will look equally clean in other media as it does in print. Heavy colors and intricate collages that look great coming off the press may be too large in terms of file size if used on the Web.

◆ Thin lines, as part of a corporate theme, can give a very sophisticated look to a brochure. But watch for these lines to give you problems if you try to transform them to video. Very thin lines can seem to jump and be distracting when viewed on a TV screen.

◆ Animated GIFs, such as rotating logos, are in abundance on the Web. If you create one, make sure that the movement is for aesthetics only and not a necessary part of the message. It will, obviously, be impossible to recreate the motion on paper when you go to print.

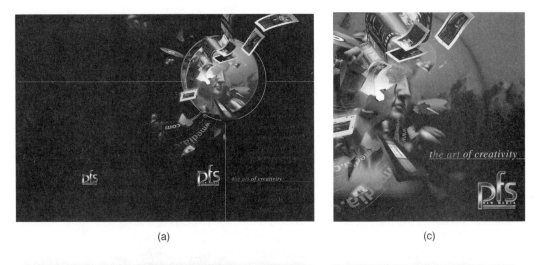

(a)

(c)

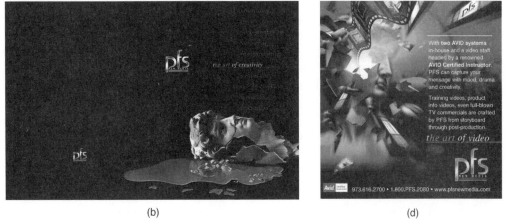

(b)

(d)

Fig. 4–32   The "David" has become a running theme for my agency, PFS New Media. He appears consistently throughout everything we put our name on, including print material, magazine ads and our website (a) Pocket folder design. (b) Brochure cover design. (c), (d) Magazine ad designs. (e) Website.

(e)

◆ If you're using subheads in your printed piece, write them in such a way that they can also be used as buttons or page topics on a future web site. This will allow you to keep your message consistent as well as the theme and layout.

◆ Create an Action in Photoshop to easily change the resolution of your images down to 72 ppi for media in electronic format. Chapter 1 of my other book, *Web Photoshop To Go*, discusses how to set an action.

Beyond Consistency: Interactivity through Multiple Media

If you are prepared to go the extra step and offer your clients more than just print media, you can play one against the other to heighten consumer interest. Advancements in technology allow you to have a lot of fun while gaining an audience. For example, let's say that you are building a web site for your client, with a print ad campaign in popular magazines to advertise the existence of the site. You could simply run ads that screamed the web address and hope to increase traffic, or you could use technology to your advantage.

What if the print ads offered readers a "secret password" to plug into the company's web site? The reader could then access the site and plug the password and their personal info (name, address, etc.) into a form on the web site. When the web site recognizes the password, they could be told that they would get a special discount on their next purchase of the company's product, or a free t-shirt, or whatever. By fusing the two media together, you have created a greater incentive for people to visit the site, increased the chance of corporate exposure to the audience, and created an easy way to track how many people have responded favorably to the print ads.

Of course that is just one idea. There are many other combinations and cross-media incentives you can come up with that can prove to have a positive effect. By understanding other avenues of advertising besides just print, you are opening up your clients to heightened exposure to a global audience. You are also opening up yourself to the possibility of increased revenue and client loyalty.

STANDARD ISSUES

So far we've covered some major aspects of designing a well-thought-out layout for a printed piece. But just like David and Goliath or Tom and Jerry, sometimes the littlest things can be the most powerful. Don't neglect to pay close attention to the standard details, such as rules, shadows, spacing, etc. If these are off, your entire piece could look out of whack.

Using Vertical and Horizontal Rules

Rules are used primarily to separate portions of your page, such as in between columns to increase legibility, or to add emphasis, like underlining a subhead. Because

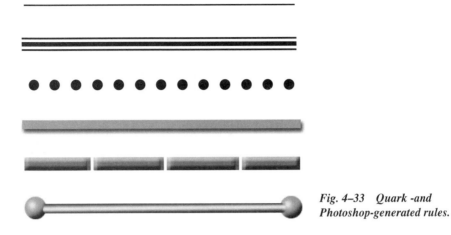

Fig. 4–33   Quark -and Photoshop-generated rules.

there can be so many variations of rules, it's important to choose a type that will work with your page layout, instead of fight against it.

If used correctly, rules can add sophistication to your piece and help keep it organized. Rules don't have to be simple black lines—they can be far more complex, intriguing, active, ugly, exciting, in fact, anything that can be made into a relatively straight line can be used as a rule.

Types of Rules

There are far too many types of rules to get into, but a quick review of a few can only help in making your decision as to which you should use. Figure 4–33 shows a number of different types of rules. The first three in the figure are standard QuarkXPress rules, while the latter three were custom created in Photoshop.

The classic solid rule, the first in the figure, is typically used to create an air of sophistication and organization. The dotted or dashed line rules can also help organize your page but are more often associated with perforations. They could make your reader think that they are meant to "cut along the dotted line."

The other rules in the figure, created in Photoshop, were created with the theme of the piece already in mind and will work in conjunction with the other graphics to create an appealing layout.

Proper Rule Sizes (Thickness)

Don't allow your rules to fight with the other portions of your page. They should be there to help readability, not become a main design feature. Figure 4–34 (a) provides an example of a page in which the rules between the columns are simply too thick. Upon first glance the reader sees the rules before anything else, and may not even know that one text column is a continuation of the other.

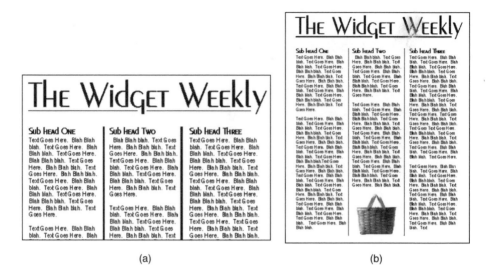

(a)   (b)

Fig. 4–34   The vertical rules on the left are too thick, and the horizontal rule is almost invisible. The layout on the right uses rules that add to the design, without detracting from the message.

Too far in the other direction can be just as bad, with the horizontal rule under the headline being so thin that is completely muted. In this instance it serves no purpose and may even be mistaken for a scratch in the film, rather than an intentional underline.

Figure 4–34 (b) shows the same page with more reasonable rules. Now the columns look organized and the rules add to the aesthetics instead of grabbing center stage. The horizontal rule below the headline emphasizes the message instead of being lost in the shuffle. By creating the thickness of your rules to be properly proportional to the page layout they are in, you allow the rules to work for the page and help the reader.

Proper Rule Sizes (Length)

Deciding on the best length for your rules can often really enhance the look and feel of your layout. Although tastes will always differ, you'll probably find more success if your rule lengths are set deliberately to work with each other or with other parts of your page.

For example, Figure 4–35 (a) shows two places on a sales sheet where horizontal rules are used. In both areas, the rules seem to be of random length. They don't necessarily detract from the page but they're not adding much either. Figure 4–35 (b) shows the same page with both horizontal rules the same length regardless of the surrounding elements, which helps to separate off the portion in between. Figure 4–35 (c) constrains the lengths of the horizontal rules to the length of the prominent item of the page closest to each rule. This not only helps to separate off the central portion but it also adds a decorative addition to the layout.

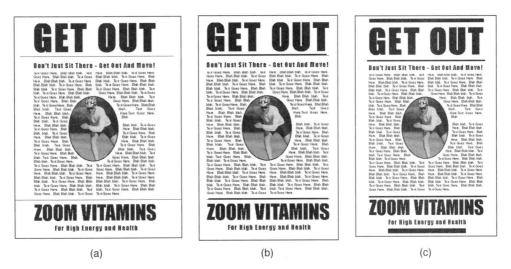

(a)   (b)   (c)

*Fig. 4–35   (a) Random length rules can be pointless or even hurtful to your piece. (b, c)
Better uses of rule lengths.*

Working in XPress: Working with Rules

To create a horizontal or vertical rule in QuarkXPress:

1. Choose either the Line tool or the Orthogonal Line tool from the tool box, shown
   in Figure 4–36. The Line tool will let you make a rule at any angle, while the
   Orthogonal Line tool will only allow you to create rules in a straight line vertically, horizontally, or diagonally at a 45 degree angle.

2. Draw a line by clicking in one area and dragging in the direction you wish to have
   your rule. The longer you drag, the longer your rule will be.

3. By default, your rule will be a thin black line. Change the look of the rule by choosing a weight from the Line Style pull-down menu in the Measurements palette, as
   shown in Figure 4–37, or from the Style –> Line Style menu item.

**The Measurements palette changes when you are working with lines
rather than text.**

4. Change the thickness of the rule by choosing a preset thickness value from Style
   menu or the Line Width pull-down menu on the Measurements palette, also shown
   in Figure 4–37. Or highlight the value shown and insert your own value manually.

5. If you know the exact length that your rule should be, you can set it by customiz-
   ing the measurement settings in the palette, as indicated in Figure 4–37. The X1
   and X2 values show where the rule starts and ends horizontally, while the Y1 and
   Y2 values show where the rule starts and ends vertically.

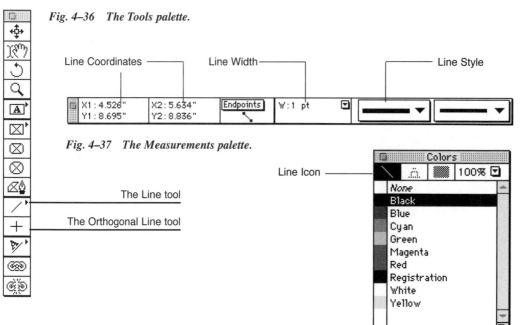

Fig. 4–36   The Tools palette.

Fig. 4–37   The Measurements palette.

Fig. 4–38   The Colors palette.

To change the color of a rule:

1. Select the desired rule by clicking on it.
2. Open the Colors palette shown in Figure 4–38 by choosing View –> Colors.
3. Select the Line icon in the palette.
4. Choose from any of the provided colors that appear in the palette. Mixing custom colors are explored later in this chapter.

To move an existing rule:

1. Select the desired rule by clicking on it.
2. Activate either the Item tool or the Content tool from the Tools palette.
3. Use the arrow keys to make short moves, one pixel at a time, or your mouse for more drastic moves (to use your mouse, you'll have to have the Item tool activated). Or, enter the desired starting and ending points on the Measurements palette.

Don't Go Crazy with Rules

It's easy to get carried away with rules. Don't. Too many rules can make your page look messy and distract the reader's eye. Ease up on rules and try to use them only when necessary for emphasis or organization.

WORKING WITH BOXES

Boxes are great tools for drawing attention to specific areas of your work. They help isolate areas of information and imply a heightened sense of importance for their contents.

Box Borders

Unless you have a specific reason directly related to the overall concept, keep the borders thin and simple. As Figure 4–39 shows, borders that are too thick or fancy draw too much attention to the borders themselves at the expense of the box's contents.

Thin boxes around photographs that are light in color can be helpful in making the picture stand out from the page, as demonstrated in Figure 4–40. A thin, black outline is usually just enough to add contrast between a light blue sky in a picture and the white of the paper behind it.

Fig. 4–39   Boxes that are too ornate and thick can draw too much attention away from the message.

Fig. 4–40   A thin black outline around light-colored photos can help them "pop" off the page.

The opposite is not always true, however. If your photograph is dark, lying on a black background, a thin white border will stand out as the primary object, much like a neon light in the dark. Figure 4–41 shows an example.

Working in XPress: Creating Box Borders

To put a border around a box:

1. Select the desired box by clicking on it.

2. Choose Item –> Frame to access the dialog box shown in Figure 4–42.

3. Enter a value in the Width value box or choose a preset width from the pull-down menu.

4. Choose a border design from the Style pull-down menu.

5. If you want to color your border (please don't—that always looks cheesy), choose a color from the Color pull-down menu.

Fig. 4–41   A thin white border on a dark background can be too jarring.

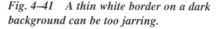

Fig. 4–42   The Frame dialog box.

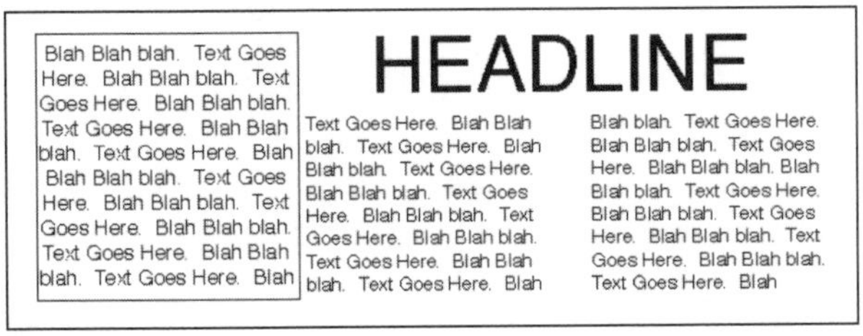

HEADLINE

Blah Blah blah. Text Goes Here. Blah Blah blah. Text Goes Here. Blah Blah blah. Text Goes Here. Blah Blah blah. Text Goes Here. Blah Blah blah. Text Goes Here. Blah Blah Blah blah. Text Goes Here. Blah Blah blah. Text Goes Here. Blah Blah Blah. Text Goes Here. Blah Blah Blah blah. Text Goes Here. Blah

Text Goes Here. Blah Blah blah. Text Goes Here. Blah Blah blah. Text Goes Here. Blah Blah blah. Text Goes Here. Blah Blah blah. Text Goes Here. Blah Blah blah. Text Goes Here. Blah Blah blah. Text Goes Here. Blah

Blah blah. Text Goes Here. Blah Blah blah. Text Goes Here. Blah Blah blah. Blah Blah blah. Text Goes Here. Blah Blah blah. Text Goes Here. Blah Blah blah. Text Goes Here. Blah Blah blah. Text Goes Here. Blah

Fig. 4–43   Text can feel cramped if there is not enough margin inside and outside of boxes.

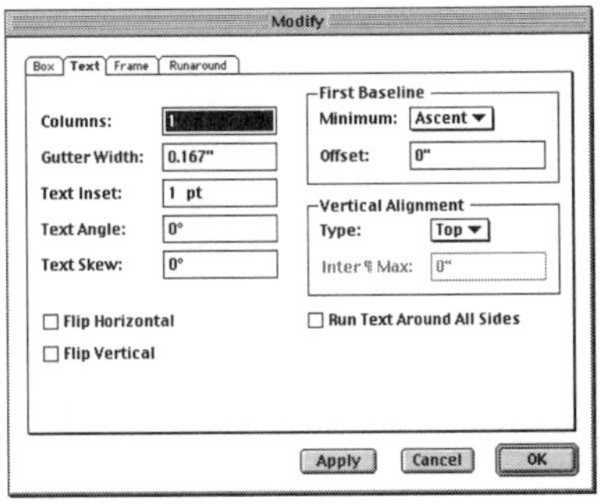

Fig. 4–44   Set the Text Inset value for margin space inside your boxes.

Box Margins

If you are going to use a text box with a border, make sure you leave enough room on both the inside and the outside. As Figure 4–43 Shows, text that is on the inside of the box but is too close to the border can feel cramped and crowded. At the same time, any text that is running next to your box on the outside needs to have a good margin also or it will look sloppy and hard to read.

In both of these cases, you'll need more of a margin the larger your font size is. As a general rule, start off with a .125" margin when working with fonts up to the standard 12 points. Add an additional .125" for each 10-point font size increase.

Working in XPress: Setting Box Margins

To set a margin inside of a box:

1. Select the desired box by clicking on it.

2. Choose Item –> Modify to access the dialog box shown in Figure 4–44.

3. Select the tab marked Text.

4. In the Text Inset value box, enter the distance from the edge that the text will lie. This will create a margin between the box edge and the copy.

To create space between the box and the remainder of the copy on your page:

1. This will seem a bit archaic, but there's really no better way to create space between a box and its surrounding copy. Choose the Picture Box tool from the Toolbar.

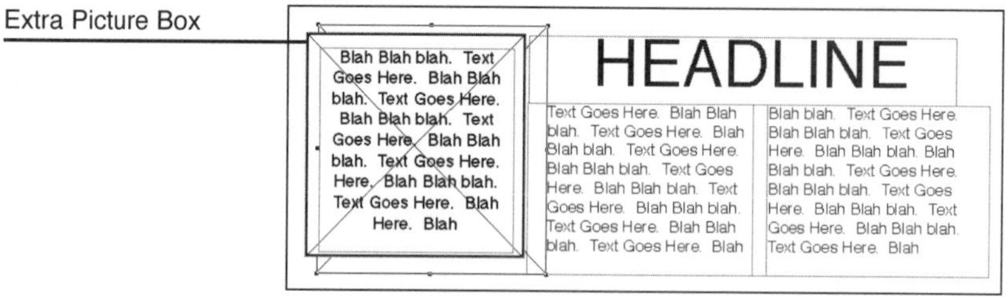

Extra Picture Box
Blah Blah blah. Text Goes Here. Blah Blah blah. Text Goes Here. Blah Blah blah. Text Goes Here. Blah Blah blah. Text Goes Here. Here. Blah Blah blah. Text Goes Here. Blah Here. Blah
HEADLINE
Text Goes Here. Blah Blah blah. Text Goes Here. Blah Blah blah. Text Goes Here. Blah Blah blah. Text Goes Here. Blah Blah blah. Text Goes Here. Blah Blah blah. Text Goes Here. Blah Blah blah. Text Goes Here. Blah
Blah blah. Text Goes Here. Blah Blah blah. Text Goes Here. Blah Blah blah. Blah Blah blah. Text Goes Here. Blah Blah blah. Text Goes Here. Blah Blah blah. Text Goes Here. Blah Blah blah. Text Goes Here. Blah

Fig. 4–45 Use another picture box to create a margin outside of the box

2. Drag a new picture box around the box that contains your contents. Make sure it overlaps the edges of the space that you want to create.
3. This new box will be white and will cover your original box. To choose your original box (now hidden behind your new box for the margins) hold down the Command + Option + Shift (Ctrl + Alt + Shift in Windows) keys and click in the area of your box. You can tell when it is selected by the handle bars.
4. Choose Item –> Bring to Front. Figure 4–45 shows an example of what all this will look like.

Box Shapes

The word "box" invokes thoughts of rectangular shapes. Boxes don't have to be rectangular, though. Standard boxes can take many different shapes, including circles, ovals, beveled corners, etc. QuarkXPress 4.0 has even included the ability to let you create practically any shape text and picture box you can imagine.

Use these box shapes at your discretion, but be careful not to get too "cute." Different-shaped boxes can get old very quickly and make your page difficult to read. If you are going to use an odd-shaped box, consider using it with photographic content rather than text. You can see from Figure 4–46 that the customized box around the picture is appealing and adds to the overall look of the image. Figure 4–47, on the other

Explore The Countryside

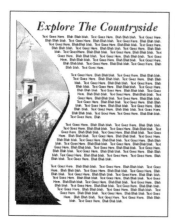

Fig. 4–46 Customized box shapes can look good around photographs…

IKE THE OWL SAYS:
SO REMEMBER WHAT IKE SAYS THE NEXT TIME YOU LITTER!

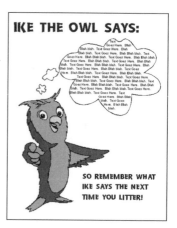

Fig. 4–47 …while they can make text more difficult to read.

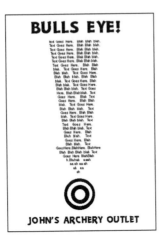

Fig. 4–48   Custom-shaped text boxes work when there's a purpose.

hand, shows that when the custom box is around text, particularly if it uses vertical indents, it becomes a bit harder to read.

Try to use shaped boxes for copy when the shape serves a specific purpose. In the ad in Figure 4–48, the shape of the box helps to mold the overall message of the page and becomes part of the design.

Working in XPress: Creating Box Shapes

To change the shape of an existing box:

1. Select the desired box by clicking on it.
2. Choose Item –> Shape and select the box shape of your choice from the menu.

To create a curved box shape:

1. Choose either the Rounded-Corner Picture Box tool or the Oval Picture Box tool from the toolbar, as indicated in Figure 4–49.
2. Drag in your canvas to create your new box.

To create a unique picture box shape:

1. Choose the Freehand Picture Box tool from the toolbar.
2. Holding the mouse button down, drag your cursor around the canvas drawing a shape by hand.
3. Close the shape either by dragging the line back to its starting point or by simply letting go of the mouse button (a straight line between the place you let go and the starting point will appear to close the shape and create a box).

or

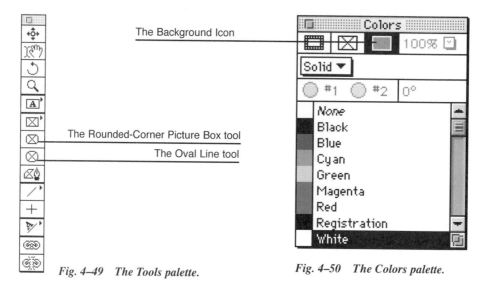

The Background Icon

The Rounded-Corner Picture Box tool

The Oval Line tool

Fig. 4–49   The Tools palette.   *Fig. 4–50   The Colors palette.*

1. Choose the Bézier Picture Box tool from the toolbar.
2. Create a box by drawing a straight or curved path between a series of endpoints. Read Chapter 5 for more details on working with the pen tool.

USING COLOR IN YOUR BOXES

Using a background color can help separate your box from the rest of the page. Be careful, though, not to make the color too dark if you're overlaying black text on it—it could be hard to read. Eventually, if your box background is too dark, you'll have to use white type.

If your using white type on a dark background, use a thick, clean font like Helvetica Bold, instead of a thin serif font like Times. White text on dark backgrounds can cause trapping problems, which could ultimately make your copy look blurry. For more information on traps, see Chapter 1.

Working in XPress: Putting Color in a Box

To fill a box with a color:

1. Select the desired box by clicking on it.
2. Open the Colors palette by choosing View –> Show Colors.
3. Click on the Background Color icon in the palette as indicated in Figure 4–50.

4. Click on your desired color from the palette. This will fill your box with that color.

5. Change the opacity of the background color by selecting a percentage from the Opacity pull-down menu in the Colors palette or by highlighting the percentage currently filled in and manually typing your desired opacity percentage.

6. Create a gradient if you want by choosing a type of gradient fill from the pull-down menu. It will be marked Solid by default.

7. Choose a color with the radio button set for 1. Click the radio button next to 2 and choose another color. The box will now be filled with that gradient.

JUSTIFYING TEXT

Justification refers to the side of a text body in which all words are flush to the same point. For example, the lines in this book are flush to both the left and right margins—it creates a squared-off appearance. Your main choices will be between left-only justified text and left and right justified text. Centered and right-only justified text will mostly be used when the situation obviously demands it, such as using right-only justification on a business card.

It's really a toss up between left-only and left and right justification of text, and there are different schools of thought on the matter. Some people think that when text is justified on both the left and the right, the blockiness of it makes it difficult to read. Others think that the jagged right edge of left-only justification creates an unattractive appearance. Personally, I'm partial to justification on both the left and the right as often as possible. It looks neater, which inherently makes it more legible.

One of the problems with justifying text on both sides is that your program will have to force spacing in between words, which might look awkward. This is more likely to happen when you are left and right justifying text that is broken into narrow columns, such as in Figure 4–51. Because the columns are so narrow, and some of the words are so long, the spacing between the words is uneven and looks like poor workmanship. Try to lay your copy and measure your columns so that this does not become a problem.

Sometimes, no matter how much measuring you do, you're going to get stuck with gaps between words when copy is left and right justified. A way around that is to use invisible letters. For example, the text in Figure 4–51 is laid over a white background. The spacing between the words is horrible—a huge gap that's destined to draw attention. Combat this by deleting the space between the words and adding any lowercase letter. Change the color of that new letter to white—the same as the background—and the spacing between the words is vastly improved, as shown in Figure 4–52.

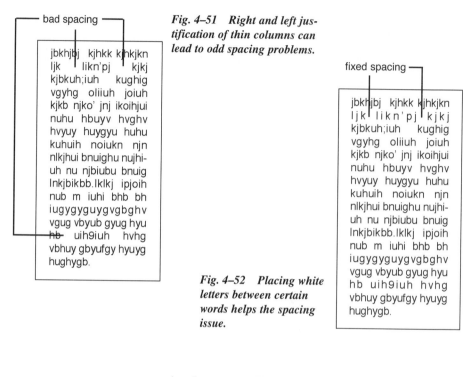

Fig. 4–51   Right and left justification of thin columns can lead to odd spacing problems.

Fig. 4–52   Placing white letters between certain words helps the spacing issue.

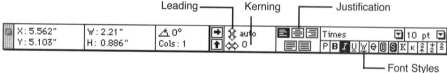

Fig. 4–53   The Measurements palette.

Working in XPress: Justifying Text

To justify copy:

1. Highlight the copy that you want to apply the justification to.

2. Choose your justification type from the Measurements palette as indicated in Figure 4–53.

BODY COPY

You can create some really good effects plus increase readability by properly working with certain text issues such as kerning, leading, and others.

Fig. 4–54   The "Sub Headline" has been kerned out for effect.

KERNING

Kerning letters adjusts the space between letters in your copy. This can be helpful if you're using fonts that may appear too close together to be read easily. It can also be helpful for creating certain types of effects, such as shown in Figure 4–54.

Working in XPress: Kerning

To change the kerning in your copy:

1. Highlight the letters that you want to kern.
2. Click on the left or right arrows in the Measurement palette as indicated in Figure 4–53. Or, if you know your desired spacing value, highlight the current value (probably Auto by defaut), and type in the value manually. Each click will kern the letters by 10 points—hold the Option (Alt. In Windows) key down to kern out by ones.

LEADING

Leading, named for the lead strips that used to be placed between lines of lead type, manipulates the space in between lines, which can be helpful when lines seem to be too close together or too far apart from each other. Leading is also an important function of separating subheads from the preceeding copy.

Working In XPress: Leading

To change the leading in a single line:

1. Place your cursor in the line *above* the copy that you want to adjust higher or lower.
2. Click on the up or down arrows in the Measurement palette as indicated in Figure 4–53. Or, if you know your desired spacing value, highlight the current value (probably Auto by default), and type in the value manually.

To set the leading between paragraphs throughout a document, use the style sheet dialog box.

HYPHENATIONS

I am just not a fan of hyphenations. At all. When they are used in a sentence—like this—that's fine. But the really bad ones are the hyphens that break up a word at the end of a line. These are always hard to read and can break up the eye's flow when reading.

Working in XPress: Hyphenations

How to change/remove the hyphenations from your text:

1. Choose Edit –> H&J's to access the dialog box shown in Figure 4–55.
2. Click Edit to bring up the dialog box shown in Figure 4–56.
3. Remove the hyphenations in your document by clicking off the Auto Hyphenation checkbox.
4. Change the value of the number of Hyphens in a Row to zero from the default of six.
5. Click OK to go back to the original dialog box.
6. Click Save to accept the changes.

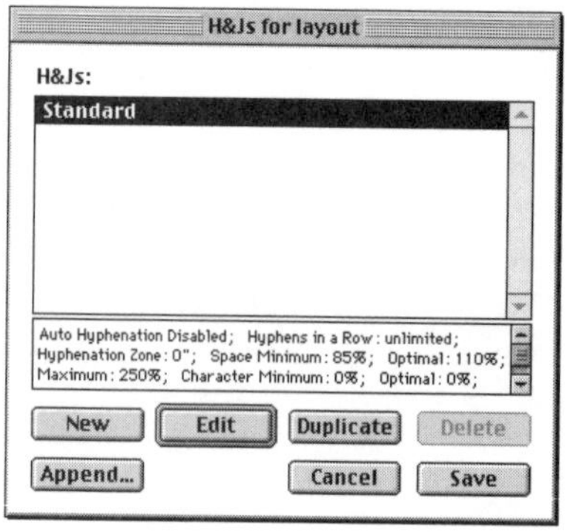

Fig. 4–55   The H&Js dialog box.

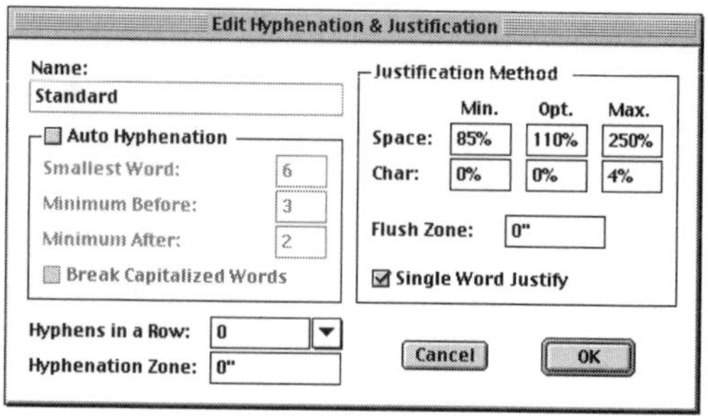

Fig. 4–56   The Edit Hyphenation & Justification dialog box.

DROP CAPS

Look at the beginning of this chapter. The first letter in the first paragraph is larger than the rest, stretching down to the second line. This is a common way to start off a document with a little flare. Quark allows you to create drop caps in practically any size you like.

Working in XPress: Drop Caps

To create a drop cap in XPress:

1. Type a sentence or a paragraph. Make sure the text box is active and that your cursor is in the desired paragraph.

2. Choose Style –> Formats to access the dialog box shown in Figure 4–57.

3. Click the checkbox marked Drop Caps to activate that area.

4. Select a value for how many characters you want to drop. XPress will start counting from the first character in the paragraph.

5. Select a value for how many lines you want the character to drop.

6. Click OK. Figure 4–58 provides an example.

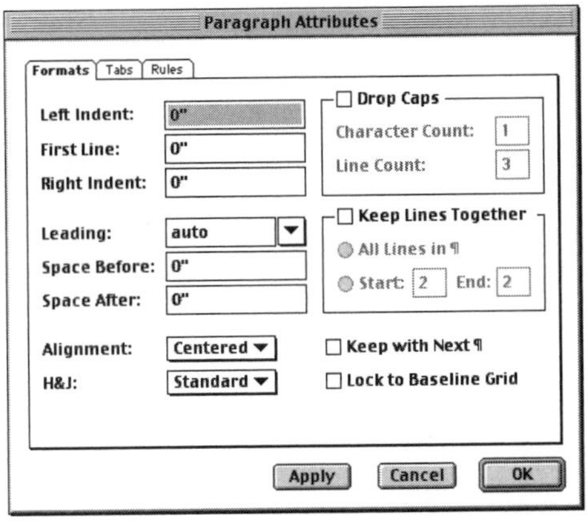

Fig. 4–57   The Formats dialog box.

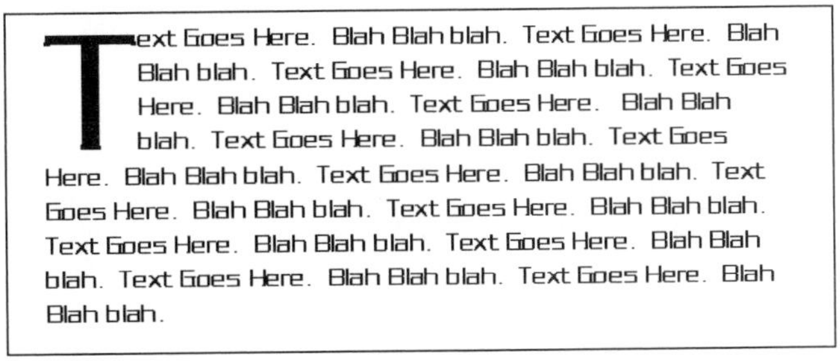

Fig. 4–58   A drop cap can add life to a paragraph.

<u>U</u>NDERLINES, **Bold,** AND *Italics*

These ar the three most commonly used type styles. Each can have a different effect on the overall page layout. None of them should be overused—in fact, as they each work to add emphasis to your page, they should be used sparingly.

Underlined text is typically the least preferable, as it makes tight text or small (12 pt. and under) copy look more crowded. Underlines are best left to other tasks, as described in the horizontal and vertical rules section earlier in this chapter.

Boldface text will usually draw the eye more immediately to a passage upon a reader's initial viewing of the page. It can be a great tool for catching attention, although it may be a bit jarring to look at, especially if overused. Avoid overusing bold text, and overusing all caps, as they may come off as shouting.

Italic text is more subtle and when buried in a paragraph, typically won't catch the eye upon first glance of the page. It does, however, add a subtle, elegant emphasis to a point while the reader is reviewing the content.

Working in XPress: Adding Style to Fonts

To add a style to text:

1. Highlight the desired text.

2. Choose a style from the options in the Measurements palette, as shown in Figure 4–53.

This option applies fake styles to the font. You should instead apply the required face of the font, rather than bolding or obliquing. Doing this, you will avoid problems when outputting to film (see Chapter 8 for more on outputting film.)

<u>D</u>ROP <u>S</u>HADOWS

The use of drop shadows has grown significantly throughout all media. In print especially, a well-made drop shadow can really help a headline or an image seem to "pop" off the page. The depth created by the shadow creates a psuedo-3D effect that lets you prioritize objects and elements on a page not only by their size, but by their relative "height" off the page.

While most page layout programs (including QuarkXPress) allow you to set a drop shadow from within the program, these are usually pretty poor. The shadow set by these programs is usually just a hard-edged, lighter version of the element that you want to cast the shadow, just a few spaces down and to the right (the universally expected placement of a drop shadow). You'll be better off if you create the drop shadow in Photoshop as explained in Chapter 5. It may take a bit longer, but as Figure 4–59 proves, the results are worth it.

*Fig 4–59   Drop shadows can add
depth to your image.*

SUMMARY

There is really no good measuring stick for good taste, if such a thing even exists at all. Good taste, as far as the print designer is concerned, rests only with how your client and the final audience will react to the piece that you create and present. This chapter has provided you with the conceptual guidelines that will help keep your clients impressed and give you a greater chance for success with your audience. Knowing what is generally accepted as "good taste," how it will translate from your computer to paper, and how to accomplish it with QuarkXPress will give you the advantage you need to get ahead in a competitive print market.

chapter 5

WORKING
WITH
ADOBE PHOTOSHOP

There are no two ways about it—if you want to be taken seriously as a graphic designer or succeed in creating print pieces with flare, excitement, and the effective use of imagery, you need to learn Photoshop. Whether you need really intense design and special effects or just simple color manipulation, Photoshop will quickly become the centerpoint of much of your work, regardless of the medium (please spare me the harassing emails pointing out that radio advertising doesn't use Photoshop—I am well aware of that).

Because of the sheer depth and strength of this program, Photoshop can take on any number of responsibilities. New users and developers of less complex projects may use Photoshop for nothing more than simple photo retouching, cropping, and color correction (that is not to say that these are unimportant features—in fact, many companies make lots of money by doing nothing more than this). Experienced designers who have the freedom to be creative in their work can take advantage of Photoshop's power to create eye-grabbing and dazzling graphic work without even touching a photograph! Of course, there are always those people who are simply unable to understand the incredible feats that Photoshop can accomplish: on first demonstrating photo-manipulation to my mother some years back, she excitedly asked "If I give you a picture of me, can you make me thinner?" I'm not sure that that's quite what Adobe's developers had in mind when they were up late programming, but that's a mom for you!

While this chapter explores the conceptual aspects of photography and graphic design as it relates to creating printed pieces, it will also provide step-by-step instruction on using Photoshop to turn these concepts into reality. It will also introduce you to

123

the exciting world of Adobe Photoshop—how it works, what the 5.0 upgrades are, and why you need to master this program. We'll explore some important color-correcting tasks, fun techniques for original graphic design work, and how to best prepare your images for your printed project.

This chapter will concentrate on using Photoshop for developing images meant for print projects. For detailed information on using Photoshop for Internet content, look for *Web Photoshop 5.0 To Go* by yours truly. And for more info on creating images for Director applications, check out Dennis Chominsky's *Director To Go* book.

WHAT CAN PHOTOSHOP DO?

The real question in terms of graphic design is "what can't Photoshop do?" Well to start with, it can't create vector images—Photoshop is a bitmap program, meaning that all images are made of a grid of pixels. It is therefore possible to have a continuous tone image with subtle gradations. The file sizes will be relatively large, however, as measured against your average vector-based file. Beyond that, when it comes to creating unanimated elements, its boundaries are somewhat limitless, and its benefits practically immeasurable.

◆ **Color Correction:** Once you have your photograph digitized in electronic format, you can use any one or a combination of Photoshop's powerful tools for manipulating the hue, brightness, contrast, saturation, darkness, lightness, and tone of your image. A more detailed description of color correction is provided later in this chapter.

◆ **Choice of Color Modes:** Depending on the type of project you're working on, you can set your image for any number of color modes, including CMYK, RGB, Grayscale and Duotone. If you're working on a piece for a specific project, say a printed brochure, for example, but do not have the necessary RAM to work in CMYK for very long (CMYK will devour more memory), you can work in one-color mode while previewing another color mode. Later in this chapter I'll discuss color modes further.

◆ **Plate Separations:** Not only can you print out each CMYK plate directly from Photoshop, but you can also manipulate the color of each plate individually in the Channels palette.

◆ **Cropping:** Each image can be cropped to order with the large array of cropping techniques available. Get rid of unwanted edges or easily crop one image to the same dimensions as another image.

◆ **Select This:** Photoshop gives you a veritable supermarket of selection tools for grabbing portions of your image. No matter how complex and detail-heavy your image may be, Photoshop will have a way for you to select your desired portion.

◆ **Layers Palette:** One of the most helpful, timesaving, and functional tools is the Layers palette. This palette acts as a storage area for each layer in your image, with each individual layer acting as a piece of acetate. You can do work on one layer without harming or affecting portions of your image that reside on other layers. And while Photoshop introduced layering in version 3.0 years ago, the rest of the world is only now starting to catch up—Dynamic HTML now allows you build web sites in layers, and Quark users are lamenting the absence of a Layers palette in the newly released version 4.0 upgrade.

◆ **Painting Tools:** All of the standard tools are available, such as the pencil, paintbrush, and airbrush tools. Other, more interesting tools in this category include the Cloning tool (aka the Rubber Stamp tool), which allows you to instantly copy, or "clone," any portion of your image to any other part of your canvas or any other open canvas.

◆ **Bézier Paths:** You can create Bézier paths with the pen tool that have multiple handles for manipulation. Plus you can create and retain clipping paths that you can import into other programs such as QuarkXPress.

◆ **Channels Palette:** The Channels palette allows you to work with each plate of color individually, as well as set spot colors and mix colors together. You can also save selections as Alpha channels within the palette for later use and creation of special effects.

◆ **Action Palette:** Simplify your life and save yourself loads of time with this palette that allows you to record and save commands and play them back, automating all kinds of tasks on any number of images. The Batch Actions feature allows you to perform commands on an entire directory full of images.

◆ **Filters:** Filters are the spirit of Photoshop. Native and third-party filters add the special effects necessary for everything from reducing noise in an image to adding a directional light source.

Of course, that's just a general description of what Photoshop can do. In practice, there are so many ways to benefit from this program that although I have been using and teaching it for years, I still find myself learning something new about it every day.

WHAT'S NEW IN VERSION 5.0

The upgrade to Version 4.0 was, in my opinion, less than spectacular. It had some new features, including the Actions palette and the fact that it forced you to use layers (which took some getting used to!) The recent upgrade to Version 5.0, however, is a graphic designer's dream! I was actually giddy for days after receiving it—gone, I guess, are the days when I was still considered "cool."

There are far too many upgrades and improvements to list and describe them all, but the following have proved to be the most functional in terms of my own work:

- **New and Improved Text Editor:** You may not want to write your annual report in Photoshop, but you sure can do a lot more with text than you ever used to. Finally you can control the kerning and leading in your copy yourself, as well as change the color of the text right from the editor. More importantly, you can set multiple font faces and sizes within one body of text. But I've saved the best for last: all text is automatically placed in its own layer and each layer retains the copy and its specifications—in other words, all copy is re-editable!

- **Layer Effects:** This new feature has leveled the playing field a bit and taken the wind out of many designers who would pride themselves on their shadow, bevel and emboss techniques. The new Layer Effects commands allow you to instantly place and customize any combination of shadows (inner and outer), glows (inner and outer), bevels, and embosses. More importantly, the layer they are applied to retains the specs for each effect—so you can go back and change the settings at any time.

- **The History Palette:** Finally, Photoshop does not limit you to just one "Undo." With the new History palette, you can have up to 100 Undos. It'll cost you in RAM, but it's worth it!

- **The Color Sampler Tool:** A new addition (one of many) to the toolbar is the Color Sampler tool. Particularly useful for the print designer, you can place up to four "marks" on your image to check the RGB and CMYK values at a particular spot. Because each "mark" holds the desired pixel, you can compare, contrast, and manipulate various areas of your image with less guesswork.

- **The Free-Form Pen:** The Pen tool, which is not unique unto Photoshop, is a difficult tool to master, no matter what program you use it in. Photoshop 5.0's Free-Form Pen tool makes it a little easier, allowing you to draw freely while placing handle bars on every turn and curve.

- **Increased Scratch Space:** As clients rapidly become more sophisticated and demanding regarding their graphic designs, the complexity and sheer size of their projects continue to grow. To help alleviate this, Photoshop has increased support by allowing for four separate drives to pitch in for up to 200GB in scratch space.

- **Spot Color:** A boon to the design community that prints two-color pieces, Spot Color Channels allow you to place spot color on an image and create a two-color separation for the commercial press.

As I stated earlier, and review more thoughly in *Web Photoshop 5 To Go*, there are plenty of other enhancements to Photoshop 5.0, including a variety of new tools. For a more complete description, check out the web site that accompanies this book, at www.phptr.com/togo.

SPECS AND REQUIREMENTS FOR PHOTOSHOP FILES

Both you and your client are going to have certain requirements and expectations for your printed pieces—at the very least you're going to demand that the colors print correctly and that the details in the image are as detailed as possible.

There are a few basic but important things you should know about your files before you begin working in Photoshop.

RESOLUTION

The term resolution is a reference to the number of pixels that make up an image, usually measured in linear (straight) inches. Basically, the higher the resolution, the more pixels there are in an image and the better the overall detail. Lower resolutions result in a reduced number of pixels and lower quality in terms of detail.

There are three different types of resolution that you need to be concerned with.

◆ **Pixels Per Inch (PPI):** Also referred to as the image resolution, this measures the number of pixels per inch in your image. The more pixels that exist in each inch, the more detail will exist in your work. More pixels per inch, though, will also equate to a larger file size.

◆ **DPI (Dots Per Inch):** also known as monitor resolution, it is the number of pixels that appear per inch on a monitor. You can usually expect that a monitor displays 72 dots per inch. Therefore, if your image is 72 ppi, it will appear as its actual size when viewed at 100 percent—one monitor pixel for each image pixel. However, if your image is 216 ppi (image pixels per inch), then a 72 dpi monitor will have to provide 3 monitor pixels for every image pixel. In this case, your image will appear three times as large when viewed on screen at 100 percent.

◆ **LPI (Lines Per Inch):** The LPI, also called the screen frequency, is a measurement of the lines per linear inch of halftone screens used to produce images. More detail on LPI and halftone screens are provided later in this chapter.

A lot of people, especially inexperienced designers, tend to confuse resolution terms and unwisely use definitions interchangeably. Don't make mistakes by taking someone literally when they want a graphic to be "300 dpi" when what they really want is "300 ppi." It is important to understand these terms to avoid confusion in the later stages of your project.

(a)   (b)

Figure 5–1   (a) The original image looks fine at 300 ppi. (b) This image, showing only a portion of the picture, is starting to break up as a result of increasing the physical size while keeping the resolution the same. (c) Reducing the physical size at the same resolution still produces a clear but smaller image.

(c)

If the resolution of an image is fixed and the physical size (width and height) is increased, the image will look blurry, jagged, or bitmapped. This is because Photoshop has to add pixels where previously there weren't any, and does not know what to fill those spaces in with. Figure 5–1 shows an example of an image that is 300 ppi, 5" x 3", and what it looks like after enlarging it to 20" x 12" still at 300 ppi. You can see how much clearer it was at the lower physical size. However, the same image, reduced down from the original size to 2" x 1.2" is still very sharp (although a little on the, well, little side). That's because when you reduce the size of the image at a fixed resolution, Photoshop simply needs to discard unnecessary information—a lot easier than adding info from thin air!

So what resolution do you use for your project? The truth is that there is no correct answer. Your best bet is to consult with your commercial printer before you start your project. But there are some good rules of thumb that you can follow:

◆   The general industry standard is to establish a resolution between 150 and 200 percent (1.5–2.0 times) of the screen frequency used by your printer. You'll have to ask your printer what screen frequency he uses (commonly between 120 lp–150 lpi). If, for example, your printer prints at 133 lpi, then your image resolution should be set between 200 and 266 ppi.

◆   Personally, in my experience I usually keep nearly all my print images at a resolution of 300 ppi. That seems to ensure a high enough quality print for superior detail.

◆ Don't Resample. Let's suppose that you have an image in Photoshop that is 100 ppi, 12" x 16". You need to print the image at 8.5" x 11", preferably at a higher resolution than 100 ppi. Open the Image Size dialog box by choosing Image –> Image Size from the main menu. Make sure that the Resample checkbox is off and change the Width from 12" to 8.5". You'll see that when you make the change, the Height automatically changes to 11.333", and the resolution increases to 141 ppi. The height is more than you wanted. You can crop a portion of it away, or otherwise manipulate it, but the idea is that you will increase the resolution of the image as you make the physical size smaller.

SETTING UP PHOTOSHOP: COLOR MANAGEMENT AND PRINT SPECS

As a designer, you may cringe at all the technical, noncreative crap that working with Photoshop entails. But it's not really crap—it's just not the fun stuff that you originally bought Photoshop for. But to really get the most out of your image when your imagination transfers from computer to paper, this section will provide some important information.

CALIBRATING YOUR MONITOR

Calibrating your monitor is kind of like flossing your teeth—you know you should do it and if certain people ask you'll usually lie and say that you have done it, but in reality, not many people actually bother. However, this is about something far more important than teeth—this is graphic design, baby! And calibrating your monitor is a way to help make what you see on your monitor look closer to what you'll see on the printed page. You only have to do it once and it's worth it.

Calibrating will bring your monitor closer to the printed page but it will never be exact, so if your client likes what they see on-screen, be wary of promises you can't keep. Even if you're working in CMYK mode, you're still seeing those colors through an RGB monitor and the colors may be off when they come off press.

The best part about calibrating your monitor is that Photoshop 5.0 makes it easy. Gone are the days when we had to hold up a piece of paper to match paper white with monitor white. Now all you have to do is the following:

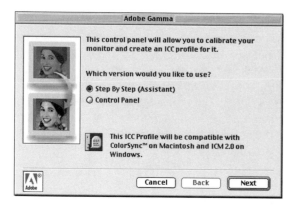

Fig. 5–2   The Adobe Gamma dialog box is your starting point for calibrating your monitor.

1. Leave your monitor off for at least half an hour before you calibrate.

2. Turn off your desktop pattern and set the background color to a light shade of gray.

3. Set the lighting in the room to the lighting that you'll most often use when working.

4. Find the Photoshop 5.0 folder in your local drive and open it. Open the subfolder named Goodies and find the folder within it called Calibration. Open this folder, and double click on the item marked Adobe Gamma.cpl.

5. The dialog box that appears is shown in Figure 5–2. The first choice you'll have to make is which version of the calibration you want to run. Step by Step is essentially the same as Control Panel, but is generally easier and will walk you through each step of the process. Make your selection and press the Next button.

6. Follow the instructions on each screen and continue to click Next when through. Most instructions will be fairly straightforward, although there may be a few questions that could stump you. If you find yourself in a position in which you don't know the answer to a question, look in the manual that came with your monitor or call the manufacturer.

ESTABLISHING COLOR SPACE

This is just not the step that anybody working with Photoshop is going to get all moony-eyed over (and believe you me, if you think this section is difficult to read, try writing about it…). But it has to be done, so let's just get to the heart of the matter and on to more interesting things.

Setting Up RGB Color Gamut

RGB has a very wide range of colors to choose from. However, the monitor that you're working on can't display all of the RGB colors—it can only show some of them. This is called its *gamut*. Photoshop allows you to work in larger RGB gamut that are

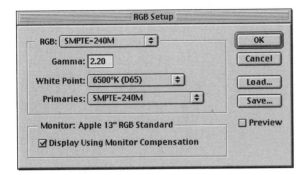

Fig. 5–3   The RGB Setup dialog box.

beyond the your monitor's color space, so that your images can utilize colors that may be able to be displayed on other monitors.

To manipulate the RGB color gamut:

1. Choose File –> Color Settings –> RGB Setup. Your monitor profile is displayed at the bottom of the dialog box, shown in Figure 5–3.

2. In the RGB pull–down menu, choose SMPTE–240M from the list provided. This is generally considered to be the best option for images that will go to print, as it includes more of the CMYK color gamut that you'll work in for printing. The Gamma, White Point, and Properties will change depending on your chosen color space.

If you're going to be doing Internet-based work, like building a web site, choose RGB for your color space, as it is used more widely as the default for many monitors, scanners, and desktop printers.

3. Click the Display Using Monitor Compensation checkbox on. This will display the images in your selected RGB color gamut in real-time.

4. Click OK when through.

Setting Up CMYK Color Space

You'll set up the CMYK color space in Photoshop to establish the way that RGB images will convert to the CMYK color mode. This is especially important if you plan on doing most of your work in RGB to save RAM and hard disk space, but will inevitably convert to CMYK for printing, and you desire a close on-screen representation of what the printed image will look like.

Establishing the CMYK color space is similar to the way you established the RGB color space:

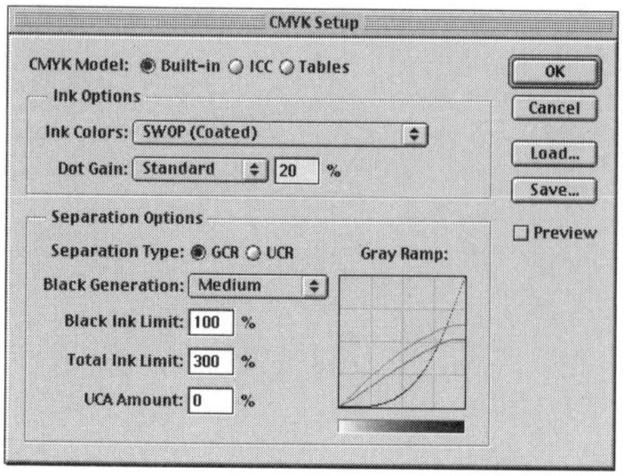

Fig. 5–4   The CMYK Setup dialog box.

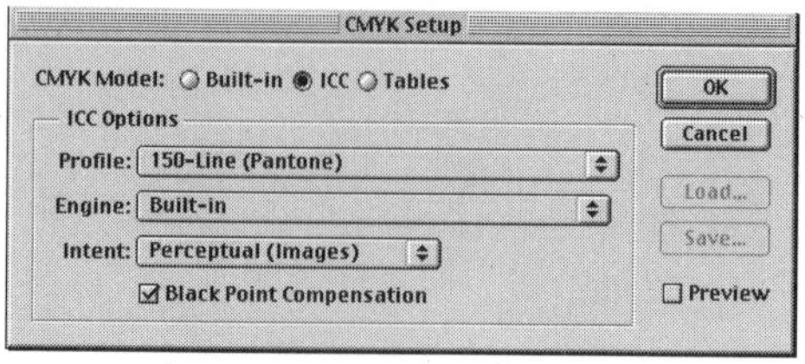

Fig. 5–5   The CMYK Setup dialog box with
ICC selected as the desired CMYK model.

1. Choose File –> Color Settings –> CMYK Setup. You will access the dialog box shown in Figure 5–4.

2. The dialog box will let you determine your own choices for how inks, printers, and paper combine to compose the final image. Unless you're really versed in color management, though, I would recommend using one of the preestablished ICC profiles instead. Do this by choosing ICC from the CMYK Model radio buttons.

3. Figure 5–5 shows the new dialog box, which has significantly fewer options. From the Profile pulldown menu, make your selection based on which printer you will be using.

4. Choose Built-in from the Engine pull-down menu to access the ICC profile interpreter that is native to Photoshop.

5. Select Perceptual (Images) from the Intent pull-down menu to maintain the way colors work together.

6. Make sure that the Black Point Compensation checkbox is checked to maintain equilibrium in neutral color value when converting from RGB to CMYK. Click OK when through.

CHANNELS: THE HEART OF PHOTOSHOP'S COLOR

At the start of every Advanced Photoshop class that I teach, I ask the students if there is anything in particular about Photoshop that they find intimidating or hard to understand. The answer is invariably "channels" (with the Pen tool running a distant second). While they may seem a bit confusing at first, you'll find that they are not only exciting to work with but will give you a great deal of control over your image once you get used to them.

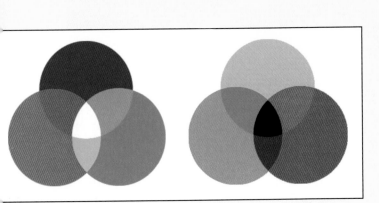

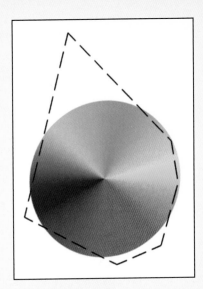

COLOR FIGURE 1
The three primary colors in light (left) and in print (right) and how they relate to each other.

COLOR FIGURE 2
The CMYK colors are not as extensive as the RGB colors.

COLOR FIGURE 3
Examples of four-color printed pieces. The four primary printing inks mix to create the illusion of other colors.

COLOR FIGURE 4

A color guide by Pantone.

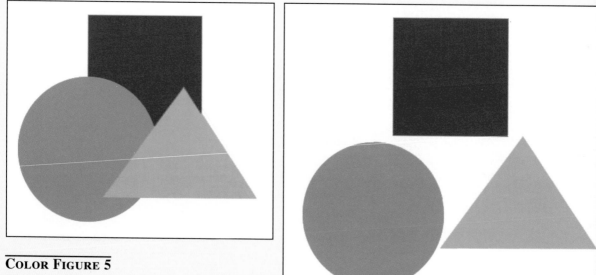

COLOR FIGURE 5

A trap is needed for the image on the left, while none is needed for the example on the right.

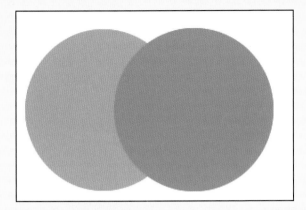

COLOR FIGURE 6

The two overlapping objects on the left need trapping as spot colors, but not when converted to CMYK, because there is a high enough percentage of Magenta and Cyan to compensate for and misregistration. The pair on the right need trapping even in CMYK mode, because there is no color that shares a high enough percentage value.

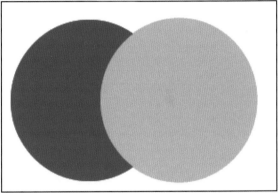

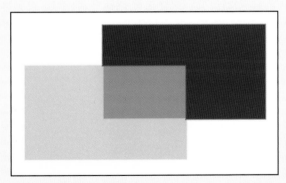

COLOR FIGURE 7

The two overlapping objects on the left show a color mix and the intersection, because they overprint. These do not need to be trapped. The overlapping images on the right are not overprinted—there is no unexpected color mix, but there is a need for a trap.

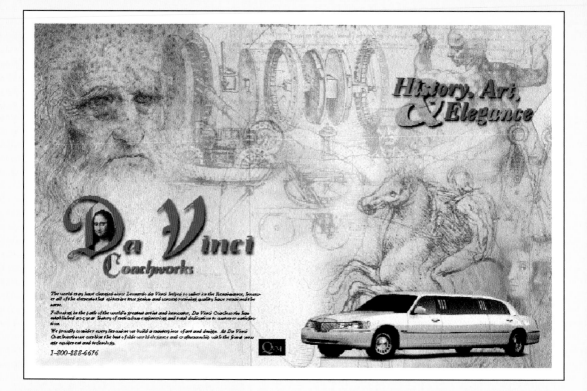

COLOR FIGURE 8

Each ad for Da Vinci Coachworks targets a distinctly different audience.

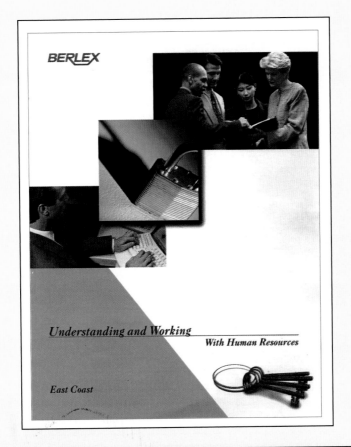

COLOR FIGURE 9

Each piece targets a different market through its use of imagery and layout.

COLOR FIGURE 10
All of the marketing pieces for my agency keep a consistent theme.

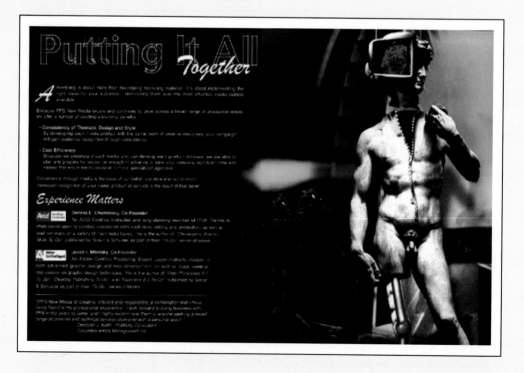

COLOR FIGURE 10
Continued

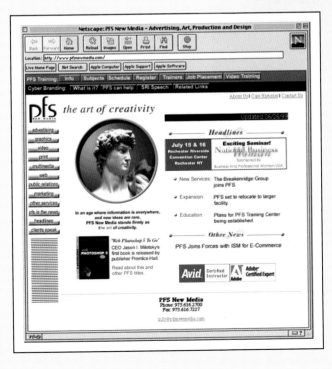

COLOR FIGURE 11
The Curves can have some wild effects on an image.

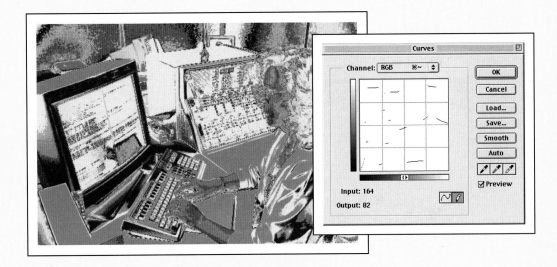

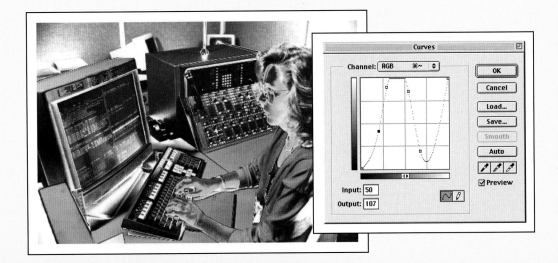

COLOR FIGURE 12

Color can play a large part in presenting your message. The poster on the left uses red to make the "hotline" standout, while the brochure below uses pastels to provide an air of sophistication.

COLOR FIGURE 13

The Color Balance can radically change your image.

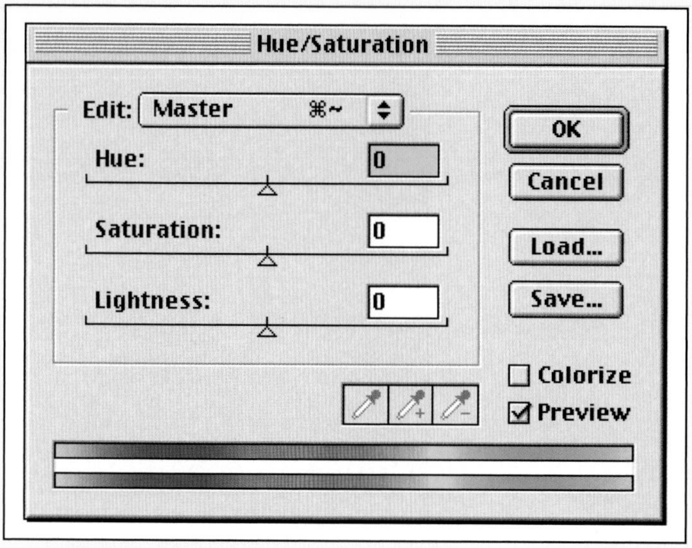

COLOR FIGURE 14
The Hue/Saturation dialog box.

COLOR FIGURE 15
This two-color brochure cover uses both duotones and spot colors.

COLOR FIGURE 16
The new Spot Channels in Photoshop 5 make it easy to create two-color images.

COLOR FIGURE 17

Duotones are not only to save money on printing—you can create some cool effects with them.

COLOR FIGURE 17

Continued

COLOR FIGURE 17
Continued

COLOR FIGURE 18
Making an image Grayscale and adjusting the level can make it more dramatic than when in color.

COLOR FIGURE 19

Changing an image to sepia tone can create a cool "aged" effect.

COLOR FIGURE 20

Add some noise to really age your image.

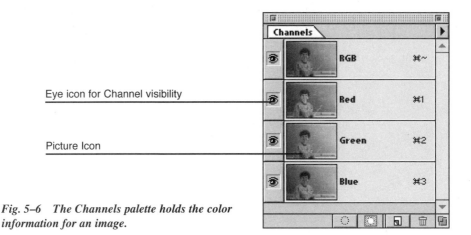

Eye icon for Channel visibility

Picture Icon

Fig. 5–6   The Channels palette holds the color information for an image.

The Channels palette, shown in Figure 5–6, is the main storage area for color information in Photoshop. Channels can also store selections that you make (called masks) so that you can refer to them later in life. But for the purposes of this section, I'll be concentrating on the color aspect (for special effects with channel masks, see *Web Photoshop 5 To Go*).

THE BARE BONES OF CHANNELS

Open the Channels palette by choosing Windows –> Channels. It will be empty until you open an image.

The color channels that appear will represent the color mode you are working in. If you are working in Grayscale mode there will only be one channel, named Black (assuming there are no Spot Color channels, as described in Chapter 6). For an RGB image, the Red, Green, and Blue channels are present, under a layer marked RGB, which is a composite of the other channels. In a CMYK image, there are separate channels for Cyan, Magenta, Yellow, and Black, all under one CMYK channel which displays a composite of the other channels.

The Eye icon on the left indicates that that channel is currently turned on or visible. You can make a channel invisible (or hide it) by clicking its eye icon. Click the empty square where the icon used to be to make that channel visible again. If all the color channels are visible, you cannot turn off the composite channel.

The highlight color in each channel indicates that all channels are currently active, meaning that any manipulation you do will affect each channel. When the composite channel is active, all of the other, individual color channels will be active as well. To make an individual color channel active, click on it. Making an individual channel active means that any manipulation you do will only take effect on that particular channel. When you activate a particular channel, you will notice the following:

◆   The highlight is removed from all channels except the active channel.

◆   The Eye icon is turned off from all channels except the active channel, indicating that they are invisible.

◆   Your image suddenly looks like a Grayscale image.

Suddenly the sirens go off and the warning flags in your head start to wave: "why, if I'm in the Red channel, is my image displaying in black and white?" Single channels will display in Grayscale primarily because it is easier to manipulate and look at an image this way. If it really makes you uncomfortable, though, you can change it to its rightful color by choosing File –> Preferences –> Display & Cursors. From the dialog box, check the box marked Color Channels in Color. Far be it from me to editorialize, but I think you'll find it much easier to leave this box unchecked and work without the color.

You can activate two channels at the same time to manipulate two distinct colors:

1.   Make an individual color channel active by clicking on it.
2.   Shift + Click on any other color channel.

When more than one individual channel is active, they are not shown in grayscale but as a mixture of the colors. When all individual channels are selected, the composite channel is also active.

HALFTONE SCREENS: WHAT THEY ARE AND HOW TO CHANGE THEM

In various other places in this book, I mention how printed pieces are made up of a series of dots. The size and spacing of these dots determine the particular shade of each color represented. In other words, a green and a light green could both be made from the same green dot—but the green color is comprised of a lot of big dots bunched together, while the light green is made from smaller dots with lots of space in between. The human eye is not usually able to see each dot without the help of a magnifying glass, so instead it sees different shades of the same color. This is called a halftone screen. The dots in the halftone screen are called halftone cells, with each cell made up of a varying number of printer pixels, organized by your output device.

Each plate in a process print piece (one for each of the CMYK values) prints a halftone at a different angle. If this is done properly, the result should look like the series of patterns (called rosettes). This type of pattern is optimal and helps our eyes see different colors and shades of colors, without drawing attention to the pattern itself. If every good thing in life has an evil counterpart, then the rosette's evil twin is the moire pattern. This pattern can be the result of a halftone being printed at an incorrect angle, and usually originates in the film provided to the printer. In Chapter 8, I emplore you not to waste your time and money setting this up on your own, but have provided instruction if you insist on it.

Halftoning is important for you to know, however in most cases your service bureau or printer will be in charge of manipulating the settings on their end. Situations may arise, though, in which you will need to make necessary changes on your end.

To change the halftone screen in Photoshop:

1. Choose File -> Page Setup. From the dialog box, push the Screens dialog box.

2. The Halftone Screens dialog box appears. To use the default settings already built into your printer, click the Use Printer's Default Screens checkbox. Leave it unchecked to manually change the following:

   ◆ **Ink:** Select which ink you want to manipulate from the pull-down menu. This option will be grayed out if your image is in Grayscale mode.

   ◆ **Frequency:** As described earlier in this chapter, the screen frequency of an image is the number of halftone cells per linear inch (lpi, or lines-per-inch). The number of pixels in each cell will determine the cell's density.

   Filling in a high number for Frequency creates a lot of small cells which will make your image look sharper, but reduce the number of shades that can be created. A smaller number for Frequency creates a fewer number of larger cells, providing more shades but a less sharp image. In most cases, you'll want to keep the frequency setting that Photoshop calculates for you.

   ◆ **Angle:** This will change the basic configuration of the lpi. Much like in the Frequency setting, Photoshop does a good job of calculating the best angle for you, so you'll most likely be best off keeping the current angle setting.

   ◆ **Shape:** You can select from up to six various shapes, although most output devices will be looking for round cells, and unless you want to create a certain effect, this is usually your best choice.

   ◆ **Use Accurate Screens:** Leave this option unchecked unless your output device utilizes PostScript Level 2 or higher. If you're not sure, check your printer manual or call the manufacturer.

   ◆ **Use Same Shape for All Inks:** Again, leave this box unchecked. Activating it will cause the same size, angle and shape specs to be used universally for all inks in an image.

You will only need to set the halftone here if you are planning on printing directly from Photoshop. Since this book is assuming that you'll be bringing files to have professionally printed, you'll most likely set the halftone screens in QuarkXPress. I have chosen to include this bit to Chapter 5, however, as Photoshop is likely to be the program tool that is most affected by an understanding of halftones.

GETTING AN IMAGE INTO PHOTOSHOP

If your specialty is web design, you'll have a lot easier time working with files and getting them into Photoshop because of the low file size requirement. Practically any desktop scanner will do. However, print is a different kind of animal and resolution is important. As explained earlier in this chapter, the resolution of an image will depend largely on the output device and medium for printing. It's worth repeating that a good resolution is 1.5 to 2 times the lpi (consult with your printer as to the lpi he'll be working with).

There are a number of different ways you can get an image into Photoshop, some of which were explored in the pre-Photoshop portion of Chapter 1.

◆ **Desktop Scanner:** Desktop scanners improve in price and quality constantly, so that by the time this book hits the shelves the market could be completely different. The following web sites and publications offer good reviews and descriptions of various desktop scanners:

www.byte.com

www.scanshop.com/scanner

www.inconference.com/digicam/scanners.html

Desktop scanners are a good option for doing comp work but not really the ideal option for print projects that rely on high quality in detail and color.

Once you hook up your desktop scanner and install the necessary software, you can begin scanning. Most scanner software allows the scanner to stand alone, digitizing images and saving them in any number of various formats. You'll most likely have better results if you scan directly into Photoshop:

1. Choose File –> Import –> TWAIN Select

2. Select your scanner from the list of import devices.

3. Choose File –> Import –> TWAIN Acquire

4. Make the scan and your image will appear directly in Photoshop. Use the manual that came with your particular scanner to change any necessary settings.

◆ **Drum Scanner:** Drum Scanners are higher end machines usually found at a service bureau. There are desktop drum scanners that can do a good job as well, but to really capture every detail of your image you'll want to find a place with a large drum to scan your image.

Getting a drum scan of your work can be expensive, but will provide you with the best resolution and detail possible. As color printing prices have dropped over the years, however, and CD Scans, computer processors, and Photoshop have become more powerful, it may not always be necessary to incur the high cost of drum scanning an image to achieve a high quality in the final print.

◆ **Photo CDs:** Photo CDs are one of the most convenient ways of getting an image into your computer. You can put your own photography on a CD or buy a CD with stock images.

◆ **Shoving a Photograph into the Floppy Disk Drive:** This never works and will almost always cause severe damage to your computer. I would dissuade you from trying this method.

◆ **Digital Photography:** Digital cameras are all the rage these days and it doesn't seem like the day is too far off that film cameras will be a thing of the past. Then again, last year I proclaimed print to be a dying medium with the popularity of the Web, and here I am, writing a book on how to print things, so what do I know?

Basically, a digital camera is one that does not use film, but rather uses a computer chip to store captured images. Rather than run to the lab to wait for processing in a darkroom, you simply connect the digital camera to the computer and literally download the images.

The digital cameras that are, as of the writing of this book, priced under $1,000 are good tools to grab images for a web site, but fairly useless if your destination is a commercial press. Currently, the resolution simply isn't there in the lower-priced cameras to get any real detail in your images. There are, however, more powerful cameras that can produce high-resolution digital photographs. Each camera will have different directions and software for downloading images onto your hard drive, so you'll want to consult the users guide for proper instructions.

SAVING AN IMAGE: WHICH FILE TYPES TO USE

When you save a file in Photoshop, you will have to choose a file type to save it as. To save a file in Photoshop:

1. Choose File –> Save As…
2. Give your file a name, and select a format from the pull-down menu.
3. Find the place in your drive that you want to save your file to, and hit the Save button. Some formats will provide subsequent message boxes that will ask you questions about your file. Answer them and your file will be saved.

The file type you choose will, in most cases, be largely influenced by what you plan on doing with your image. There are 20 different formats native to Photoshop to save your files, not including the GIF 89a format available if you change your coler mode to Indexes Color. After years of designing and teaching, I still haven't had a need to use all of the formats. Some are meant specifically for the web (see Chapter 3 in *Web Photoshop 5.0 To Go*), while others are meant more for transferring files from one system or platform to another.

While there may be times that you need to use other file formats, for the purposes of understanding electronic desktop publishing we'll concentrate on just a few: the native Photoshop format, TIFF, and EPS.

THE PHOTOSHOP FORMAT

This may seem like an about–face from the previous paragraph, but the Photoshop format is not meant for printing. It is an important format to understand, however, since you'll be using it while you are working on many projects.

Although there are other programs that can read the Photoshop format (.psd on Windows), it is really meant to be used just in Photoshop. Currently, this is the only format that Photoshop offers that can save both layers and channels, as well as compress a file without destroying information. (TIFF can compress this way as well, but it can't save layers.) So let's say that you're working on a file that has a lot of layers in it, and you want to save it to work on later. When you choose File –> Save As you'll only have one option available to you, which is the Photoshop file format. Click Save to retain the layers and you can resume working later.

Layered files, especially hi-res layered files, can have a very high file weight. Don't waste more hard drive space than is actually necessary. Photoshop is also saving a flattened version of your file so that it can open it in Photoshop 2.0 and earlier versions, which did not have layers capabilities. When, if ever, will you have to work in Photoshop 2.0? Choose File –> Preferences –> Saving Files and click off the checkbox for Include Composited Image with Layered Files. You could end up reducing the file size by a third!

While the Photoshop (.psd) format is primarily used for work in Photoshop, Web designers have found a huge benefit in opening layered files in Image Ready (Adobe's for-web-users-only program) to create animations. Again, at the risk of sounding like a commercial, you can read more about this in *Web Photoshop 5 To Go*. (I only mention this as reference—not to suck more money out of you. Chances are you're sitting in the café at Barnes and Noble or Borders, reading this book for free, anyway.)

THE EPS FORMAT

The EPS (Encapsulated PostScript) format is a popular one for print designers. It is meant primarily to save images whose destination is an object-oriented application, like Illustrator (Chapter 7), or QuarkXPress (Chapters 3 and 4), and will be output on a PostScript device. (For more information on PostScript, see Chapter 1.)

One of the benefits of using the EPS format is that you will allow the original application (in this case, Photoshop) to change the image information into PostScript at the source. This is a preferred alternative to allowing your page layout program to be responsible (you know what they say: "if you want something done right, you've got to do it yourself"). There will be less of a chance of a color shift or problem when sending the project through the output device.

Another benefit is the ability to save clipping paths. Clipping paths allow you to silhouette a portion of your image so that that portion can be imported into QuarkXPress or Illustrator without inclusion of an unwanted background.

The downside of the EPS format is that because of the way it saves information, without benefit of a dynamic compression technique like the LZW compression you'll read about in the TIFF file format section, it has a very large file size attached to it. Large file size relative to what you may get with a compressed TIFF, anyway. The large file size could cause your file to RIP more slowly.

When you save a file as an EPS, you will be faced with the dialog box shown in Figure 5–7. The Preview pull-down menu allows you to choose how you would like your image to appear when placed in another application like QuarkXPress. The TIFF (8 bits/pixel) default option will allow you to see your image in 256 colors.

 Remember that the color palette has been reduced for the preview only when you import the image into another program. It'll look like crap compared to how you see it in Photoshop, but it's only a preview. It will print as sharp as you see it in Photoshop (as long as you use a good printer).

```
╔══════════════ EPS Options ══════════════╗
║                                          ║
║  Preview: [ Macintosh (8 bits/pixel) ▲▼ ]   [   OK   ]
║                                          ║
║  Encoding: [ Binary                  ▲▼ ]   [ Cancel ]
║                                          ║
║         ☐ Include Halftone Screen        ║
║                                          ║
║         ☐ Include Transfer Function      ║
║                                          ║
║         ☐ PostScript Color Management     ║
║                                          ║
╚══════════════════════════════════════════╝
```

Fig. 5–7 The EPS Options dialog box appears when you save an image as an EPS..

The other options in the Preview pull-down menu are designed to reduce the file size in case your computer is low on disk space. It's a minimal difference, though.

You'll want to choose Binary form the Encoding pull-down menu most often. This will compress the file size using the Hoffman compression technique. Most of the programs you will use, and all of the ones covered in this book, support Hoffman encoding, so it's fairly safe. If you are working in some other application that you know does not recognize Hoffman, you'll have to choose ASCII, which is a text-only format. The final selection is to save your image using JPEG compression. The editors of my last book already know my attitude toward JPEG files, so I won't get into an editorial debate. (I am in a minority on this one, so be careful who you repeat that to.) Bottom line: don't use this option. It will destroy image information and reduce the overall quality.

If you have changed the halftone screens yourself and want that halftone information to be attached to your image when going to the printer, put a check in the Include Halftone Screen checkbox.

Click the Include Transfer checkbox if you have customized the Transfer Setting. You can customize the Transfer settings by choosing File –> Page Setup, and pushing the Transfer button. Within the next dialog box, you can manipulate how the brightness of your image relates to the shaded areas. Playing around in this dialog box is hazardous, and it will cause the overall brightness and shading of your image to be altered, sometimes with an unexpected effect. If you are doing your own outputting, you may want to explore the Transfer function as a means of compensating for any deficiencies in your output device, but otherwise I would recommend that you leave this alone, and let your service bureau handle this for their output devices if necessary.

Leave the PostScript Color Management checkbox unchecked unless you are familiar with the output device. It only works with PostScript Level 2 and 3 printers and will attach a color profile (discussed in chapter 4) to your image for better color management when printing.

If your image is in Grayscale mode, the latter two checkboxes will be unavailable, replaced with a checkbox marked Transparent Whites. Click this box to make the white pixels in your image transparent. Be careful that you don't have white highlights that will be made transparent with this checkbox.

THE TIFF FORMAT

The TIFF (Tag Image File Format) is my personal favorite for a number of reasons. The first benefit of using TIFF has little to do with printing directly—it's a great format for transferring between platforms. When you save an image as a TIFF, you get a very simple dialog box, shown in Figure 5–8. It will ask you perhaps one of the easiest question you will ever be asked: which platform will you be using when you next open this image? Click either the radio button for IBM PC or the one for Mac. Pretty simple.

Fig. 5–8   The TIFF Options dialog box appears when you save an image as a TIFF.

The other option on the dialog box reveals another benefit to TIFF: the LZW Compression compresses your image to a significantly reduced file size, yet doesn't harm your image at all or discard data. This is a major boon especially to designers who have limited space left for saving files.

In previous versions of QuarkXPress, it was always a good idea to use EPS if you wanted a clean silhouette. The clipping paths that EPS supports provide for that. TIFFs, on the other hand, didn't do so well—although a TIFF image will automatically translate white pixels to transparent, designers often found that Quark would cause TIFFs to print with jagged edges. The new version of Quark, however, deals with TIFFs much better. Save the selection around your object as an Alpha channel (by choosing Select –> Save Selection.) This channel will knock out the background of your picture when you import it into XPress.

SUMMARY

Photoshop is not an easy program—you would need far more than a short chapter to fully learn it. However, the parts that were touched on here are vital to not only giving you the necessary overview of the program but to ensuring high quality for print graphics. What the design looks like—it's draw, it's impact—that's up to you and your imagination. How it looks on paper, that's up to Photoshop, Quark, and your printer.

chapter 6

ADDING "POP" TO PRINT WITH PHOTOGRAPHY

There is no better way to get a point across than with the proper use of photography. Printed pieces, regardless of their intended audience, almost universally share the common truth that they need to include photography. In some instances, it's for pure aesthetics—an eye catcher to grab attention. In other cases, it's hard necessity—how many vacationers would an ad for a tropical island resort attract if all it did was describe the long white beaches and crystal blue waters? Probably not many. But throw in a color photograph of that same beach and now you've got people's attention.

Photographs add a certain level of realism to your printed pieces. People will be more likely to trust and pay attention to your work if it is accentuated with photography. They will also be much more likely to recall the piece in the future because images create memories. For example, think about any major advertising campaign or even historical event that you are familiar with. What do you see? Chances are, you are associating your memory with an image. Who can remember the Oklahoma City bombing without seeing that incredible photograph of the fireman carrying the baby? Or the 1998 baseball season without remembering Mark McGuire's 70th home run swing? The images of these and other events permeate our consciousness like nothing else can. And while it's a relatively rare occurrence for an advertisement or collateral piece to be recalled and passed down through the generations, there is at any given time a crowded battlefield of ads, catalogs and brochures all vying for a desensitized audience's attention. Photography can be, in most cases, your greatest weapon in this battle.

But while the importance of photography is an easy theory to prove, it is not necessarily as easy to implement. How you use your photography will prove to be as important as the subject of your photographs. Matters like relative sizes, contrast, brightness, and other such issues are important considerations when designing your layouts. This chapter will outline the basic rules of using photographs, and provide tips on how to get the most out of your images. I'll also further explore Adobe Photoshop, the industry's most widely relied upon tool for graphic design and photographic manipulation. The Photoshop portion of this chapter will concentrate primarily on setting up the program for print projects and the utilization of the color correction and photo-retouching commands.

WHERE TO GET PHOTOGRAPHS

You have a number of choices when it comes to obtaining photographs. Which methods you choose will depend on a number of different factors, including budget, deadlines, and the type of project you are working on.

CUSTOM PHOTOGRAPHY

Often you will need photographs that are specific to your particular project, such as product shots for a catalog, or a group shot of a company's staff. When a particular subject like this is called for, you'll have to arrange for a custom photo shoot. You may opt to do this yourself if you have any talent at all behind a camera or you can hire a professional photographer to do the shoot for you.

Commercial photographers are a very different breed of artist, especially when it comes to the rigidity of their contracts and how money and rights will be ultimately transferred. In most cases you can expect that they will retain all rights to any photographs that they take and they will be, in essence, *leasing* the use of that image to you for your project.

PHOTO CDs

Photo CDs are a popular way to import images into Photoshop because of the relative simplicity involved. Put the CD in your computer's CD drive and copy the image. (If your computer doesn't have a CD drive, you can pick up an external drive up at any computer store or mail-order outlet at fairly reasonable prices.

So now the only question is how do you get a photo CD? The answer depends on what type of pictures you want to use.

YOUR OWN PICTURES

If you have your own pictures that you want to digitize and use in your work, getting them onto a CD is just a matter of a little time and money. (Doesn't that seem to be the formula for everything in life?) While your local one-hour photo processing center can usually take care of this for you, they'll probably have to send it out to be done. They could take more time than you might be willing to wait and may not even be able to provide the scan resolution your project needs.

You'll be better served finding a more advanced photo lab that does the work on location. If you don't know one, you can ask your service bureau if they can point you in the right direction (they might even do the work themselves).

Provide the lab with your photograph—they'll tell you what they need, but try and get them either chromes or slides. Positives will work but probably won't yield the best results.

Photo labs will probably be able to scan to practically any resolution so that an 8.5"x 11" 300 ppi file that takes up 72 Megs would not be unreasonable. Depending on the number of scans you have, many labs can complete your job within a couple of days. As of the writing of this book, you can expect to pay between $2 and $6 per scan depending on the resolution, and between $20 and $30 per CD. You can also expect for the back of your CD case to be printed with icons of all the photographs on the CD for easy reference.

If you want to save yourself some money, fill up all of your CDs. Each writable CD holds 650 Megs of information. If you put a few photographs on one CD and a week later have to scan more images, tell the lab to put the new images on the old CD. You'll save yourself between $20 and $30 for a new CD change each time you do this.

STOCK PHOTOGRAPHY

Stock photographs are another good way of getting high-quality images into Photoshop, and a great way to get both general and specific shots for your work. The downside is that while tons of images are available on the market, there are always a few that become really popular and nothing is more frustrating than using a stock image in a brochure just to see the same image on a billboard somewhere for an entirely different company.

Stock images can be purchased either individually or by ordering a CD-ROM with hundreds of hi-res images on them. There are plenty of images out there for you to use for practically every subject you can imagine. Check out the following companies and their respective web sites for a sample of the types of images that they offer:

www.photodisc.com

www.eyewire.com

www.digitalstock.com

CONCEPTUAL ISSUES: WHAT LOOKS GOOD AND HOW TO ACHIEVE IT

Well, that was a particularly long introduction to the world of photographs, and how they relate to your printed pieces. It's all a necessary part of producing quality pieces, however, and it's part of the inalienable truth: Photoshop is not an easy program to learn. Hopefully, though, with the combination of technical information in the previous chapter, and conceptual issues discussed in this chapter, you'll have a good head start in understanding the necessary key issues.

SUBJECT MATTER

This is the most important issue but one I can barely help you with, save bringing it to your attention and increasing your awareness of it. Because the imagery that you'll include in your work will be the most visible and arguably tell the most accurate story to your audience, choosing the subject matter should be taken seriously. If you're creating an ad for a brand of cola, what's going to be more effective: a picture of the can, or a picture of a happy, attractive person drinking from the can at a really fun party? Keep the following issues in mind when choosing your photographs:

◆ **Mood:** What's the overall feeling of the picture? Dark shades and shadows could cast a morose, somber feeling over your piece, while bright shades could help give an upbeat feeling.

◆ **Scene:** Is there anything happening in the scene of the piece? Oftentimes subtle background imagery can be more important than the primary subjects.

◆ **Action:** Does the picture require movement? A shot of a racing car speeding to a win over the finish line could have a more dramatic and exciting effect than a dull shot of the driver standing in a room with his trophy.

◆ **Expression:** Are you using imagery of people? Subtle facial expressions, such as a lifted eyebrow, a nostril flare, or leaning too far in one particular direction can send subliminal messages to an audience about the person's character.

◆ **Angle:** In most cases, a photograph that is looking up at the subject matter portrays that subject as majestic and powerful. Photographs that are angled down on the subject portray that subject as small and weak.

All of these issues should be taken into deep consideration when developing your piece.

Fig. 6–1   Dust, scratces, and other problems are apparent on my scan.

PHOTO RETOUCHING

There will likely be any number of problems with a photograph when you first start to use it, especially if digitized by a scanner. You'll want to retouch these problems before moving on to any real color correction or graphic design issues.

Dust, Scratches, and Tears

Figure 6–1 shows a number of problems with a photograph that was scanned in using a desktop scanner. The dark areas in the corner show dust from the scan bed as well as small scratches and an ugly tear in the original photograph. These problems are common—even for photos that are drum scanned or scanned to a CD—and you should take extra care to check each scan thoroughly before working them into your layout. Dust on black looks especially bad coming off a press and can greatly detract from the overall effect.

Working in Photoshop:
Removing Dust, Scratches, and Tears

The best way to remove dust and other problem elements resulting from poor scans or damaged photographs is to use the Rubber Stamp tool:

1. Choose the Rubber Stamp tool as indicated in Figure 6–2. The Rubber Stamp lets you instantly clone one area of your image onto another area.

2. Hold the Option key (Alt in Windows) and click in an area of your image that has the same color value or pattern as the area you want to fix. This is the area from which you will clone.

Fig. 6–2   The Rubber Stamp tool in the Toolbar.

Rubber Stamp

Fig. 6–3   The Rubber Stamp tool at work fixing scan problems.

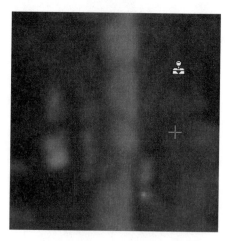

3. Place the cursor over the area you want to fix. Click or click and drag, and you'll cover the problem area with a clone of the area you clicked on originally. As Figure 6–3 shows, there will be two cursors when you do this—one cursor where you are stamping to, and a cross hair to indicate the area you are stamping from.

You can adjust the size and edge of the pixel area you're copying by choosing different brushes from the Brushes palette.

Try not to clone from an area that is too close to the area you want to fix, especially if you are cloning from a pattern. If you're not careful about this, it may be obvious where the clone came from.

Problems with Dot Patterns

Another problem that you'll probably encounter when scanning an image into Photoshop is seeing the printing pattern of dots in your image. As Figure 6–4 shows, these dots can practically destroy any value that your image may contribute to your layout.

Working in Photoshop:
Removing Patterns

You can remove patterns from scans by using the Gaussian Blur filter:

1. Choose Filter -> Blur -> Gaussian Blur to access the dialog box seen in Figure 6–4 (b).
2. Alter the Radius setting as desired. The minimum setting is .1 and the maximum setting is 250. The higher the setting, the greater the blur—typically you can remove a scanning pattern with a very slight Gaussian blur. Depending on the severity of the pattern, a blur of just a few tenths of one pixel can often be enough. The higher blur values will blur your image into nothing more than a mix of colors or gray shades.

Keeping Photographs in Focus

Unless you're going for a certain effect, blurry pictures, such as the one displayed in Figure 6–5, can be distracting and reduce the overall quality of your layout. You're going to want to use photographs that are crisp and sharp, to help the subject of the shot stand out and send a message. The best way to do this is to try and get it in focus on the initial photo shoot. This isn't always possible, though, especially if the budget isn't available to hire a professional photographer for the job.

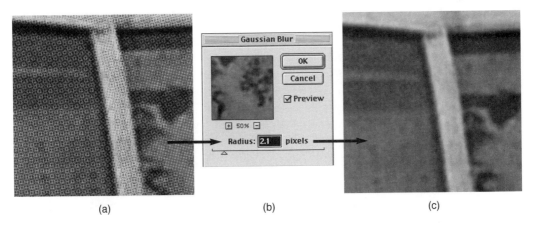

(a)   (b)   (c)

Fig. 6–4   (a) The dot pattern can ruin a picture. (c) The same portion of the picture after using the Guassian Blur filter.

Fig. 6–5   This picture is too blurry to be effective.

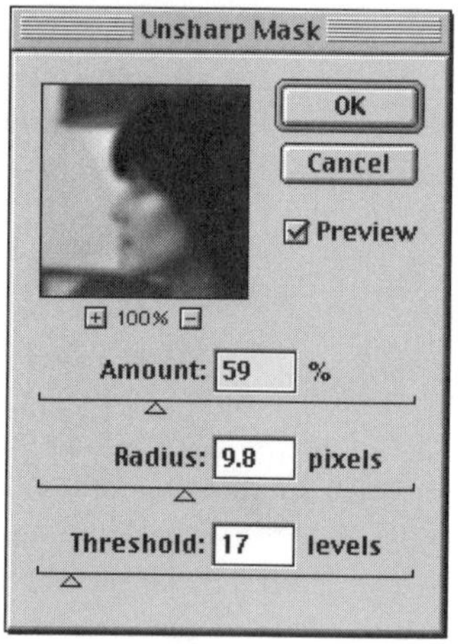

Fig. 6–6   The Unsharp Mask filter.

Working in Photoshop:
Sharpening Blurry Photographs

The best way to sharpen a blurry photograph (besides reshooting it) is to use the Unsharp Mask filter. The Unsharp Mask filter sharpens your image by increasing the contrast between congruent pixels.

1. Choose Filter -> Sharpen -> Unsharp Mask to access the dialog box shown in Figure 6–6.

2. Adjust the settings as desired. The Amount setting is a value between 1 and 500 percent, indicating the intensity level that your image will be sharpened. Lower percent values have a less severe effect than higher percent values. The Radius setting, measured in pixels, controls the thickness of the edges in your photograph. Higher radius values will create thick edges with greater contrast. The final control in the dialog box, the Threshold setting, works the opposite of the other settings. Measured in levels, the value entered is the minimum brightness differential between two pixels that needs to exist before they can be sharpened. Lower values will affect a greater number of pixels, and higher values will affect fewer pixels.

3. Hit OK when you are satisfied with your settings.

Fig. 6–7 The picture after applying the Unsharp Mask.

Figure 6–7 shows a sample of how the Unsharp Mask filter can affect a picture. Notice that you have lost some of the blur but also some of the detail. Filters can have unwanted side effects so keep your finger near the undo.

Excess Image and Dramatic Effect

Not all portions of your image are necessary to tell the story that you need told. Figure 6–8 (a) is a good example of a picture that has an obvious subject but a lot of excess imagery that adds little if anything to the point of the shot. This excess, if left in your image when you do your layout, will confuse your reader as well as detract from any power that your picture may have.

Another benefit you'll derive from eliminating excess portions from your image is drama. Drama in an image, brought about by a close-up of a facial expression, a tight shot of a product, or something else, can provide mood, tone, and add a sense of importance. Figure 6–8 (b), for example, shows how extracting the main subject from its background so tightly that is runs off the edge creates a much more focused, dramatic message.

Working in Photoshop:
Cropping

The Crop tool allows you to quickly eliminate unwanted areas of your photograph.

1. Choose the Crop tool from the Toolbar. It's the last option in your Marquee tool.

2. Drag a marquee selection around the area of your image you wish to keep. Anything that falls outside of the selection will be cropped away. Notice that the bounding box that appears around the selection has handlebars on the sides and corners.

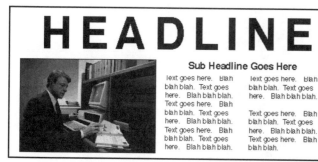

Fig. 6–8   (a) The picture loses power because of all the unnecessary elements around the subject. (b) Cropping to the essentials.

3. Drag the handlebars to change the size and shape of the crop area. Drag inside the bounding box to move the entire crop space and drag outside to rotate the crop selection.

4. Push Return (Enter in Windows) or double click inside of your crop selection to accept the crop. The Esc Key unselects without cropping.

Size Effects

As I emphasized in Chapter 4, the size of your images relative to other images and elements in your layout can have a significant impact on how your audience views your work. Larger images will usually command the most attention on a page and be interpreted as being representational of the primary message. In Chapter 4 this was discussed primarily as a layout issue. However, when it comes to sizing photographs, the real work should be done in Photoshop.

Working in Photoshop:
Resizing Photographs

In general, the basic rule of sizing images is that you can easily resize an image smaller and maintain quality, however you cannot resize larger without losing detail. To resize an image:

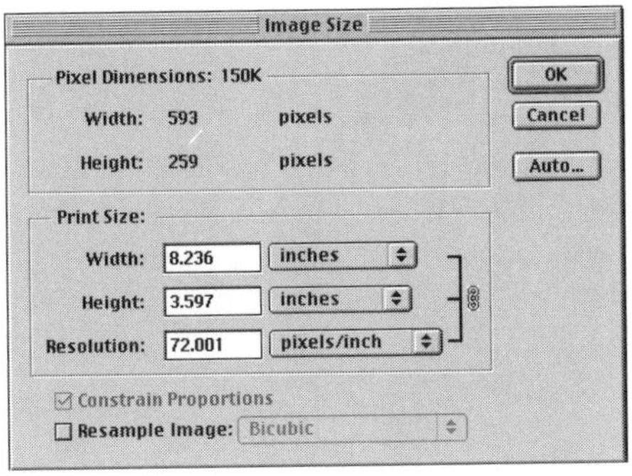

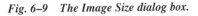

Fig. 6–9   The Image Size dialog box.

1. Choose Image –> Image Size to access the dialog box shown in Figure 6–9. The top portion shows the width and height of the image as measured in pixels, while the bottom portion shows the dimensions in inches, centimeters, or other units of measure, and the resolution (ppi—pixels per inch).

2. Turn off the Resample Image checkbox and turn on Constrain Proportions. The pixel dimensions will remain fixed and the measurements in the Print Size will all be linked together, as indicated by the chain link icon.

3. Increase either the width or the height. The other will increase proportionately and the resolution will decrease. Alternately, the resolution of the image will increase as you enter smaller values for either the width or height.

4. Click OK when through. Figure 6–10 shows the result of resizing an image with the Resample Image checkbox off.

or

1. Turn on the Resample Image by clicking on its checkbox. If the Constrain Proportions checkbox is also checked, the chain link icon now only connects the Width and Height in the Print Size section, and the Width and Height in the Pixel Dimensions (which you can now manipulate).

2. Increase the width or height in either the print size or pixel dimensions. The other will increase but the resolution will stay the same.

3. Click OK when through. Figure 6–11 shows the result.

If you are forced to increase the physical size of an image and are concerned about the blurry effect this has on your photograph, use a slight Unsharp Mask (described earlier in this chapter) to counteract the problem. It's not a perfect solution, but it will help. Remember that what you see on a monitor will always look better for low-res images than what you finally print.

Fig. 6–10   With Resample off, the image increases in resolution as the physical size is reduced and vice-versa.

Fig. 6–11   With Resample on, the resolution stays the same as the physical size changes. Notice how the image quality gets worse as the size is increased.

PHOTO EDITING

Once you have retouched any problems with your photographs and cropped or resized them to your desired dimensions, you can begin the intensive work of image enhancement and color correction.

SHADOWS AND HIGHLIGHTS

Shadows and highlights are responsible for picture depth. Without them, your photos will look flat and uninteresting, diluting much of the image's impact as it relates to your piece. Figure 6–12 shows the differences in impact when the shadows and highlights in an image are dull versus intensified. Use this difference to increase the power of your print projects.

Working in Photoshop:
Increasing Shadows and Highlights with Levels

The Levels command gives you limited control over the shadows, midtones, and highlights of your image. To use the Levels command:

1. Choose Image -> Adjust -> Levels to access the Levels dialog box shown in Figure 6–13. The first thing you'll notice about this is the histogram in the center, which measures and displays the brightness value for every pixel in your image (or selection). The histogram is wide enough to chart each of the possible 256 brightness values. The shadows, or black pixels, are represented on the left and gradually transition to the white pixels, or highlights, on the right. The gray pixels in the center are called the midtones. Each of the vertical lines show how many pixels exist in your image or selection at any particular brightness value.

Fig. 6–12   Shadows and highlights can make a world of difference to an image.

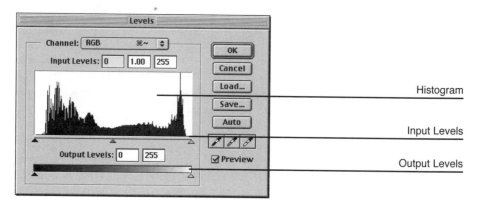

Fig. 6–13   The Levels dialog box.

2. Select which channel you wish to make adjustments to if you do not want to make universal changes to the composite image.

3. Change the contrast of the image by moving the sliders below the histogram or enter a numeric value in the corresponding Input Levels value area. The slider begins at the far left of the histogram—as you move it right, your image will darken as all the pixels it leaves behind will become black. For example, if you adjust the shadow's slider from 0 to 100, any pixel whose color has a brightness value less than or equal to 100 will become black. The reverse is true for the highlight: as you move the slider from the right, you will be turning higher valued pixels white. The center slider, which represents the midtones, will darken or lighten the grays in an image, darkening them as the slider is moved to the right, and lightening them as the slider is moved to the left. Figure 6–14 shows how adjustments to the Input Level can affect your image.

4. Adjust the Output Levels to reduce the severity of the darkest and lightest pixels. The slider provided works almost in the opposite direction as the Input Levels: when you pull the triangle on the left, which represents the darkest pixel, over to the right, you will be lightening the darkest pixels. As you pull the triangle on the right, which represents the white pixels, over to the left, you will be darkening the lightest pixels. Figure 6–15 shows the results on my image of manipulating these controls leaving the Input Levels at the values used in figure 6–14 (b).

Working in Photoshop:
Increasing Shadows and Highlights with Curves

The Levels command is some pretty powerful correction stuff—you can see the vast differences between the adjusted images and my original in the samples provided. But you've been driving around in an automatic Plymouth compared to the manual Porsche you're about to jump into.

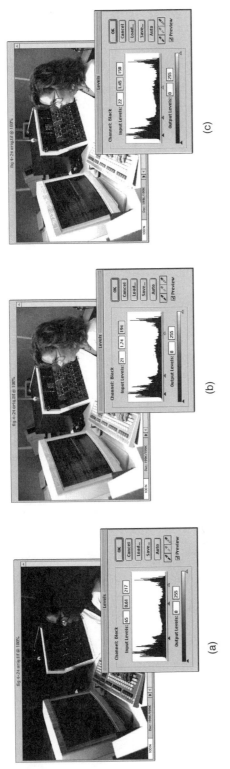

Fig. 6–14 Effects that the Input Levels can have on an image.

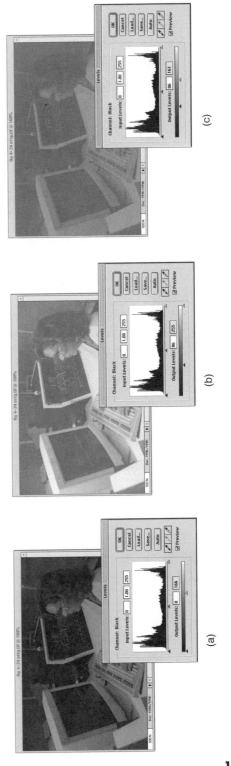

Fig. 6–15 Effects that the Output Levels can have on an image.

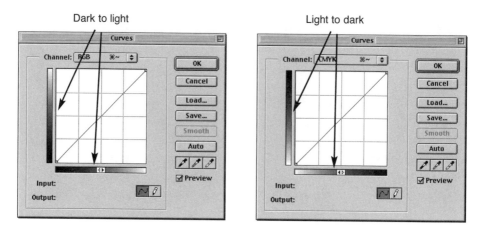

Fig. 6–16 *The Curves dialog box—notice the difference in how Curves measures dark and light between and RGB and a CMYK image.*

1. Choose Image -> Adjust -> Curves to access the dialog box shown in Figure 6–16.

2. If you do not want to work on the composite image select the channel you wish to apply your manipulation to from the Channel pull-down menu.

3. That big graph in the middle of the dialog box is where you will be doing the bulk of your adjusting work. The gradient bar on the left (the vertical axis) measures the output levels, and the gradient bar at the bottom (the horizontal axis) measures the input levels. The curve, which starts out as a diagonal line from bottom left to top right, describes how each output level value measures against each input level value. Exactly how your image will change when you alter the curve will depend upon what color mode you're in:

   ◆ In RGB mode, the values will be measured as brightness values and the point of origin (the bottom left, where both input and output values are equal at 0) will be black (no brightness). Both the input and output gradient bars will gradate from black to white outward and upward, so that the further along the curve you go, the brighter your image is. Figure 6–16 shows how the Curves differ.

   ◆ In CMYK (and Grayscale) mode, the curve will measure the ink coverage in an image. Both gradient bars are opposite their RGB counterparts, as the point of origin now measures the level of ink applied to an image (0 percent at point of origin) and increases to full ink coverage as you move outward along the curve.

4. There are two tools that you can use to change the shape of the curve. The default is the Point tool, which allows you to place points on the curve by clicking on it. Place a point and drag it upward (increase the value) and your image will become darker. Drag it downward (decrease the value) and your image will become lighter. You can set as many points as you'd like to manipulate your image at different levels. Figure 6-17 and Color Figure 11 show a number of manipulations to my image,

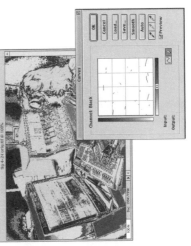

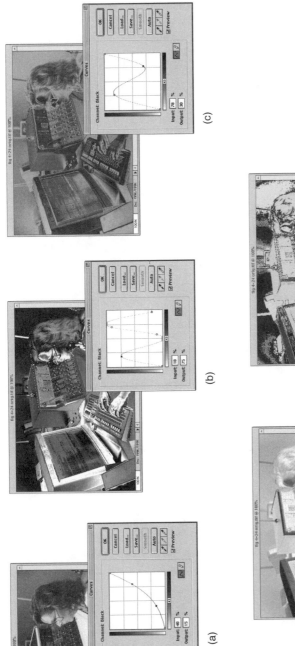

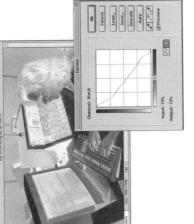

(a)

(b)

(c)

(d)

(e)

Fig. 6–17   Curves can have some wild effects on an image.

159

and their respective curves. You can also use the Pencil tool to draw a customized curve. Click on the Pencil tool in the dialog box to activate it. To use it, simply draw a curve freehand through the graph, which may or may not be one continuous line. You can get some pretty crazy results from it, though, as Figure 6–17 and Color Figure 11 demonstrate.

5. Click OK when through.

BRIGHTNESS

Photographs in print benefit from having a good balance between being bright and dark. Unlike shadows and highlights, which affect the dark and light pixels in your image respectively, brightness deals with the light and dark values of all the pixels. Figure 6–18 shows how a picture can be unuseable if it is either too bright or not bright enough.

Working in Photoshop:
Changing Brightness Values

To change the brightness values in an image:

1. Choose Image -> Adjust -> Brightness/Contrast to access the dialog box shown in Figure 6–19.

2. Adjust the sliders. Higher values (to the right on the slider) increase the brightness and contrast.

3. Click OK when through.

Fig. 6–18   The image on top is a good balance, while the image on the left is too dark, and the image on the right is too bright.

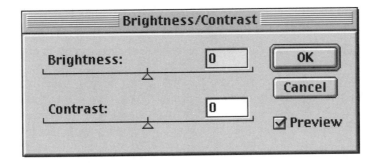

Fig. 6–19   The Brightness/Contrast dialog box.

THE POWER OF COLOR

Color not only adds significant life to your piece but can also affect how your images play into your audience's subconscious. Red and yellow, for example, grab attention and convey a sense of urgency. Blue and green are typically reserved for more conservative pieces and promote a more subdued, corporate message. Pastel colors, such as subdued browns, oranges, and greens can give a whispy, light feel to your piece that might work well in a spring apparel catalog. Color Figure 12 shows a few samples of how colors can play a major part in overall design.

While four-color (CMYK) print pieces are largely considered to be the most effective in terms of power and effectiveness, they are also the most expensive. Depending on your client, four-color printing may be well out of your budget. In addition, some designers would argue that grayscale images are as powerful as color, if not more.Of course a two-color piece, properly done, can also send an exciting message without a significantly restrictive price tag.

FOUR-COLOR DESIGN USING: CMYK

Color in your print pieces can be either manufactured patterns and textures for backgrounds, designs or other elements, or continuous tone for photographic images. Designs that you make from scratch can be practically any color you desire (any printable color, that is), depending upon your audience and intended use. Photographic images, unless you are trying to achieve a certain special effect, should be as close to realistic in color as possible. Even slight variations can lead to a poor overall result for your print piece.

Chapter 1 explained how the CMYK color mode is used when printing. This will be the mode you will most often work in when developing images for print. As explained earlier, images worked on in RGB mode could be deceiving, and lead to disappointing print results due to the smaller CMYK color gamut.

Working in Photoshop:
CMYK Color Mode for Four-Color Work

When you're creating a full-color (or rather, four-color) image for print, you'll want to work in the CMYK color mode. Do this by choosing Image ->Mode -> CMYK. This will separate all of your colors into Cyan, Magenta, Yellow, and Black. Open the Channels palette by choosing View -> Channels. You'll see that there are four color channels already created—these channels will contain all the color information for your image and later separate into individual pieces of film for your printer to create plates from. (See Chapters 8 and 9 for more information on plates and color separations.)

There are a few hazards that are part of working in CMYK mode:

◆   It can be a beast in terms of file size. An 8.5" x 11", 300 ppi image newly created in RGB mode can be 18 Megs in size. Turn it into a CMYK image and the file size jumps to 24 Megs—before anything is even on the canvas! And obviously, the larger the file size, the more RAM you'll use while working on it.

You'll be somewhat limited in your selection of colors. As we discussed in Chapter 5, the range of colors for any particular mode is called a gamut. As shown in Color Figure 2, the RGB color mode has the most colors available and the CMYK model has far fewer. Colors that fall outside of the CMYK color range are said to be *out of gamut*. There are a number of ways you can check if whatever colors you are using are out of gamut. These methods are explained later in this chapter.

CHANGING COLORS

Because of imperfections in scanning technology and the need for changing color mode to CMYK, you will likely need to adjust colors within your images. These adjustments may be minor, requiring only slight color enhancements, or could be vast color manipulations for either correction purposes or special effects.

Working in Photoshop:
Adding and Subtracting Colors with Color Balance.

The Color Balance is an especially useful tool for enhancing color or removing color casts that may become a factor after scanning. Although you can make radical changes with it, you'll probably find that this tool will serve you better for more subtle corrections.

1.   Choose Image -> Adjust -> Color Balance to access the dialog box show in Figure 6–20.

2.   From the radio button options, choose whether you want to manipulate the shadows, midtones (default), or highlights.

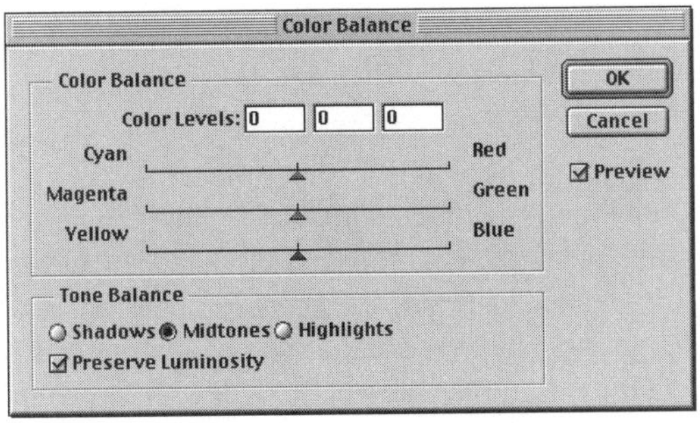

Fig. 6–20   The Color Balance dialog box.

Fig. 6–21   The Hue/Saturation dialog box.

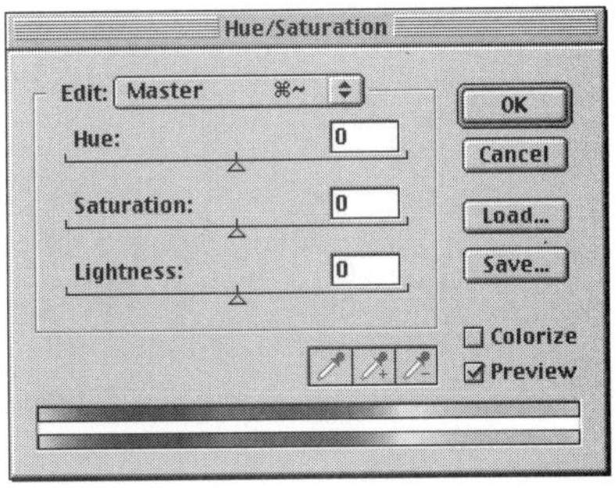

3. Move the sliders to alter your colors. Working off of the theory that RGB values should translate directly to inverse CMY values (remember that the Black component is only added to print because of imperfections in ink), increasing cyan decreases red, increasing magenta decreases green, and increasing yellow decreases blue.

4. Click OK when through. Color Figure 13 shows how an image can be affected by the color balance.

Working in Photoshop:
Changing Colors with Hue/Saturation

The Hue/Saturation dialog box, shown in Figure 6–21 allows you to alter the colors of your image by—take a wild guess—the hue and saturation. It also gives you control over the lightness of your image, although apparently this feature isn't exciting enough to have made the title.

The *hue* is the full-intensity RGB color wheel that you played with in art class back in third grade. It's measured in a 360 degree circle and is shown in Color Figure 14. The specific colors that you can adjust individually in the Hue/Saturation dialog box are at the following positions on the color wheel:

Red:	0 degrees	Cyan:	180 degrees
Yellow:	60 degrees	Blue:	240 degrees
Green:	120 degrees	Magenta:	300 degrees

Other colors fall in between those indicated, which are mixes of two colors. Orange, for example, is in between red and yellow at approximately 30 degrees. And you can find a rich orange between Magenta and Red at around 330 degrees.

The *saturation* is the strength of any particular color. It is measured from –100 to 100. At the point of lowest saturation, your image will be devoid of color and look like a Grayscale image. At the point of highest saturation, your image is at full color purity, often looking almost blurred with the colors bleeding significantly.

1. Open the Hue/Saturation dialog box by choosing Image –> Adjust –> Hue/Saturation.

2. Select the color you'd like to adjust from the Edit pull-down menu. You can choose to manipulate a particular shade of color, or all of them at the same time by selecting Master. The Color Range control will isolate your desired color tones on the gradient bars. You can increase or decrease the range by stretching either side of the control bar. Only the colors that fall within the isolated range will be manipulated.

3. Adjust the hue by pulling the Hue slider to either side.

4. If you want, adjust the saturation and lightness to their desired position.

5. Click OK when through.

Working in Photoshop:
Color Correcting Using Adjustment Layers

Using layers in Photoshop is a must—you simply can't avoid it. In practically every file you work on, Photoshop will force you to use the Layers palette. Unfortunately, a quality layers discussion is too involved for the purposes of this book. In short, the Layers palette (shown in Figure 6–22) allows you work on one portion of your image without affecting other portions.

An adjustment layer lets you make color corrections to your image without making those corrections permanent. Because the adjustment is on its own layer, it can be discarded, turned off, or altered with ease at any time. To create an adjustment layer:

1. Open the Layers palette by choosing Windows -> Show Layers.

2. In the Layers palette, choose New Adjustment Layer from the pull-down menu (push the triangle in the upper right-hand corner to access the pull-down menu).

3. In the Adjustment Layer dialog box, shown in Figure 6–23, select your desired color correction tool from the Type pull-down menu.

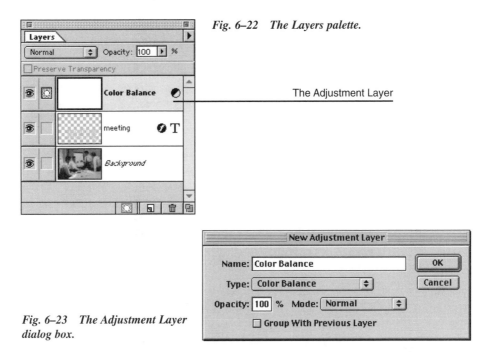

Fig. 6–22   The Layers palette.

The Adjustment Layer

Fig. 6–23   The Adjustment Layer dialog box.

4. Adjust the settings as you desire and click OK. You'll notice that there is a new layer in the Layers palette containing your chosen adjustment.

To see your image without the adjustment, turn the Adjustment Layer off by clicking on the eye icon on the left. To change the settings, double click on the Adjustment Layer, and the dialog box for your desired tool will reappear.

Working in Photoshop:
Checking for Nonprintable Colors

Still working in RGB? Don't worry—I do it all the time. I'll usually pay for it later, though, when I send it out to get an IRIS proof and find out that my colors are all washed out.

If you want to continue working in RGB mode (either for increased speed, reduced file size, or to utilize some of the cool filters that are only available in RGB mode), there is hope. You can do a couple of things to protect yourself:

◆　Check for the out-of-gamut icon [🔺] when selecting colors from the Color palette.

◆　Choose View –> Preview –> CMYK to view your image as it would appear in CMYK mode. If you're short on RAM, though, don't keep this feature on because it will take up memory.

◆ Choose View -> Gamut Warning. You may see a portion of your image turn gray. These are the areas that are out of gamut and need to be corrected before they go to the service bureau for output.

Any one of these options will help save you at the very least a bunch of unwanted headaches, and at the most significant dollars for re-outputting film.

CLASHING COLORS

Unless there is a specific reason for it, clashing colors will detract from your images. This is especially true when trying to attract a corporate audience. As for other audiences, the verdict is still out as to whether the loud, iridescent clashing colors overused in the last six to seven years to grab the attention of Generation X actually ever worked as an advertising strategy. My own personal opinion is that with the exception of the rare campaign or magazine design that was quirky enough to pull it off, Generation X was largely bored by a wild mix of loud colors, and remained unmoved by these attempts.

TWO- AND THREE-COLOR PRINTING: SPOT COLORS, DUOTONES, AND TRITONES

If the budget for your project doesn't quite allow for four-color printing but does leave room for something more than a one-color job, you can create images with just two or three colors. You can do this either by using spot colors or duotones/tritones (or a combination of them).

Although the printing price will be pretty much the same regardless which method you choose, the aesthetic differences between them are quite great. Color Figure 15 show a print piece, printed in two colors, using both a duotone and a spot color.

In either case, if possible, try to create your design so that there is an obvious reason that only two colors were used—such as a sepia tone for an antique look. Unfortunately, if there is no apparent reason for using two colors, much of your audience will interpret its use as "cheap" and assume a lack of financial stability in your client. This is not to condemn two-color projects, but this is a four-color world and people are always ready to assume the worst.

Spot Colors

Spot color refers to colors on an image that stand alone. In other words, they don't mix with other colors in your image. In older versions of Photoshop, designers who used spot colors either placed the color in a page-layout program like Quark or PageMaker or placed the spot color in Cyan, Yellow, or Magenta and then later told the printer what PMS ink to substitute in its place.

Photoshop 5 has made life easier for the two- and three-color designer with the inclusion of Spot Channels. These are channels that hold color information strictly for PMS colors. Spot channels are particularly useful when a client has a specific PMS color for their logo that would otherwise be difficult to recreate.

 The letters PMS stand for Pantone Matching System, and refers to a set of premixed colors manufactured by a company called Pantone. These premixed colors are typically impossible to recreate using the traditional mix of CMYK, and can often compensate for the metallic and neon colors that fall outside of the CMYK spectrum. Other companies, such as Dic and TruMatch also manufacture colors, but Pantone is by far the most widely used and recognized.

Working in Photoshop:
Creating a Spot Color Channel

To create a two-color image with a spot color channel:

1. Choose Image –> Mode –> Grayscale and hit OK when Photoshop asks if you want to remove the color information.

2. Open the Channels palette by choosing View -> Show Channels.

3. There should be one channel in the palette, Black, indicating that this is currently a grayscale image. From the palette pull-down menu, choose New Spot Channel.

   The New Spot Channel dialog box will appear as shown in Figure 6–24. Click on the Color box and then click on Custom to access the Custom Colors dialog box.

4. From the Book pull-down menu, choose Pantone Coated (one of the more common premixed spectra) and type in your desired PMS color. Type it quickly to make sure you get the color you want (Photoshop apparently thought it'd be more fun to make us poor typists try and get the number right in a hurry rather than provide a text area and Enter button). When your color is selected, hit OK.

5. Back in the New Spot Channel dialog box, fill in 100 for the Solidity percentage. The percentage you fill in will only affect the way the image appears on-screen, not the way it will print. Click OK.

```
┌─────────── New Spot Channel ───────────┐
│                                         │
│  Name: PANTONE 176 CVC        ┌──OK──┐  │
│                               └──────┘  │
│  ┌─ Ink Characteristics ──┐   ┌─Cancel┐ │
│  │                        │   └───────┘ │
│  │  Color: ▢  Solidity: 100 %          │
│  └────────────────────────┘            │
└─────────────────────────────────────────┘
```

Fig. 6–24 The Spot Channel dialog box.

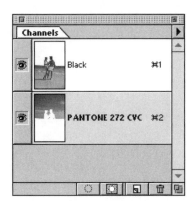

Fig. 6–25   The Channels palette with the Spot Channel at the bottom. The Spot Channel, by default, is named with the chosen Pantone color name.

6. Notice that the Channels palette now has two channels—the original Black channel, and a new channel, named whatever Pantone number you selected. With the Black channel active, select the portion of your image that you want to apply the spot color to. Cut this section by choosing Edit -> Cut.

7. Make your new Pantone channel active by clicking on it. Choose Edit –> Paste to paste the selection from your clipboard into this channel, as shown in Figure 6–25. You'll notice that the color you chose is now applied to the portion of your image that you pasted. Color Figure 16 shows a sample of what my image looks like after this stage. Notice, too, that unlike most instances when you paste an object into Photoshop, a new layer is not automatically created in the Layers palette. In fact, you'll even notice that the shading on the active layer is now grayed out and the palette is rendered temporarily inactive until you leave the spot channel.

You can create shades of your PMS color. While in the Pantone channel, reduce the color value percentage in the Color palette and then fill in a selection.

DUOTONES AND TRITONES

With a duotone you can create a two-color image in which both of the colors mix together to create a mixture with depth. This type of depth would be nearly impossible using just spot colors.

Working in Photoshop:
Creating Duotones and Tritones

To create a Duotone or Tritone:

1. Choose Image -> Mode –> Grayscale and agree to remove the color information.

2. Choose Image—Mode –> Duotone.

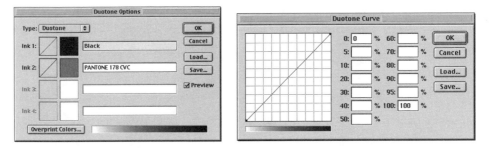

Fig. 6–26   The Duotone Options dialog
box. Use this to select and mix your colors
for two- or three-color work.

Fig. 6–27   The Duotone Curves dialog box.
This allows you to change the intensity of the
color at any brightness level.

The Duotone color mode option that is available now was
previously grayed out. You cannot go directly to Duotone from either
RGB or CMYK mode—you need to change your image into
Grayscale first.

3. The dialog box that will appear is shown in Figure 6–26. By default, the Type will
   be set to Monotone and the ink color in the first box will be black. We'll mix black
   with a new color chosen from the Pantone Coated color wheel.

4. Choose Duotone from the Type pull-down menu, and click on the empty (white)
   box directly under the black box.

5. Choose your desired Pantone color by typing in the number quickly or by scrolling
   through the spectrum provided. As you click on each color, you'll see your image
   change to the mixture of that color and black. I chose PMS color 178. Make your
   selection and click OK when through.

6. You'll see that the Pantone color you selected is now filed in for Ink 2 in the dialog box. The gradated bar at the bottom shows the range from highlight to shadows
   created by this particular ink mixture.

7. To manipulate how the new ink will blend with the black, click on the box immediately to the left of your PMS color (it will have a diagonal line going through it). This
   will give you access to the Duotone Curves dialog box as shown in Figure 6–27.

The Duotone Curves dialog box will illustrate how the brightness values that you see
on your monitor translate to print shades. The default diagonal line shows that the shade
percentage that will print is equivalent to its on-screen brightness value. To make your
image darker, fill in a higher number for a lower percentage: for example, you can make
the inks translate to a darker shade by filling in a 90 percent print value at the 6 percent
on-screen brightness value. Notice what this does to your curve, to the gradated bar in
the Duotone dialog box, and to your image. Color Figure 17 shows a few duotone
results and their associated curves.

You can do the same thing with three colors by choosing Tritone from the Type pull-down. You can add a fourth color by selecting Quadtone, but at that point, unless you have a specific effect in mind, you might as well take advantage of a full four-color process—the price will be the same.

Photoshop will print the inks in Duotones, Tritones and Quadtones in the order that they are placed in the dialog box. To increase the sharpness of your highlights and shadows, arrange your colors in order from darkest to lightest.

One Color Printing: Grayscale Images

On the other extreme, pieces that are made up of only one color are usually produced with black and shades of gray. This type of image is called a Grayscale image in Photoshop, or more commonly referred to as black and white in photography.

Black-and-white pictures have three distinct benefits:

1. They're cheap to print, at least relative to two-, three- and four-color pieces.

2. You're likely to have fewer headaches touching up black-and-white images than you will with color images. There is also a slimmer chance of being disappointed with the result off the press in black and white, since no RGB to CMYK conversion is necessary.

3. Done properly, black-and-white images in print can be dramatic and highly effective.

Color Figure 18 gives an example of an image both in color and black and white. You can see that in the color version, the image is attractive, but somewhat unappealing. The black-and-white version, however, with some adjustments to the shadows and highlights, is quite a bit more powerful.

Working in Photoshop:
Creating Grayscale Images

Grayscale images are smaller in file size than either CMYK or RGB images, which makes them an attractive alternative if you have limited RAM or hard disk space. They are also far cheaper to print since there is only one piece of film for the service bureau to output and one color for the printer to run.

Grayscale images don't need to be confined to black and shades of gray. You can direct your printer to substitute any PMS color for black when it goes to film. Oftentimes using any color other than black can tend to look somewhat flat, lacking any serious depth, but if you're creative you can make it work.

To create a Grayscale image:

1. Choose Image -> Mode -> Grayscale. Photoshop will ask if you really want to discard the color information. Click OK to continue into Grayscale mode (if you decide later that you want your color back you can always use the History palette).

2. If you have layers in your image, Photoshop will also ask you if you want to flatten your layers. If you still have work to do on your image, click the Unflatten option.

ENHANCING GRAYSCALE IMAGES

Beyond adjusting the shadows and highlights in Grayscale images, I find that in many cases adding a bit of noise to the image can heighten the drama and visual effect. *Noise* is randomized pixels that keep the image from being clear. You've probably seen this as "snow" on your television when you're tuned into a station that you don't receive.

Figure 6–28 shows a black-and-white image, once with and once without noise. The version with noise gives it a certain grainy feel, which, considering the subject matter, adds to the overall message.

Fig. 6–28   The Grayscale image on the right uses noise to add a grainy, gritty effect as opposed to the smooth image on the left.

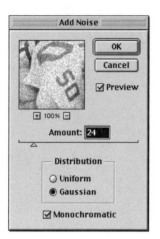

Fig. 6–29 The Add Noise dialog box.

Working in Photoshop: Adding Noise

You add noise to an image in Photoshop by:

1. Choosing Filter –> Noise –> Add Noise to open the dialog box shown in Figure 6–29.
2. If you're adding the noise to a color image, click the Monochrome checkbox to create black-and-white noise. If you're working in Grayscale mode, this won't matter. Adjust the slider to the amount of noise you wish to add. The further to the right, the more noise you'll apply.
3. Click the radio button for Uniform or Guassian to change the pattern and distribution for the noise.
4. Click OK when through.

Whichever method you choose (CMYK, spot color, black and white) and for whatever reason (budget, effects, message clarity), the colors that you use or don't use in your imagery will play as major a roll as the choice of images themselves. Take the time to understand how your color choices will affect the overall project before you end up with a disappointing piece or the responsibility of having to print something again.

PICTURE EFFECTS

Many of the effects that you see in printed pieces are done directly in the image editing program—most likely Photoshop. While Chapter 4 showed you a few things that you could do to enhance your pictures in Quark, such as importing them into custom shaped boxes, there is far more that you can do directly in Photoshop. And although you

Fig. 6–30   This ad layout benefits from the faded image in the background.

won't want to go overboard applying every type of effect imaginable (remember, the point is to draw attention to the message, not the design), many of the pieces you will create could potentially benefit from a few well placed special effects.

FADING PICTURES

Having colors appear ghosted in the background can create a nice effect for more corporate pieces. Almost like a more visible watermark, pieces such as the one shown in Figure 6–30 benefit from an almost subliminal enhancement of their message to the audience.

Be careful when you fade images, however, that you achieve the proper opacity. Images that are faded but still too opaque may interfere with any copy that is written over them. Images that are too transparent may be only slightly perceptible, causing you to incur the extra film expense while not gaining any real benefit.

Working in Photoshop:
Changing Image Opacity

As with most anything else in Photoshop, there are a number of different ways to go about accomplishing any given task. Making images transparent is no exception. The following is my personal favorite way to go about this:

1. Select your entire image by pushing Command + a (Ctrl + a in Windows).
2. Place your image on a new layer by selecting Layer -> New -> Layer Via Cut. This will place your image on a new layer, named Layer 1 by default. By working on a layer other than the background layer, you can adjust the opacity of the image.

The Background layer will be filled with whatever color is set as your background color. So if your current background color is red, for example, then your Background layer will be filled with red after the image has been moved to a new layer. This is important, since the Background layer will momentarily show through your image. Use white as your background color to make your faded image lighter and black to make the faded image darker.

3. With Layer 1 the active layer, change the opacity by clicking on the small arrow next to the opacity value. Adjust the slider to its desired position (as you move the slider further to the left, the image becomes more faded.)

4. Get your image ready to import into XPress by choosing Flatten Image from the Layers palette menu. Save your image as an EPS or a TIFF.

SOFT EDGES

A nice effect that can really help highlight the subject of your image is to fade the edges around them. The severity and shape of the fade can also add to your message. Figure 6–31 shows an example of how soft, faded edges can really help your audience focus on the message of the picture.

Fig. 6–31   Fading the edges around your subject can help highlight the important parts.

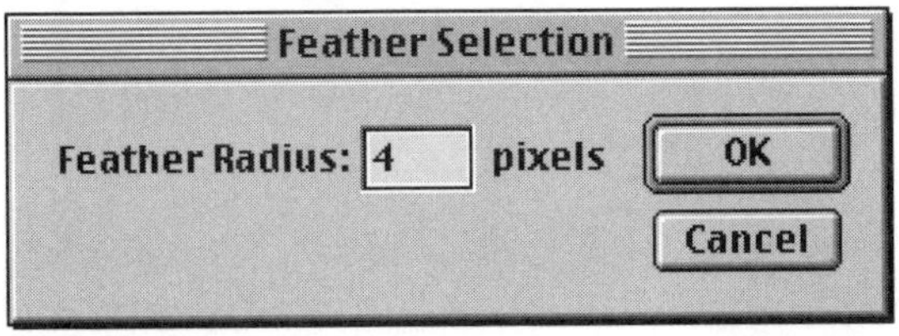

```
┌─────────────────────────────────────────┐
│ ═══════════ Feather Selection ═══════════ │
│                                           │
│  Feather Radius: 4   pixels  ┌──────────┐ │
│                              │    OK    │ │
│                              └──────────┘ │
│                              ┌──────────┐ │
│                              │  Cancel  │ │
│                              └──────────┘ │
└─────────────────────────────────────────┘
```

Fig. 6–32   The Feather Selection dialog box. Feathering softens the edges of your selection.

Working in Photoshop:
Fading Edges

To fade the edges around the main subject of your picture:

1. Create a marquee selection around the subject within your image. This selection can be any shape—circular, oval, rectangular, or you can use the Lasso tool to customize the shape.

2. Choose Select -> Inverse Selection.

3. Choose Select -> Feather to bring up the dialog box shown in Figure 6–32. Set the desired pixel value. The higher the value, the softer the edge will be. Click OK when through.

4. Push Delete or Backspace on your keyboard. The perimeter of your subject will be replaced with the current background color (you'll most likely want it to be white). The edge around your desired subject will be soft, helping the reader's eyes focus directly on its implicit message.

ADDING DROP SHADOWS, BEVELS, AND EMBOSSES

Drop shadows, bevels, and embosses make portions of your image seem to "pop" off the page. Drop shadows especially help give an image the appearance of floating off the page and relieve the reader of the static two dimensional confines of paper.

Keep the shadows and bevels to a minimum throughout your work, as their main benefit is to draw attention to a specific area, such as a headline or an image. If they are overused, their entire effect can be lost. Figure 6–33 shows a few samples of how shadows and bevels can be used to increase visibility.

In general, these effects are created as light and/or dark areas placed in specific portions of your image. The idea is that an imaginary light somewhere in space is shining on your selection, casting a shadow, or lightening one part of your image (the part in the light) and darkening another part of your image (the part out of the light). Although you can put this imaginary light anyplace you want, it could seem odd if it's placed outside of what most people have come to accept as the universal norm. This "universal norm" is the belief that light should, in most cases, come from the upper left and cast a shadow down to the lower right. Figure 6–34 gives an example of an image in which light seems

Fig. 6–33   Shadows and bevels help make images "pop" off the page.

Fig. 6–34   When light is hitting an image from an odd direction, the bevels and shadows can make it look strange.

to be coming from another direction. You can see that this is somewhat jarring. It takes focus away from the message and places it on what appears to be a mistake in the design.

Working in Photoshop:
Creating Drop Shadows, Bevels, and Embosses with Layer Effects

Special effects that were once as common as the sunrise are every bit as common today, just significantly easier. Photoshop 5.0 has made the creation of drop shadows, bevels, and embosses so quick and painless that if not for their invaluable benefit to the printed piece, they might soon become clichéd.

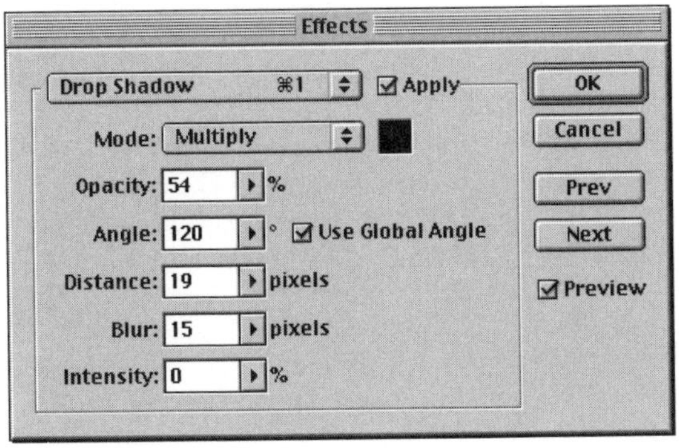

Fig. 6–35   The Layer Effects dialog box for creating a Drop Shadow.

To create a drop shadow, bevel, or emboss in Photoshop:

1. Place your text or image on its own layer. The following effects will not work on the Background layer. For drop shadows and certain bevels, you'll need extra space, so make sure that you have extra canvas room around your image.

2. Choose Layer –> Effects –> Drop Shadow to access the dialog box shown in Figure 6–35. You'll likely want to leave the Angle value alone, as it sets the angle that the light is coming from at the universally accepted angle by default. Change the Distance, Opacity, Blur, and Intensity accordingly. As a rule, if you increase the distance of your shadow from the image, you should also increase the amount of Blur and reduce the Opacity, as would likely happen in nature.

3. If you want to apply just the drop shadow, click OK. To add a bevel or emboss, choose Bevel and Emboss from the Effect pull-down menu.

You don't have to select Drop Shadow first—or at all. I did that for the sake of this description. You can instead choose Bevel and Emboss directly from the Layer -> Effect menu.

4. In the new dialog box, check the box marked Apply to activate the commands.

5. Choose your desired effects from the pull-down menu and adjust the settings accordingly. Increasing the Depth will make your bevel or emboss more severe, while increasing the blur will make the edges more round.

Because the maximum depth that you are allowed to bevel an object in this dialog box is only 20, the Bevel and Emboss effects work much better on low-resolution images like those made for the Web. High-resolution images, which you'll be working with for print, utilize far more pixels per inch and thus are not as affected by a 20-pixel bevel.

6. Click OK when through.

7. Alter your settings at any given time by double clicking on the small "f" on the layer in the Layers palette.

Working in Photoshop:
Deeper Bevels—Creation without Layer Effects.

As mentioned in the preceding "Note," bevels from Layer Effects will only go so far in a high-resolution image. To create a deeper bevel:

1. Place your desired image or text on its own layer.

2. Select the image or text by Command (Ctrl in Windows) + clicking on its layer.

3. Create a new layer by clicking on the New Layer icon at the bottom of the Layers palette.

4. Choose Select –> Modify –> Contract.

5. Set the desired amount of pixels to contract your selection by. The amount you select will be the width of your bevel.

6. Choose Select –> Inverse Selection.

7. Confine your selection to the intersection between it and the desired image by Shift + Option + Command (Alt + Ctrl in Windows) + clicking on the layer with your image in it.

8. Paint with black in the right and bottom portions of your selection and with white in the left and top portions. Reduce the opacity of your layer to make the bevel more realistic. Figure 6–36 provides an example of this type of bevel.

TORN AND BURNT PAPER

Creating edges that seem to be torn or burnt can help emphasize a title or a portion of your page, such as a sidebar. In actuality a ripped page is nothing more than a creative use for a drop shadow and burning it is a simple touch addition of paint, but as Figure 6–37 shows, it can be a very effective method of adding highlight and aesthetic flare.

Working in Photoshop:
Tearing and Burning the Edge of an Image

There are many reasons and areas for which you can create a torn or burnt edge. How you go about creating them will conceptually be the same, with a few slight modifications for different tears. For this explanation, I'll assume that the edge you will be tearing will belong to an image.

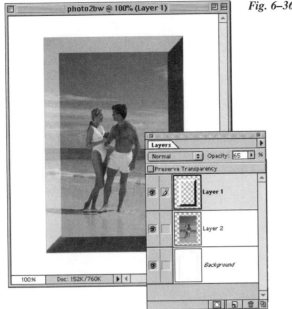

Fig. 6–36   A handmade bevel using Layers.

1. Place your image on its own layer with the background color white.

2. Use the Freeform Lasso tool to create a rough selection around the portion of your image that you want to tear off. Figure 6–38 shows an example.

3. Hit Delete or Backspace to remove your selection. The white background shows through.

4. Create a new layer between the Background layer and your Image layer.

5. Create the selection of your image by Command (Ctrl in Windows) + clicking on the image layer.

6. With the arrow buttons, move your selection so that it moves out past the image.

7. Choose Select –> Feather and set the feather value to about 4 pixels.

8. Fill your selection with black and reduce the opacity to about 65 percent for a more realistic-looking shadow. Figure 6–39 provides an example of what this should look like at this point.

9. To burn the edge, activate the layer with your image. Click the Preserve Transparency button in the Layers palette.

10. Choose the Paintbrush tool, and in the Options palette (choose View –> Options), click the checkbox for Wet Edges.

11. Using a hard-edged brush, paint the torn edge of your image. The Wet Edges will create the effect that the edge has been burned by a small fire.

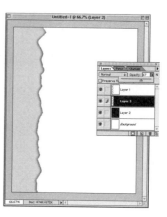

Fig. 6–37   A torn paper edge can create a cool effect for your printed page.

Fig. 6–38   Use the Freeform Lasso tool to create the torn edge.

Fig. 6–39   Set a realistic shadow on its own layer with a decreased opacity.

FLIPPING IMAGES

In Chapter 4, I described how the direction that your image faces plays an important part in how much attention the audience pays to the rest of your layout. If the image is facing away from the page, then your reader's eyes will tend to follow and move off the page as well.

But while flipping images in XPress is a simple matter, I also described a situation in which XPress was not the best program for this job. Figure 6–40 reprints the XPress example, showing that the flip not only changed the direction of the image but also made the text within the image backwards and unreadable. In this instance, however, the image has been corrected.

Look around your image carefully for even the slightest hint that something looks wrong when flipped. Words, numbers, logos, even the buttons on a man's jacket (which should be on the right) could give away an unnatural image flip.

Working in Photoshop:
Flipping Images

Flipping images is an easy task in Photoshop, although saving type or other issues can be a bit more challenging:

1. Choose Select –> All while in the layer of the image or object you want to flip.
2. Choose Edit –> Transform –> Flip Horizontal (or Flip Vertical).

Fig. 6–40   This reprint from Chapter 4 shows the problem with flipping some images. The text has been corrected in Photoshop.

3. If there are words or other portions that make it obvious that the image has been flipped, use a combination of the Rubber Stamp tool, the Free Transform function, and other tools to correct the situation. Unfortunately there are so many problems that could occur as a result of flipping that it would be impossible to give one standard way to fix them.

SAMPLE EFFECT: TURNING NEW INTO OLD

You have a brand new picture but you want to make it look like an old picture, like the ones from the turn of the century. You have two choices: you can let it sit around for a hundred years or so or you can digitize it and use some color manipulation tools (and a filter or two) in Photoshop:

1. Open your image. It won't matter for this example if it's RGB or CMYK.

2. Choose Image –> Adjust –> Desaturate. This will make your image look as though it's in Grayscale mode, but will still retain the color channels of RGB or CMYK (whichever you are currently working in).

3. Increase the shadows and the highlights—much early photography seemed to emphasize each considerably more than we're used to today. From the Layers palette pull-down menu, choose New Adjustment Layer.

4. Select Levels from the Type pull-down menu to access the Levels dialog box.

5. Manipulate the Input Levels by dragging the shadows slider to the right, and the highlight slider to the left. Continue this until you achieve a good sense of depth in your image. (See Photo Editing: Shadows and Highlights earlier in this chapter for more info on this). Hit OK when through.

6. Create a new Adjustment Layer again, except this time choose Color Balance from the Type pull-down.

7. For each of the shadows, midtones, and highlights, add a good amount of yellow, and just a hint of red, until you get an old looking sepia tone as shown in Color Figure 19.

8. Make the *Background* layer active by clicking on it.

9. Choose Filter –> Noise –> Add Noise to access the Noise dialog box. This will help give the image a grainy, aged appeal. Experiment with the slider to achieve your desired effect—the higher the resolution your image is, the more noise you'll have to add to see any real effect. The slight noise in my image is shown in Color Figure 20.

SUMMARY

It's true that a picture is worth a thousand words, but we all know that words can be quite harsh. A bad image, with weak colors, mistakes, dust, or other problems could be worse than having no image at all. Make sure that you take care and pride in the images that you intend to use in your print pieces. Understanding what looks good in print and how Photoshop can help you achieve these goals is the first major step.

chapter 7

CREATING

ILLUSTRATIONS

AND LINE ART

Standing in the Metropolitan Museum of Modern Art not too long ago, my friend Michali was marveling at the genius behind the brush strokes of a particular painting. I shrugged as I said that I could produce the same piece in Illustrator and probably faster. (I'll admit that I enjoy baiting her).

"Computer art doesn't count," she sneered.

And thus the debate began, as my friend, the voice for a dying breed of traditionalists and artistic purists, made her case for not accepting computer illustration as a viable art form. But the truth is that computer art programs, Adobe Illustrator in particular, are blurring the lines of what has historically been considered to be fine art.

In the advertising and digital publishing world, there is practically no room for hand-drawn art any longer.

This chapter will explain conceptually what type of illustrations you should consider using in your projects, and what elements can make them successful. Chapters 4 and 6, not only provided conceptual considerations but followed each with a "how-to" in that chapter's program of choice. That format is more limited here. That's because when discussing the benefits of keeping photographs in focus, for example, there is really only one method to accomplish this in Photoshop—the Unsharp Mask filter. This filter wouldn't work, however, if your goal is to change the color of the grass in a photo of a meadow. But Illustrator is different—the basic creation methods, namely paths, are needed regardless of what you are designing. Because of this, step-by-step methods for using Illustrator to accomplish any given conceptual goal would be limited and pointless.

This chapter will explain what Illustrator is and how to set it up for print production. An overview will provide the basics of how to use Illustrator, why it has such a strong foothold in the industry, and how to best prepare artwork for printing.

TOOL OF CHOICE:
ADOBE ILLUSTRATOR

Adobe Illustrator, while certainly not the only illustration program on the market, is far and away the most powerful tool of its kind. Works produced in Illustrator can range from simple minimalist pieces to complex, detailed mechanical drawings, to cartoon-style illustrations. Unlike Photoshop, which (normally) creates a final image using a pre-established element (photograph) as a base to begin work, Illustrator pieces are more commonly built from scratch, appearing on a blank canvas directly from the artist's mind. The lack of a safety net—the idea of starting from scratch rather than having a defined point of origin—can be very intimidating to some designers and has probably contributed to some of the anxiety that many novice graphic designers feel when learning Illustrator.

The Pen tool, of course, is the other reason.

Although newer versions of Illustrator have included alternate tools, such as brushes, to let you make free-form paths, the pen tool is still the most powerful. And, unfortunately, the Pen tool is also the most frustrating to learn. But this tool and the paths it creates are the heart and soul of Illustrator and little work of value can be created without them. We will discuss the Pen tool and how it works later in this chapter.

SAME CHEF, DIFFERENT MEAL:
ILLUSTRATOR AND PHOTOSHOP

Chances are if a designer is going to know one graphics program, it is going to be Adobe Photoshop. The incredible success of this program can be attributed to the fact that it appeals not only to professionals using it for practically any medium, but also to amateurs and hobbyists who are spellbound by Photoshop with every new color correction tool they learn.

That's not to say that Illustrator is the forgotten cousin by any means. It's a vastly powerful program itself, overshadowed only by the extreme popularity of Photoshop.

Given today's visual society, more lured by continuous tone photographic imagery, this is not much of a surprise. But line art has its place, too, and when the need is there, Illustrator excels.

Unlike Photoshop, which is a bitmap program (meaning that files are comprised of pixels) developed to deal with photographic imagery, Illustrator is a vector-based PostScript drawing program, meaning that it utilizes a mathematical equation to develop high-quality line art. Because of this, images in Illustrator are made up of separate *objects* of lines, text, and shapes, which can retain their independence from each other. Illustrator files will also print with well-defined edges and detail. And, because its formation is mathematical, you can zoom in on the image without fear of it breaking up, as would a Photoshop image.

While the ability to zoom in on an area of an image to see details is important for making corrections, some programs use this as an active feature. Macromedia's Flash, for example, is a vector-based program for creating web content. The fact that a Web surfer can zoom in on a Flash piece without losing resolution is a huge benefit to Web development.

If you read through Chapter 6, which provides a significantly deeper look at Photoshop, you'll notice that Illustrator is barely even mentioned, yet so far in this chapter Illustrator has only been described in terms of how it compares with Photoshop. That is because like a glass of merlot complements tenderloin, the great chef Adobe has continued to season Illustrator in such a way as to make it a perfect complement to Photoshop. To begin with, the interface is increasingly similar to Photoshop's, making it an easier psychological transition from one program to another. For many who are unfamiliar with either program, they might look like the same program at first glance. Figure 7–1 shows the interfaces of each, side by side, and the interface of an Illustrator version prior to 7.0. (I used 5.0.) You can see the dramatic improvement in the environment of the upgrade, and how much easier it is now to switch gears between Photoshop and Illustrator without having to think too much about it.

In addition, although Illustrator is a vector-based program, it can work with bitmap images to create photograph/illustrative conglomerations such as the one in Figure 7–2. It doesn't work the other way around, though. Photoshop can *import* Illustrator files, but will *rasterize* them, turning them into bitmap files. Once converted, they lose their vector-based properties.

The ability for Illustrator to handle bitmap files makes Illustrator an extremely powerful tool and an increasingly important application to master.

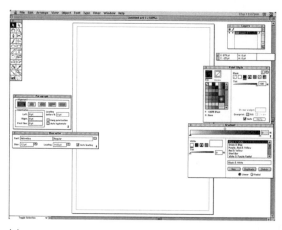

(a)

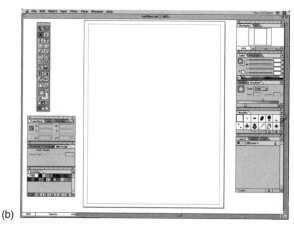

(b)

(c)

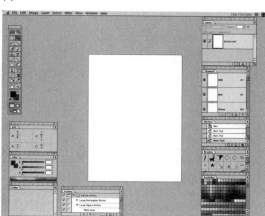

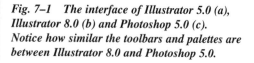

Fig. 7–1   The interface of Illustrator 5.0 (a),
Illustrator 8.0 (b) and Photoshop 5.0 (c).
Notice how similar the toolbars and palettes are
between Illustrator 8.0 and Photoshop 5.0.

Fig. 7–2　An image made from a combination of Illustrator and Photoshop imagery.

ILLUSTRATOR 8.0: NEW ADDITIONS

As with any other program, the new version of Illustrator has enough bells and whistles that you'll happily dole out more money to purchase the upgrade. The following are just some of the changes that were incorporated into Illustrator 8.0:

◆ **New Palettes:** Both the Navigator palette and the Actions palette, strong additions to recent versions of Photoshop, appear in Illustrator 8.0. The Navigator allows you significant freedom to zoom in and out of your image and move freely around your illustration. The Actions palette is a total time saver that lets you set up recipes of production that can be automatically applied to other parts of your image or other images.

◆ **Real-Time Blending:** Illustrator can now automatically update any color change, move, or edit that you make to a blend. It may not sound like much just to read about it, but you won't realize how much you've missed it in previous versions.

◆ **Free-Transform:** Again borrowing from Photoshop, the Free-Transform tool allows you to do all of the transform tasks at once. It may, in fact, be a step ahead of Photoshop, since Illustrator's transformation options are arguably cooler than Photoshop's.

◆ **A Better Blend:** Illustrator now lets you apply a gradient over more than just two paths and in far more than just a linear configuration. Now you can apply a gradient over an unlimited number of paths, both closed and open, compound and grouped, etc. In addition, these gradients aren't restricted to being straight—they can curve to fit practically any shape.

The Gradient Mesh tool is a great new tool for adding the sparks, shadows, and highlights of color that can really make an image "pop." This tool lets you add a new color to a path that is already filled with color. The new color will automatically blend in with the original color with just one mouse click. Pretty cool, huh? Figure 7–3 shows an example of how this tool works.

◆ **Links Manager:** A pretty handy feature for those inclined to place a lot of images into an Illustrator file. The Links Manager, shown in Figure 7–4, helps keep them organized, allowing you to locate them quickly, modify newly updated files, etc. This can be an important palette to refer to before you go to the service bureau for output (see Chapter 8 for more information on service bureaus).

◆ **Smart Guides:** These could possibly win the award for "Most Annoying New Feature" if you didn't have the ability to turn them off when you know you don't want them. When you do have them on, though, they can provide some welcome help in rotating, scaling, or otherwise transforming a tool. Smart Guides will appear when needed to help you make your change more accurate.

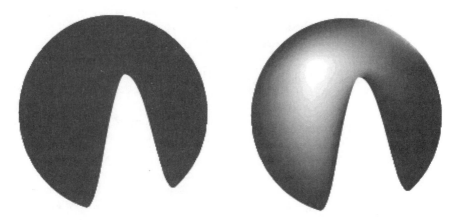

Fig. 7–3   The Gradient Mesh tool, new to version 8, can create a gradatient from one color into an already-existing color.

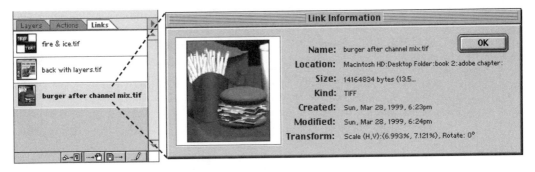

Fig. 7–4 The Links Manager helps you keep track of imported objects. Double clicking on a link provides detailed information about the object.

◆ **New Brushes:** New Illustrator brushes allow you a new range of versatility in control—from extracting certain shapes from an object to replacing a path with a stretched object or calligraphic line.

Of course there are more changes than just the ones listed here. Both major and minor adjustments can be found everywhere in Illustrator 8.0—far too many for the purposes of this book. For more information on new features to Illustrator, check out *Illustrator 8.0 To Go.*

ADJUSTING COLOR FOR PRINT

Having read Chapter 5, your head may still be spinning from color profiles and CMYK conversions and you're probably thinking that Web design is an attractive medium.

Well before you give up on desktop publishing and settle in with my other book, Illustrator color is far less complex and involved. In fact, one of the most important uses of preadjusting the color settings in Illustrator is so that when you import Photoshop files the colors will appear largely the same.

If you haven't already, you should calibrate your monitor. It's kind of a pain, and it horrible to have to do, but it will provide at least a little help in seeing colors true to life. For more information on calibration, see Chapter 5.

Some of you out there, though, might wonder why Illustrator has the Color Settings options included. The truth is, its main goal is to not scare the hell out of you with wide color shifts on-screen when you import Photoshop images into Illustrator, and to help ensure that you see your illustrations as true to life as possible. But it doesn't really work all that well and it's enough of a pain that I would recommend you skip it. But for the masochists out there that are intent on using this feature, here goes:

1. Since the main point in all this is to provide consistency between Photoshop files as they're seen in both Photoshop and Illustrator, you're going to have to do this in both programs to make sure that the profiles are identical. If you haven't already done so, go back to Chapter 5 and set up your RGB color space in Photoshop.

   You'll want to save your profile after you set it up. Mac users should save it in your System folder/Preferences/ColorSync Profiles folder. Windows users should save it in the Color folder in the System directory. For those of you with short-term memory problems (myself included), save the profile using a name that you'll recognize later.

2. Do the same for the CMYK profile.

3. Open Illustrator (if it's already open when you are doing all of this, quit and restart the program).

4. Choose File –> Color Settings. The dialog box that appears is shown in Figure 7–5.

5. From the Monitor (RGB) pull-down menu choose the RGB profile that you just created in Photoshop. Select the CMYK profile you created from the Printer (CMYK) pull-down menu.

6. Choose Perceptual (Images) from the Intent pull-down menu.

7. Leave Use Embedded ICC profiles unchecked. Since you will be using CMYK from Photoshop on your own system and have set up the color profile for both Photoshop and Illustrator, there won't be any conversion between the programs. If you will be importing images from an outside source (either Photoshop from an unfamiliar system or another program entirely), you could make a case for checking this box, which will cause the CMYK settings to convert to Illustrator's color space. Or you could just ignore this option altogether—like I said before, I'd opt to skip this whole process.

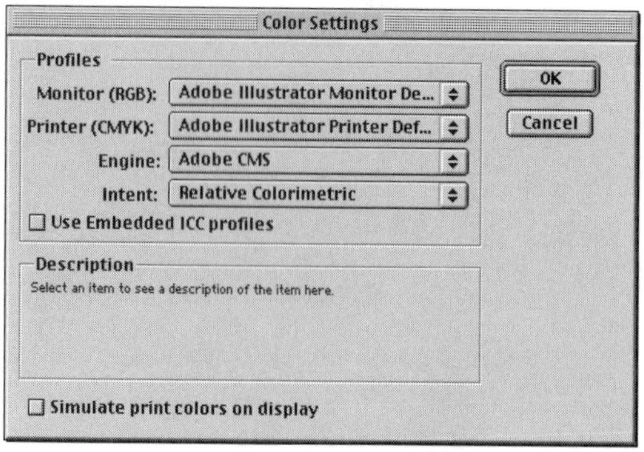

Fig. 7–5   The Color Settings dialog box.

CHANGING FROM RGB TO CMYK (AND GRAYSCALE, TOO!)

Illustrator allows you to change the color mode of any image. To change an image to RGB color mode choose Filter –> Colors –> Convert to RGB. The same path would be taken to convert an image to CMYK or Grayscale, except your last choice would be Convert to CMYK or Convert to Grayscale. A more detailed discussion of Color Modes appears in Chapter 1.

If you're planning on importing an image from Photoshop to Illustrator, you should make the conversion to CMYK while still in Photoshop. The color conversion in Photoshop is more accurate and any corrections you may need to make are better off made using Photoshop's tools.

Because Illustrator is a PostScript program and does not base its images on pixels, file sizes are relatively insignificant when compared to Photoshop files. So, while in Photoshop it might pay to work in RGB to save RAM and hard disk space, working in CMYK in Illustrator is not going to cost you much in file size. If the end result of your project is a printed piece, you'll be better off working in CMYK the whole time. (Or Grayscale for one-color pieces).

CREATING AND USING COLORS IN ILLUSTRATOR

The main items you'll need to become familiar with are the Fill and Stroke icons in Illustrator's toolbar, the Color palettes with the slider bars, and the Swatches palette. When you *fill* something, you are placing a body of color in its interior area and when you *stroke* something, you create an outline for it. Paths do not need to be closed in order to be filled or stroked. Each of these features is displayed in Figure 7–6 and can be accessed via the Windows menu. The two palettes are where you will mix, select, and save your colors and gradients. The toolbar lets you select how you want to use those colors—either filling your path with them or adding an outline or "stroke" to it.

MIXING A COLOR: THE COLOR PALETTE

You mix colors in Illustrator by manipulating the sliders in the Color palette—one slider for each color. The number of sliders available depends, obviously, on the color mode you are mixing in. You can select your desired color mode to mix colors in from the palette pull-down menu. Once in your desired mode, do the following to mix a color:

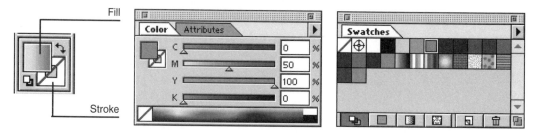

Fig. 7–6   *The Fill and Stroke icons, Color palette, and Swatches palette are important to know when it comes to Illustrator color.*

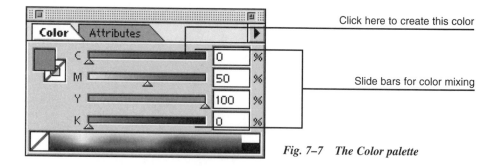

Fig. 7–7   *The Color palette*

1. Click on the portion of the spectrum bar (marked in Figure 7–7) that is the closest to the color of your choice.

2. Create a more specific color by moving the triangles below each slider to increase the amount of any specific color. You can also change the current values of each color by manually entering in new numeric values in the input boxes.

   ◆ The colors on each slider are there to help you select your colors more quickly and exactly. By looking at the bars, you can know in advance the color you will create by moving the triangle to that point. Once the triangle has been moved and the slider manipulated, the colors will be updated on the sliders automatically.

If there is a color on the slider that you like particularly, you don't have to hurt yourself moving the slider to it—just click on it and that color will be selected.

   ◆ Change the tint of the colors by holding the Shift key down while sliding or clicking. The tint will adjust through all colors that have a value greater than zero.

3. Change your color to black or white by clicking on the black or white buttons, in the spectrum bar.

If you are in Grayscale mode, you will only have one slider. You can choose white by moving the slider to the extreme left (0 value) or black by moving the slider to the extreme right (100 value).

If you are mixing colors in RGB mode, you may periodically see the same yellow triangle with an exclamation point that you see in Photoshop. This is the out-of-gamut warning to let you know that your chosen color is not available in CMYK mode. In other words, if you try to print with this color, you're likely to be disappointed.

4. You can choose a color from the Swatch palette (discussed in the next section). If you choose a process color, the slider adjusts to the proper setting for mixing that color and a new slider appears for adjusting the tint. If you select a spot color, you're limited to just one slider—to adjust the tint of the color.

WORKING WITH THE SWATCHES PALETTE

The Swatches palette is a storage center for process colors, spot colors, gradients, and patterns. Illustrator starts you off with a few predefined creations of each that appear when you open the palette. Typically, unless you change the order, process colors are in the first row, spot colors in the second row (each has a white triangle with a small dot in the lower right hand corner), and gradients and patterns are in the third row. To work with the palette:

1. Add a color that you created in the Color palette by either clicking on the New Swatch icon (indicated in Figure 7–8) or choosing New Swatch from the palette pull-down menu. New colors show up at the end of the swatch palette. To place your new color in a certain spot, drag the color from the Color palette to the Swatches palette and place it where you'd like it to go. Drag your new color in between two existing swatches to add a color. Option (Alt in Windows) + drag it onto an existing color to replace it.

2. Make two of the same swatch by dragging a swatch onto the Duplicate Swatch icon at the bottom of the palette or by highlighting it and choosing Duplicate Swatch from the pull-down menu.

3. Option (Alt in Windows) + drag one swatch in the palette onto another swatch to get rid of one (the one you are dragging onto will disappear).

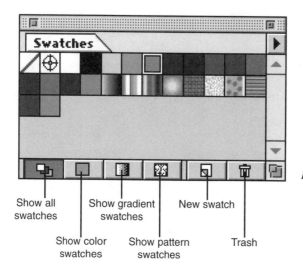

Fig. 7–8   The Swatches palette.

Show all swatches

Show gradient swatches

New swatch

Show color swatches

Show pattern swatches

Trash

4. You can also get rid of a swatch by dragging it to the trash can icon at the bottom of the palette or by clicking on the swatch and choosing Delete Swatch from the pull-down menu.

Unless you're really sure about it, choose the latter way of getting rid of a swatch to allow for any last-minute change of mind. The first way described just gets rid of the swatch with no warning. (Although you can always change your mind with the Undo button).

DESIGNATING A PREMIXED COLOR

As you read in Chapter 1, the CMYK color gamut doesn't include many of the colors that you can otherwise achieve from a mix of RGB colors. Metallic and neon colors in particular are counted among the missing. To compensate, companies such as Pantone, Trumatch, and others manufacture premixed colors that, for the most part, cannot otherwise be replicated with a combination of CMYK colors.

Illustrator, like Photoshop and QuarkXPress, allows you access to many color libraries of premixed colors. To access these libraries, choose Window –> Swatch Library and select your desired third-party premixed color library. The colors in this library will show up in a separate palette, which will be available to any open illustration.

Since these palettes will eat up RAM, and you will probably not need any more than a few of these colors for your illustration, add the ones that you need to your regular Swatches palette. To do this, Command (Ctrl in Windows) + click on the colors that you want and choose Add to Swatches from the palette's pull-down menu.

ADDING COLOR TO YOUR IMAGE

You can apply a fill or stroke to your path or object by doing the following:

1. Select a specific path from your canvas.

2. Make either the Fill or Stroke icon active by clicking on either one (the one that is active will be on top, see Figure 7–6).

3. If you are working with the Color palette, the color of your object will change as you manipulate the sliders or accept any manually entered numeric color value.

4. If you are working with the Swatches palette, simply click on any color to apply it to the selected object.

5. You can drag a swatch onto either the Fill or Stroke icon to apply that color to the object. The slim benefit of this is that you can drag the swatch onto either icon—it doesn't matter which is active. It's kind of picky, though—if you don't place it right in the center of the icon it doesn't always work. Personally, I'd say you're better off using the keyboard command to switch active icons (push the x key) and then just click on your choice of color in the Swatch palette.

6. To change the color of an object that is not selected, drag a color from the Swatches palette onto it. Whatever icon is currently active (Fill or Stroke) will be the recipient of the color change. Hold the Shift key down while dragging the color swatch to apply the color to the opposite of whichever icon is active.

OVERPRINTING SPOT COLORS

Chapter 1 went into detail as to what, exactly, an overprint color is, as well as how it works. If you haven't done so already, you may as well go back to Chapter 1 and learn it—the subject is going to appear both here and in QuarkXPress. Basically, when Overprinting is turned on, any two colors that lay on top of one another will mix together. With Overprinting turned off, the color that lies below the other is sacrificed to allow the overlaying color to print untainted. For example, if you have a blue square overlapping a red square, keeping Overprinting on will create a purple color where the squares overlap. Turning Overprinting off will only show the blue square, knocking out the red portion that lies beneath.

To turn Overprinting on, select the adjoining objects or paths that you want to affect and open the Attributes palette (shown in Figure 7–9) by choosing Windows –> Show Attributes. This palette gives you two checkboxes (among other things that don't have any relevance to this section). It's probably self-explanatory what will happen if you turn on the options for Overprint Fill and Overprint Stroke.

As was mentioned in Chapter 1, when you overprint colors, the mixture doesn't show up on screen. This could make it difficult to determine what color will be produced when it comes time to print. To see the mix of colors, you can choose Object –> Pathfinder –> Hard. This command will turn the intersection of two overprinted paths into its own separate path, then calculate and fill it with the result of the color mix.

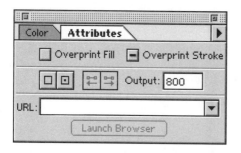

Fig. 7–9   The Attributes palette.

 While the Hard command is good for creating a mix of colors and displaying them on screen, the rest of your images may be off. Hard will also remix all of your spot colors to reflect their closest CMYK match. This, in many cases, largely defeats the point of using spot colors in the first place.

If you want to Overprint black for purposes of trapping, there is a separate filter for this. I'll go deeper into this in the section of this chapter concerning Traps.

FILE FORMATS FOR SAVING IMAGES

For the purposes of printing and what you're learning in this book, there are two main types of formats you'll need to be concerned with.

NATIVE ILLUSTRATOR

There's actually more than one kind of native Illustrator format, and I'm doing an injustice by bunching them all into one category. Illustrator 8.0, the current Version as of the time of this writing, has eight separate forms of Illustrator file that you can save your image as. It is important to remember that if you create something in version 8.0 to be compatible with earlier versions, you will lose any aspect that is unique to the Version 8.0 upgrade. The eight available formats are:

- Illustrator 8
- Illustrator 7
- Illustrator 6
- Illustrator 5
- Illustrator 4
- Illustrator 3
- Illustrator 88
- Illustrator 1.1

It is outside the scope and purpose of this book to provide a detailed explanation of each, and besides, I think you can probably figure out most of them just by their name. The exception being the Illustrator 88 format, which seems to be the odd man out. This was a longstanding standard format a number of years back, but is so ancient (relative to modern computer graphics) that you will lose many of the important features you're likely to use in your image when you save this way.

Illustrator EPS

This is the format you're going to use if you plan on laying out an ad or brochure in QuarkXPress or PageMaker, (which I'm assuming you plan to do, if you're reading this book). Figure 7–10 shows the dialog box you get when you choose to save in the Illustrator EPS format.

Make sure that the CMYK PostScript checkbox is checked, since your image will eventually be printed. Once again, the compatibility options are somewhat obvious—if you plan on opening the image again in Illustrator, just click the radio button that corresponds to the version number you will be using—most likely 8.0.

For Preview you have five choices, again fairly obvious:

◆ **None:** The only option that is cross-platform. It is also the smallest of the preview options in terms of file size. When you place the image in a layout program such as QuarkXPress, the program will only display an X where the image should be. When you print it, however, your image will appear on paper.

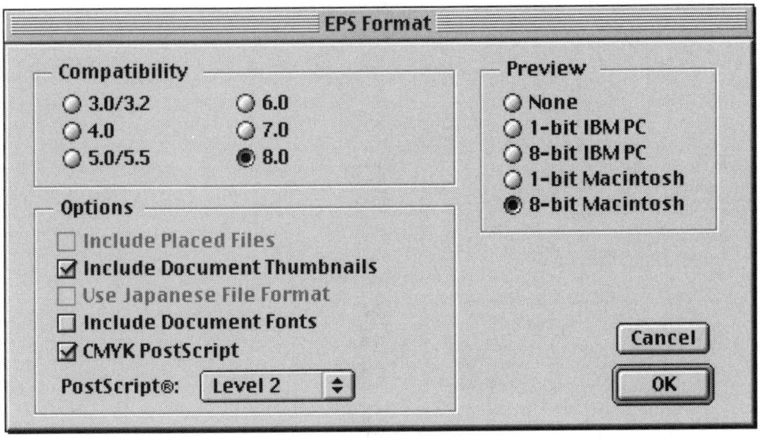

Fig. 7–10 The EPS Format dialog box

◆ **1-bit IBM PC and 1-bit Macintosh:** This option will preview your image in other programs as a crude black and white picture.

◆ **8-bit IBM PC and 8-bit Macintosh:** This will create a preview for other programs in 256 colors. These options will create the largest EPS files in terms of file size.

THE HEART OF ILLUSTRATOR: CREATING PATHS

If you are new to vector graphics, there are two basic truths you should know:

1. You will need to learn how to create paths.
2. You will probably do anything in your power to avoid learning how to create paths.

Paths are difficult to learn—no two ways about it. They can be one of the most frustrating aspects of graphics to really get control over, but they appear in a majority of graphics applications. In some programs, such as Illustrator, they play such an integral role as to be unavoidable. And, when all is said and done, after you finally master it, you'll find it to be such an important part of life you'll wonder how you ever lived without it.

Figure 7–11 shows a few simple paths. Each path that you create has at the very least the basic combination of two end points (also called *Anchor Points*) and a line between them. There are different types of Anchor points to use, and the type of Anchor point you use will decide the type of line that is created between them. Every path can have as many Anchor points as you desire and the number of points will play a role in how the path gets manipulated.

You can create paths a number of different ways in Illustrator, ranging from the "Have Illustrator do it for You" category—creating them from marquee selections or

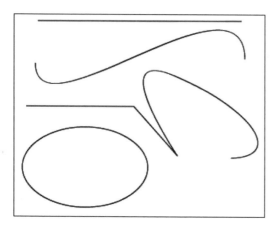

Fig. 7–11: Simple paths in Illustrator

text—to the seemingly impossible Pen tool. The Paintbrush and Pencil tools fall in between the two extremes in complexity of use. Illustrator 8.0 has made each more effective for creating paths. This does not mean you're off the hook when it comes to creating paths with the Pen tool—sorry, you still have to. It's the most precise and functional and it's the more universal method of creating paths.

PIERRE BÉZIER: AS TWISTED AS THEY COME

No matter where you are in the industry, you have at the very least heard the term *Bézier Curves*. These are the mathematical formulae from which a vector program such as Illustrator bases the curvature of a path. They were created by Pierre Bézier in the 1970s, in the hopes of torturing young graphic designers.

Actually there were more important reasons involved. Either way, the result was the mathematical structure that allowed for a curve to be created by the placement of two endpoints (Anchor points) and two random points on the path. These points could be shifted, moved, and manipulated to create virtually any form of curve. By combining two or more of these curves, one could create virtually any shape. In Illustrator, all of the mathematics responsible for this minor miracle are calculated behind the scenes, where they won't bother anybody.

 Bézier Curves were thought by Adobe engineers to be the most effective way to create curves on a page. They used this mathematical structure as the basis for all the curved shapes possible in PostScript.

CREATING WITH THE PEN TOOL

Okay, we've procrastinated long enough. It's time to rev up the motor and see what this baby can do. The following examples will give you hands-on experience with using the Pen tool to create straight, curved, and compound paths, as well as how to stroke, fill, and even wrap text around them.

CREATING A STRAIGHT LINE PATH

To create a simple path made up of straight lines:

1. Choose the Pen tool from the Tools palette. When you move the Pen Tool over the canvas, there is a small *x* next to it to indicate that it is about to start a new path.

2. Click a spot on the canvas. You'll see a dot, or an Anchor Point, at the place you click. This Anchor point is black because it's active. You'll also notice that the *x* next to the Pen icon has gone away, indicating that there is a path currently being built.

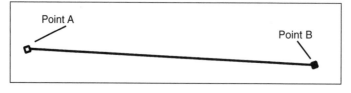

Fig. 7–12   Each path is bounded by two endpoints.

3. Move the pen somewhere else on the canvas and click on that spot. As Figure 7–12 indicates, Illustrator automatically draws a straight line segment from the starting point (point A) to the new point (point B). Notice that point A, which was black, is now an open square. This is because it is no longer the active point in the path. Point B is black to show that it is currently active—the line segment to the next point will come from point B.

4. Click somewhere new on the canvas. There is now a new straight-line segment from point B to the new point (point C). Point C is now the active point (it's black) and the next line segment will stem from it. Points A and B are now both open since they are inactive. Point B, in fact, is *really* inactive—since there are already two line segments connected to it, there can't be any more.

5. Click somewhere new on the canvas. There is now a new straight-line segment from point C to the new point (point D). Point D is now—okay, this can go on for a while. You get the idea, right? New segments appear between the active point and the new point and that new point then becomes the active point. This can go on forever—literally, until your fingers get tired of clicking the mouse or your computer just explodes. A path can have as many points as you want it to, until you end the path. Which leads us to…

Ending a Path

Before you can start a new path, you have to end your current one. You can end a path by doing any one of the following:

◆ Choosing Edit –> Deselect

◆ Command + click (Ctrl + clicking in Windows) on any area of your canvas away from your path.

◆ Clicking the pen tool in the toolbox.

◆ Closing the path that is, return to your starting point.

For the purposes of finishing the previous example, we'll go through the motions of closing the path:

6. When you're done connecting the dots all over the canvas, end the path by clicking on the point of origin, point A, the initial point. When you place the Pen tool over the initial point, the cursor changes, and includes a small *o* to indicate that it's about to close the path. Click on point A and the final segment will be drawn between the active point and the starting point.

7. You can now begin a new path anywhere else. If you move the cursor to a new spot on the canvas, you'll see that the icon again has a small *x* in it, indicating that there is no path currently being created.

Creating Curved Paths

Okay—straight lines were simple, right? Maybe all this talk about the Pen tool being tough to learn is just an extreme overexaggeration. Well, keep telling yourself that ... it'll make you feel better as you learn to draw curved paths.

1. Make sure your Pen tool is active. If you want, start a new document to begin creating your curves without interference from the path in the previous example.

2. Click on any point in your canvas to place the first anchor point, much like you did in the previous example. This time, though, do not just click the mouse button and release. Instead, click and hold the button, and drag the mouse upward. You'll notice that as you drag, you're creating a long solid line with a small dark circle at the end, as displayed in Figure 7–13. This is called a *handle* and we'll use it to set and adjust the direction and shape of the curve.

3. Click a new point (point B in Figure 7–14) approximately a quarter page to the right of your original point (point A). Again, don't just click and let go—click and drag your mouse downward, to create another handle. Your path should look like a semi-circle, similar to the one shown in Figure 7–14. There are a few other things you should note about the path that will help you understand how they work:

   ◆ The beginning of the curve is moving in an upward direction—the same direction that you originally dragged your mouse from point A.

   ◆ The path at this stage ended by moving downward to point B—the same direction in which you dragged the handle bar from point B.

   ◆ The extremity of the curve was directly related to the length of distance you pulled your handle bars.

   You may want to recreate this path again with these points in mind. In simple terms, curved paths will begin and end in the same direction that you drag the handles. The length of these handles will dictate the curvature of the path.

4. Create a new point on your canvas and drag your mouse in the direction of your choice. Without letting go, drag the handle bar to different areas on your canvas to see how it affects the curvature of your path.

Fig. 7–13   Handle bars from an endpoint determine the direction and shape of the curve.

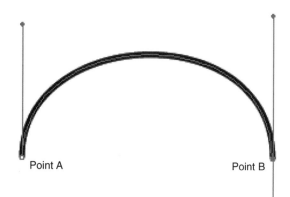

Point A   Point B

Fig. 7–14   By pulling handle bars, you can manipulate the curved path.

Notice that only the path segment between point B and your new point is being affected—the path segment between points A and B remains still.

FILLING AND STROKING YOUR PATH

Any path that you create can be a candidate for filling or stroking. Text, marquee selections, and paths like the ones created in the previous exercise can all be used.

Fill a path by doing the following:

1. Choose the Selection tool from the Toolbox and click on your path to activate it.

2. Select a color from the Color palette, the Swatches palette, or the Gradient palette.

3. Click the Fill area in the toolbar, shown back in Figure 7–6.

Stroke a Path by:

1. Choosing the Selection tool from the toolbox and clicking on your path to activate it.
2. Selecting a color from the Color palette, the Swatches palette, or the Gradient palette.
3. Using the Stroke palette to set the weight and other attributes for your stroke.
4. Click the Stroke icon in your toolbar, also shown back in Figure 7–7.

More (and More General) Path Info

Up to now you've been given the basics (the *very* basics) of what you need to know to start creating paths in Illustrator. The following will provide you with a general description of what else you can do regarding paths and the power they command over computer illustrations.

Joining Paths

You can join two open paths together to create one complete open path or one closed path. This allows you to apply effects to them as a single path and work on them as one item.

Compound Paths

A Compound Path is when two or more paths intersect each other and eliminate the area in which they intersect. This area can be left empty, or can be available to be filled with an alternative color, gradient, pattern, or type. Figure 7–15 shows an example of a compound path and the area dropped out in the intersection.

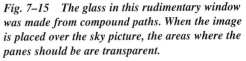

Fig. 7–15   The glass in this rudimentary window was made from compound paths. When the image is placed over the sky picture, the areas where the panes should be are transparent.

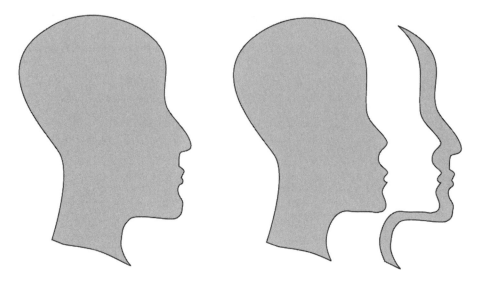

Fig. 7–16   By cutting a path, one face becomes three.

Cutting a Path

You can split a path into pieces, which is useful for other type of effects and image creation. Paths can be either at an Anchor point or a path segment. Figure 7–16 shows a sample of different paths that have been cut.

AND THAT'S IT FOR PATHS!

If you believe that, then please email me—I have a bridge you might be interested in. Paths and the Pen tool do not instill nightmares in new designers for nothing. There is far more that you can do with paths, curves, points, and all the rest, that is beyond the scope of this book. But these last few pages should have given you the head start that you need to get the feel for Illustrator, and decide what part it will ultimately play in your work process. For more information on Illustrator, check out *Illustrator 8.0 To Go*.

SETTING TRAPS

If you read through Chapter 1, you may have noticed the subtle suggestion that you pay someone to set your traps for you, as opposed to doing them yourself. Traps are a tricky business and none of these software programs is a wizard at this process. Setting traps can be so important, in fact, that entire technologies, including Scitex, TrapWise, IslandTrapper, and others, have been developed—some with the express purpose of setting your traps properly.

True, paying a service bureau can cost you—but the costs are negligible compared to setting the traps improperly and having to run your project through the press again. Chapter 1 details what trapping is, when you need to worry about it, and why it can be so bad if not taken seriously.

There are those, I'm sure, who'll still insist on doing this step for themselves. If you fall into this category, let me offer you my sincere wishes for the best of luck and the following directions.

When setting traps in Illustrator, you have to set them individually instead of universally throughout your document. This makes sense considering that each set of paths that need trapping could need different treatment, depending on its attributes. Chapter 1 describes which situations are the right ones for setting traps.

 You can only trap paths that are filled with a single color. Gradated paths won't trap, nor will patterns of images brought into Illustrator from another program such as Photoshop. Text and stroked paths won't trap either, but there are workarounds for these.

To set a trap around text:

1. Select the text to which you want to apply the trap.
2. Choose Type –> Create Outlines to change the text into paths.

 Your copy will be uneditable as paths—you can manually change the shape by moving the endpoint, handle bars, or segments, but you won't be able to change the wording with the Type tool.

To set a trap around a stroked path:

1. Select the path to which you want to apply the trap.
2. Choose Filter –> Object –> Path –> Outline Path to change the stroked path to a filled path.

In Illustrator, you can establish paths by selecting the paths in question and choosing Filter –> Object –> Pathfinder –> Trap. The Trap dialog box is shown in Figure 7–17. If it's active when you open it, then chances are the paths you have selected are good candidates for traps. If it's not active (all areas are grayed out), then you can assume that the paths don't need a trap set or that you've selected text, gradients, stroked paths, etc. that cannot have a trap applied.

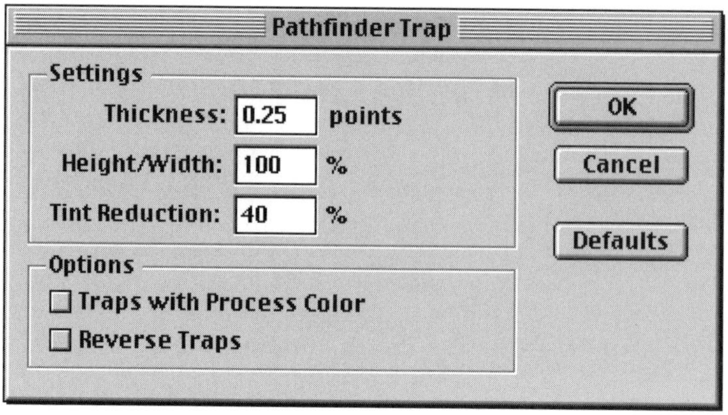

Fig. 7–17   The Trap dialog box.

The dialog box has the following commands:

◆ **Thickness:** This option allows you to set the width of your trap in terms of points. The default is a quarter of a point, which is really pretty low. In my opinion, you'll want to increase this. If you have confidence in your printer, you may want to increase it just a bit, maybe a tenth to .35. If you aren't so sure, increase this up to a point. If you have such a lack of confidence in your printer that you feel the need to go beyond a point, then you want to consider finding another printer.

Just to be on the safe side, discuss the project with your printer and ask him how thick the trap should be.

◆ **Width/Height:** You can use this to set the width to height ratio of your trap. At 100 percent, the trap will have an equal thickness throughout. The thickness was set in the previous value control. The horizontal thickness will always be equal to the Thickness value, while the vertical thickness will change relative to the Width/Height value. Raise the value to increase the vertical thickness, and lower the value to decrease the vertical thickness.

◆ **Tint Reduction:** This option lets you set the tint percentage of the lighter color between the paths in question. When the paths in question are each filled with process color, Illustrator will create a trap color by mixing the full intensity tint (100 percent) of the darker color with a lighter tint (the percent value that you set in this command) of the lighter color.

If the two paths that you are trapping are filled with spot colors, then Illustrator will set the path with the percentage tint that you choose of the lighter color.

◆ **Traps with Process Color:** Click this on to fill the trap with CMYK color, even if both of the lighter of the paths is a spot color. Since you generally don't want to have the darker color print over the lighter spot color, you'll usually want to leave this box unchecked.

◆ **Reverse Traps:** Although sometimes it's fairly obvious which color is lighter and which color is darker, other times it's more of a judgement call. Navy Blue and Forest Green, for example can really go either way. If Illustrator chooses the Navy Blue as the lighter color, and uses a tint of this to set the trap, but you think that the Forest Green is really the lighter of the two, click the Reverse Traps checkbox to force Illustrator to switch between them.

SETTING TRAPS BY OVERPRINTING BLACK

As you read in the Overprinting Spot Colors section of this chapter, overprinting with black has its own special filter. Remember that Overprint = mix, so that when you are overprinting two colors, you are, in essence, mixing them together. I also noted that one of the inherent problems in terms of spot colors is that you really can't be *sure* how the mixed color will look when it comes off the press. Even the Hard command is actually mixing the CMYK equivalent of the spot colors, which can be significantly different. That's not as much of a problem with overprinting black—it doesn't take a brain surgeon to guess the result of black mixed with any other color.

In my opinion, it's almost always a good idea to overprint black—especially if you're working with small, thin letters. Serif fonts are particularly strong candidates for overprinting, as the serifs can get particularly thin at certain points.

To overprint black, select the objects (these can include text, unlike setting Traps) in which you want black to overprint, and choose Filters –> Colors –> Overprint Black. Figure 7–18 shows the dialog box that you'll encounter, which has the following commands:

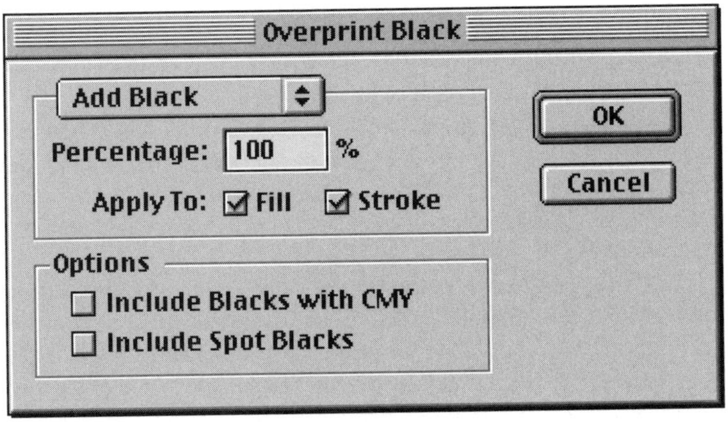

Fig. 7–18   The Overprint Black dialog box.

◆ The, um, pull-down menu: I don't know why they didn't give this a name, so for now we'll just refer to it as the, um, pull-down menu. Choose either Add Black or Remove Black. Remove Black is if you had already set black to overprint and want to remove the overprint command.

◆ Percentage: Overprinting black doesn't have to apply only to full blacks—you can control the percentage of blacks that you want to overprint. All of the blacks at this exact percentage in your objects will have overprinting applied.

◆ Apply to Fill and Apply to Stroke: As I said earlier, I think these are somewhat self-explanatory. If you can't figure these out on your own, please consult with a physician.

◆ Include Blacks with CMY: As an equal opportunity overprinter, Illustrator has provided this checkbox. Leave it off to ignore objects whose matching percentage of black is part of the larger CMY component. Click it on to make sure that even these objects will overprint.

◆ Include Spot Blacks: Check this box if you want all colors to be printed as spot color. Checking this box will allow all spot blacks in your image to overprint.

CONCEPTUAL ISSUES: WHAT WORKS IN ILLUSTRATION

Different illustration types conjure different messages. As you can see, illustration has a wide range of styles, all potentially wildly different from one another.

LIGHTENING THE MOOD WITH CARTOON ILLUSTRATIONS

In the past it would have been easy to define a cartoon. The word itself invokes thoughts of bubbly characters, happy faces, and artwork that inherently makes you laugh—Garfield, Bugs Bunny, Fred Flintstone. But go to your corner newspaper stand and look at any of the new comic books on the stand. Batman is an increasingly morose character, often with sharp edges, dark shadows, and more drama than a soap opera on the Fox network.

But whatever type of cartoon you create, be it funny and light or dark and serious, one characteristic sets them into a class by themselves: they are almost never realistic. In some instances, the features are distorted. In other instances, the coloring is off, such as the comic staple of using blue for dark hair highlights. Sometimes the drawings are just too simplistic to be mistaken for real likenesses.

Fig. 7–19   Cartoonish illustrations give a light, fun feel to the piece.

Whichever elements are different though, the stand-out style of cartoons gives your print work a lighter feel, less realistic and possibly less serious. Because of this, you'll likely want to stay away from cartoon illustrations when working with corporate material. However, as Figure 7–19 shows, cartoons are perfectly at home in print pieces whose topic is more lighthearted and fun.

While there is no definitive way to demonstrate how to create cartoons in Illustrator (once again, it's all in how you place the paths), it's worth noting that Illustrator is the perfect vehicle for cartoons. That's because as a vector-based program, Illustrator is incapable of creating continuous tone color, such as you find in a photograph. Instead, it uses large patches of colors or relatively simple gradients. This color limitation makes Illustrator the perfect program for creating great cartoons, comics, and spoofs of real life.

Realistic Illustrations

For a more serious tone to your print piece, try illustrations that more closely resemble real life, such as the ones shown in Figure 7–20.

These illustrations can be used to reinforce a point, or depict a real person, place, or situation.

Why, you might ask, would anyone choose a real-life illustration to a photograph for inclusion in a print piece? There are a couple of reasons why:

◆   Photographs are not readily available of your desired subject matter.

◆   You or your client prefer this style over photography.

◆   The subject cannot be photocopied, such as a house under construction.

Fig. 7–20   Realistic illustrations can add a more serious tone.

Most realistic illustrations tend to be black-and-white line art, without the addition of color. This is especially true for computer-generated illustrations that are realistic in nature.

Abstract Illustrations

Besides cartoons, abstract artwork is what Illustrator does best. Really, any conglomeration of shapes and squiggles that can be seen as a random work by a heavily drugged psuedoartist can be labeled "abstract." (You can see that I have a very honest view of modern artistic practices and the amount of crap therein.)

Abstract art does work, however, for very traditionalist clients and, even though there is typically a lot of color, for corporate work. As abstract pieces are typically thought of as "high art," many corporations can forgive the use of wild abandon of shape and color and happily adorn their brochures, annual reports, and other material with them.

The great thing about abstract art, such as that shown in Figure 7–21, is that it is purely subjective. Unlike realistic illustrations, which either look right or don't, abstract art is purely in the eyes of the designer and the audience. What one person would hang on a refrigerator, another would hang on the wall of a museum. And Illustrator, with its paths, shapes, spot colors, and gradients, is the perfect tool for abstract creation.

Technical Drawings and Diagrams

Technical drawings, like the ones shown in Figure 7–22, are really more for information than for aesthetics. Found primarily in any brochure or catalog created for hi-tech or complex engineering firms, they give a graphical representation of how something, such as a car or an electrical switch, works underneath the outer shell.

Illustrator is a fine tool for creating technical drawings that have some color and life to them, making the information easier to absorb. However, truly detailed drawings are more likely to be developed in a program like AutoCad, which concentrates more on the technical side than the aesthetics.

Fig. 7–21   Abstract illustration, often used in obscure corporate work, is purely subjective.

Fig. 7–22   Technical drawings provide details about a product or concept.

SOME TYPE OF FUN

Type is an inherent component of practically every print job you do. Of course there will be the rare occasions where your work will be so outstanding that it will stand on its own without a need for copy at all, but by and large the written word will usually make its way onto your page. Body type, which gives the details and meat of your message, is usually uneventful save a few layout techniques as described in Chapter 4. Titles, headlines, and other key words or phrases can draw attention by becoming a part of your image. And while every program discussed in this book allows you to set type (QuarkXPress has integrated many cool, Illustrator-like features in Version 4.0), designers have religiously turned to Illustrator for type placement.

The reason is that while there are many cool things you can do to words in Photoshop, they are dwarfed by what you can do to type in Illustrator. Being a vector-based program, Illustrator lets you twist, turn, fold, spindle, and mutilate type in ways Photoshop can only dream about. There's nothing stopping designers, of course, from setting their type in Illustrator and importing it into Photoshop for more photographic effects, which is exactly what most do.

Type Along a Path

Who says type has to be in a straight line? Straight can be useful, but too much of it can be as boring as watching Al Gore debate, well, anyone. The reader's eye deserves a break from the straight and narrow once in a while, and, as long as it's not overdone or seemingly random in its path, type that has a funky direction to it can add a touch of fun and ingenuity to your work.

You can use type in odd directions to your advantage. If you read Chapter 3, you know that the eye will move in certain patterns over a printed page. Usually, providing there are no obstructions, a one-page layout will be read from the top-left corner to the lower-right corner. But an example was also given of an image that was ill used: the person in the photograph was facing away from the rest of the page and the reader's eye followed the person's gaze right off the page and away from the message. The same holds true for text—if it's running in an odd direction, the reader's eye will follow it.

Working in Illustrator:
Setting Type Along a Path

To set type along a path in Illustrator,

1. Create a path using any one of the path creation tools, such as the brush described earlier. For the sake of this example, make sure that the path is curved. It doesn't matter if the path is open or closed.

2. Choose the Type Path tool, as shown in Figure 7–23.

3. Click on the path with the Type Path tool. A cursor will appear.

4. Begin typing. As you type, the text will follow the shape of the path you created.

5. The type you create will appear on the top of the path. To make it appear below the path (but stay right-side up and running in the proper direction), open the Character palette shown in Figure 7–24 by choosing View —> Show Character.

6. Use the baseline shift function to lower your type as far down as you want.

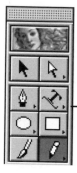

Fig. 7–23   The Type Path tool.

Type Path tool

Fig. 7–24   The Character palette

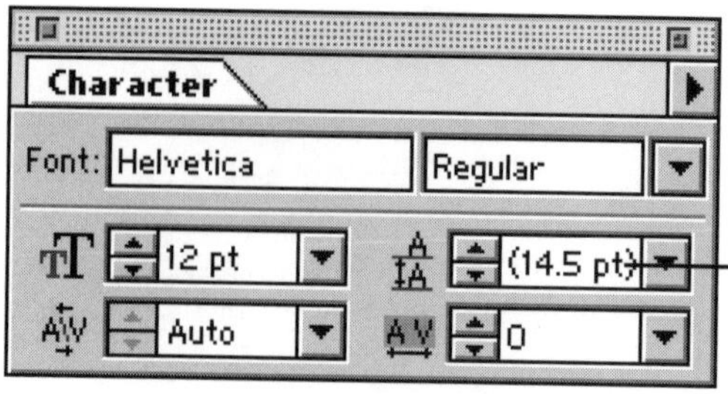

Baseline
Shift

Turning Text into a Path

There can be more to text than just the way you place it. What if you could actually start with a base font style and then easily manipulate the outline? You'd be able to create very cool-looking logos, headlines, and type-like graphics. A few samples are shown in Figure 7–25.

Working in Illustrator:
Turning Text into a Path

Turning text into a path is easy—it's what you do with it afterward that's up to you!

1. Set your type however you'd like it.

2. Select the type with the Selection tool. Having the type selected with the Type tool will not work for this example.

3. Choose Type –> Create Outlines. Your text will look like the text shown in Figure 7–26, with each letter now its own editable path. Any "holes" in letters, such as in "b" or "d," will be transparent.

Fig. 7–25   *Type after being turned into paths.*

Fig. 7–26   *By turning type into paths, you can manipulate it into cool-looking logos and pictures.*

Make sure that all spelling is correct before you turn your type into a path and edit it. Once it's done, the only way to go back is to hit the Undo command—there is no way to change a path into type, so you'll be stuck with either living with a typo or starting over again.

In Chapter 8 I discuss how I would never, ever, disobey the copyright law and simply hand over fonts to my service provider. Really, that is not sarcastic. Not at all. Other moral souls out there, who do not want to provide their service bureau with fonts they might not have, can use the Create Outlines feature to set type and give the layout to your bureau with no copyright infringement.

PRINTING FROM ILLUSTRATOR

If you read the end of Chapter 6, you already know what I'm about to say. But it holds doubly true for Illustrator, because designers (new? cheap?) are more likely to try and lay out their entire project in Illustrator than they are in Photoshop. Hey, it's a PostScript program, right? What you see is what you get, right? Maybe, but remember, Illustrator is a *drawing* program. That's pronounced "draw-ing"…not "lay-out." While you may be able to lay out a page in Illustrator, you're going to gain a lot more functionality, control, and respect from the service bureau if you lay things out in QuarkXPress like you're supposed to. It may be a somewhat expensive tool, but as I warned you in Chapter 1, prepress design is not a cheap endeavor.

SUMMARY

Illustrations are effective ways to add the kind of life, vibrancy, and effects that photographs often can't provide. Whether your need is for a cartoon, a diagram, or even just a colorful collage, illustrations are a proven tool of success. While this chapter has far from provided an exhaustive manual on how to use Adobe Illustrator to accomplish these illustration needs, it has given you the information you need to get started and a springboard into any further research.

chapter 8

PREPARING FILES
FOR PRINT:
WORKING WITH A
SERVICE BUREAU

The service bureau sector of the industry has grown significantly over the past few years. It's no coincidence that this growth has coincided with the recent popularization of computer graphics and the deconstruction of hand drawings and mechanicals as the standard for advertising design.

The service bureau typically performs a variety of functions. How much a part of your life they become will really rely on what type of projects you are working on. There are many instances in which you will need a service bureau, such as:

◆ You need to provide a client with a high-quality proof, like an IRIS or a Fiery for an initial draft of your project.

◆ Your desktop printer or computer breaks down and you need to change or print something in a hurry.

◆ You need to have chromes, positives, slides, or other material scanned in at a higher resolution and quality than you can get from your desktop scanner.

◆ You are creating a project such as an annual report, brochure, or flyer that will be reproduced in large quantities and you need to present film to your printer.

◆ You are designing an ad for a client that will run in a magazine and the publication requires you to provide color separations.

◆ You need a final, close-to-exact color proof like a Matchprint to have your client sign off on.

◆ You have an intense longing for some really in-depth conversations about Star Trek or just feel like geeking-out with a discussion of last year's MacWorld convention. (I try to keep away when these things are occurring.)

You would probably not have much of a need of a service bureau if:

◆ You are working on things for yourself and precision of color in your drafts is not vital to you.

◆ You are working with a client whose budget simply doesn't allow you to spend money on high-quality proofs.

◆ You are creating projects such as internal company newsletters or flyers where the demand for quality is such that you can get away with using your desktop printer.

◆ You are creating projects that will have a low enough print run that you can utilize the services of a digital press (otherwise called *direct to press*).

◆ You really, really hate Star Trek and MacWorld has never really impressed you.

If any of that last set of circumstances applies to you, you can probably skip this chapter, and jump right ahead to Chapter 9. If your work falls into the first set, you'll probably want to read this chapter rather thoroughly.

A BRIEF OVERVIEW OF PRINTING AND THE SERVICE BUREAU'S PLACE IN OUR WORLD

Although Chapter 9 is dedicated in full to the science and art of printing, the process actually starts here, at the prepress stages. If you read through Chapter 1, you understand that pieces get printed with a mixture of four primary printing colors: cyan, magenta, yellow, and black. When you are looking at your project on screen, you are seeing a composite of these colors—or what your image looks like when the CMYK colors are mixed together.

 Remember, even if you are working in CMYK color mode, you are still seeing images in RGB—the monitor you are looking at uses phosphors to shoot red, green, and blue light into your eyes.

For a four-color project, a printed piece reaches completion after having gone through a process in which the paper travels through a printing press, and each of the four primary printing colors is laid on, one at a time, in a series of dots. The intensity of these dots, their angle, and their proximity to one another determine what color and shade of color your eye will be fooled into seeing.

The printer uses *plates* that go on the press to apply each color (see more about plates in Chapter 9). He makes these plates from the film that the service bureau provides to him—one piece of film per CMYK color per page of the project. The service bureau outputs this film and, if the budget allows, a Matchprint (or *color key*) for the printer to follow and use as a visual aid when printing.

THINGS YOU SHOULD KNOW WHEN CHOOSING A SERVICE BUREAU

Like anything else, you have to shop around when trying to find a good service bureau. Service bureaus are like auto mechanics—the mass populace has little idea what's going on behind their doors. Some are honest, and provide great work and reasonable pricing. Others arn't and they'll take advantage of you if you give them half the chance.

Following is a list of some of the things you should find out about a service bureau. Some may seem obvious, but they're important enough to warrant a review:

◆ What is the extent of their services? Not all bureaus offer the same services and you'll be better off knowing exactly what they do and do not handle.

◆ Do they prefer to receive raw files or Postscript files? (This is explained later in this chapter.)

◆ Are their systems calibrated, and if so, how? Do you need any special software to calibrate your system to work with it properly?

◆ What is their pricing policy? Are there price breaks for separating a large amount of film, or price reductions for providing the PostScript files instead of raw files (again, this is explained later in this chapter).

◆ What is their turn-around time for various projects?

◆ Are they willing to talk to your printer directly? This may be necessary if you are unavailable and the bureau needs to find out a line screen, paper type, etc.

◆ Will they check the film for errors before they send it out for print? Even better, will they check your files before they output anything and call to warn you of potential problems?

There are a few other questions along the same lines as the last two, such as what they are responsible for in terms of mistakes, and what you are responsible for. But many of these issues come down to one simple issue: money. Most service bureaus are small shops with a relatively small staff, rather than big service bureau chain conglomerates. Every dollar counts to these guys. If I can be so bold—if you plan on using your service bureau often, try to pay them either as soon as the project is done or at least within ten days. The better you treat them, the better they'll treat you. The better they treat you, the more money you'll save from frivolous mistakes and problems.

Every service bureau is different and each works in a different way. So let me take this opportunity to save myself hordes of angry email and tell you that much of this chapter is recommendations stemming from my own individual experience. You'll want to keep these points in mind when you discuss things with your service bureau, but understand that what I am writing may not apply to every shop and every situation.

How Do You Find a Service Bureau, and Do You Need More Than One?

Unfortunately, you probably can't just open up the yellow pages and look up "service bureau" expecting to find anything. If you don't already know of one, you can usually get the name and number of a couple by asking your commercial printer—they usually stay in close contact with service bureaus in the area.

You may be wondering whether or not your printer can provide some of the same services as a service bureau. While I can't say this for all printers, the answer is that the majority of them do not offer these services and rely on outside bureaus. In my experience, the ones that have provided services such as outputting film or printing IRISs typically don't do a great job of it. These services are very exacting and are typically left to those who are not otherwise involved watching over a Heidleberg press.

Besides your printer, you can also give a call to your local SCORE chapter, which are groups of retired business men and women who try to help up-and-coming businesses with advice, information, or whatever else, or call your local Chamber of Commerce.

As for whether or not you need more than one service bureau, it depends on what the different bureaus offer and what they're good at. For example, when I need IRIS proofs to provide drafts to my clients, I use Pro-Set Color (see Acknowledgments). Their IRISs are so far superior to any others I've seen that I can rely on them to be within a fraction of a shade of what the final printed piece will look like. But when it comes to outputting film and Matchprints for the printer, I send all my files to ElectroType (profiled in this chapter). I haven't found another bureau yet that can match their quality of film, speed of service, and prices.

DOES PLATFORM MATTER?

Not really, and as the days progress, it's becoming less and less important which platform you use. The predominant platform at the service bureau is still Macintosh, but since designers are slowly beginning to take advantage of Windows NT, service bureaus are starting to add more Windows capabilities. Don't be surprised, though, if you give your service bureau Windows files and they charge you a little extra—most have not yet made a full conversion to Windows and it's a hassle for many of them to output these files. You'd also be wise to be available for each phase of the conversion if you use Windows files—certain unwanted shifts in layout could happen that could cause problems, and extra money.

While most bureaus are still Macintosh-based, at the time of this writing, many are still using QuarkXPress 3.3 instead of the newer version. This is because the initial release of 4.0 was so buggy that most of the free world immediately removed it from their systems. Although most of the problems have since been fixed, bureaus have been gunshy about reinstalling it. This book is written referencing Quark 4.0.4 because bureaus are likely to switch to the new version of XPress en masse more quickly than they are likely to embrace Windows.

GETTING FILES READY FOR OUTPUT: A TALE OF TWO CHOICES

I remember once when I was younger, maybe about eight or nine years old. I had been to a friend's house while he was mowing the lawn. He was sweating, he was tired, and he complained that he'd rather be playing, but he said it was something that he did practically every week, and (unbeknownst to me) so did many of our friends. I had never mowed the lawn at my house—was I missing something?

I went home immediately and asked my dad why he had never shown me how to mow the lawn. "I didn't know you wanted to learn," he said. "Come on—I'll show you." I beamed a smile—finally, I was going to get to sweat and work and be miserable just like my friends! My dad took me to the kitchen. "Here's how you mow the lawn," he started. "First you open this drawer and take out the big yellow book. Open it to the L page and look at all the titles until you find one that says 'Lawn Care.' Pick a name, dial the number, and when someone answers, say 'come mow my lawn.' And that's all there is to it."

I had to admit—that was easier.

Besides being a cute recollection of my childhood, there actually *is* a point to that story: it is analogous to the choice you have when preparing files for the service bureau. Basically, when you are getting ready to have your project output to film, you have two choices, each with certain pros and cons:

◆   You can give your service bureau a PostScript file. This means that you can plan on what could amount to quite a bit of work. In presenting the PostScript file, you will be saving your layout, fonts, images, colors, etc. into one compact file, already configured to your service bureau's output device. You will have to set your own traps, eliminate unwanted Quark colors, set the line screen, and go through a number of other steps before your file is totally prepared for delivery.

   The benefits of this are that you are in total control of your files, which some people prefer, and that if you consistently output a large quantity of files to film, you can expect a reduced price (usually) for setting up the PostScript file for the bureau. The negatives of doing this are that while you are in control, you are also liable for anything that goes wrong—all the service bureau will do is push the print button and any mistakes will be your fault (costing extra dollars). Another, more succinct negative is that it's just a pain to set up.

◆   You can give the service bureau all of the individual files that go into your project—fonts, images, etc.—and let them take care of all the work for you. The bad part about this method is that you are giving them some control of your project and it may cost you a bit more for them to set it up for output. You also have to remember to provide all the necessary ingredients or things could get ugly. But the benefits are great—you are not liable for most mistakes, and it's far, far easier.

Those are your two basic options. I'll describe each of them in this chapter, but my recommendation would be to opt for the latter of the two choices. It may seem like the easy way out and the lazy way of doing things, but the way I see it, it's simply a question of mathematics:

1.   Read about what is involved with both providing the Postscript file and providing the raw files later in this chapter. You'll need to know both to properly use the equation we'll derive.

2.   Take your hourly charge and call it *x*. If you or your company work with project pricing rather than hourly rates, estimate what an hourly charge would be.

3.   Try to guess at how long it would take you to finish the job using one or the other of the delivery methods. Call this figure *n* and express it as a decimal.

4.   Multiple *x* times *n*.

5. Figure out what the approximate percentage chance is that you'll screw something up while setting up the file(s) for whichever method you are currently estimating for (whichever method you chose in Step 3). Express this as a decimal and call it *r*.

6. Call your service bureau and ask the price for outputting film (plus color proof if desired—this will be discussed later in the chapter). Find out prices for both delivering the Postscript file or the raw files. Call this amount *q*. Multiply *q* times *r*.

7. Here's the equation for your total cost for the project (I'm no mathematician, but this equation has worked for me):

$$x(n) + r(q) = \$\text{your cost}$$

8. Do this again for whichever method you did not already try. For example, if you just went through this equation and plugged in values based on you providing PostScript files, go back and recalculate the values based on providing raw files.

For my situation, there is no question: financially it makes more sense to provide the raw files. There is, of course, the argument that you lose control of your files, subjecting them to reflow, font substitutions, etc., and that it's very, very difficult to find a really good service bureau. My response: like any industry, it's not always easy to find a person or a company who can do the job well. Not all dentists are great dentists, but you still go and you try to find the best one—you don't take a drill and start going to town on your own teeth, do you? Find a service bureau who is reputable and can do a good job for you, provide them with the proper files and paperwork (see next section) and you should be okay. You might even be able to save your client a little money in the process.

PROVIDING RAW FILES

Although this is my favorite way of providing files to my service bureau, there are a number of things that you have to remember to collect for delivery.

The Quark Files

First of all, make sure that you check over all your files carefully. This is probably obvious, but it never hurts to be reminded again to check your spelling, spacing in your layouts, bleeds, etc. The checklist at the end of this section provides a full list of the things you need to watch out for.

QuarkXPress does not use the actual images in its layout. Rather, it uses any previews of your photographs, graphics, or illustrations that were created when you saved them originally. These previews are typically 8-bit representations of your images, which is why your graphics never look as good in Quark as they do in the original creation program. In order for your project to output properly, Quark needs to have all of the images available to reference. You'll need to collect these into a file to present to the service bureau.

Quark has a handy little command that can be very helpful when it comes to collecting images for output. It's called, cryptically enough, "Collect for Output" and is found under the File menu. When you select this option, Quark will ask you to either find a current folder or create a new one. It will also ask you to name the report which will provide a valuable description of the fonts used, trapping information, images used, etc. Once you name the report, or decide to keep the default name (also cryptically named "report"), QuarkXPress will race around your computer, finding all the images and text documents that are embedded in your file. This may take a bit longer than collecting the files yourself, but you'll be assured that you won't miss anything.

Fonts

Besides needing the images and text documents from your QuarkXPress layout, the service bureau will also need the fonts that you used. It goes without saying that if you have used a relatively obscure font, they probably don't have it. If you have used a font like Helvetica or Times, though, it's pretty much guaranteed that they have it.

Personally, though, I don't trust using anyone else's fonts—even simple ones like Helvetica and Times. Maybe I'm paranoid, but different systems, releases, corrupted files, or other problems could account for a change in appearance, even the slightest of which could cause severe shifting and reflow of your work. The service bureau will need you to provide both the screen fonts and the printer fonts to output the film correctly.

If you read the above TIP about using QuarkXPress's Collect for Output command, you should know that while this feature will gather all of your images and text documents, it will *not* collect the fonts. Quark wisely wants no part of any copyright infringement problems.

Provide a Sample Printout:

In almost every conceivable circumstance, your service bureau will require a hard copy. Make a quick print from your desktop printer to send along with your files. This way your service bureau will know in advance what the end result should (kind of) look like and can make any last-minute adjustments that might be necessary. Providing samples and spending a few minutes to review these samples with the service bureau could also reduce your liability for fixes should anything go wrong.

Providing a List of What's on the Disk:

If you're sending your files to the service bureau on a disk, discussed later in this chapter, you should give them a list of everything that is on the disk. Again, this will not only help them to have better success when outputting your files but leaves a further paper trail to reduce your liability in case of a problem.

On a Macintosh, you simply have to have the desired window open, and choose File –> Print Window. On a Windows computer, you first need to take a screen shot of the window by holding the Alt button and pushing the Print Screen button. Paste the image (now on your clipboard) into either a paint program or a text editor. Print from there as you would any other document.

CHECKLIST FOR PRESENTING RAW FILES

The following list provides a suggested agenda to follow before taking a disk with raw files over to the service bureau. Don't worry—even with the list you're sure to forget something, but after you go through that hell enough times, you'll learn to get it right the first time.

Review All Files: Did You Check...

◆ Spelling? Choose View –> Check Spelling –> Document to check the spelling for the entire document.

◆ That your layout is the way you want it?

◆ That your're sending the most up-to-date version of the project and not an old draft? You'd be surprised at how often this occurs. It is the cause for significant embarrassment and money.

◆ That none of the graphics have Suppress Printout turned on.

◆ The bottom of all the text boxes to make sure that none of the text has fallen below the confines of the box.

◆ That none of the images have been updated since you last saved your QuarkXPress layout? To check this, Choose View -> Usage to get the information box shown in Figure 8–1. Choose the tab marked Picture and check to see if any of the images are listed as Modified or Missing. If any of them are marked as such, click on them and push the button marked Update. For Modified images, XPress will ask you if it's OK to update. Hit OK. For images marked Missing, you'll have to find them on your computer for XPress to reference.

◆ That no images or text boxes are outside of the canvas that shouldn't be? Figure 8–2 gives an example of this. These extra elements can throw off the output.

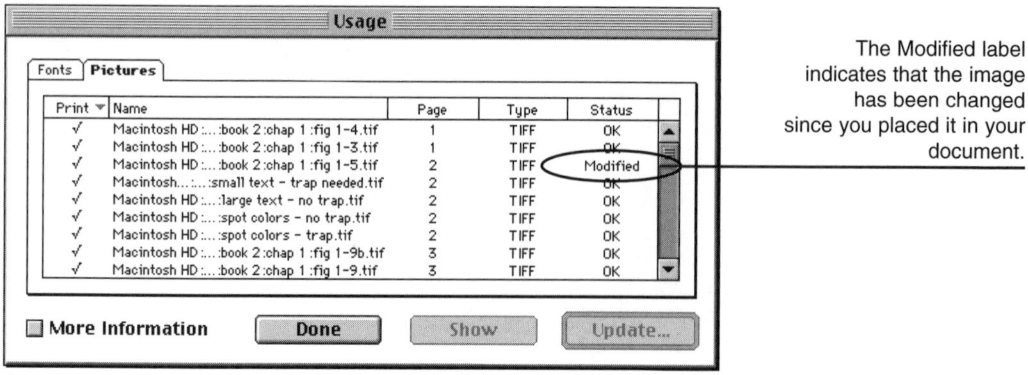

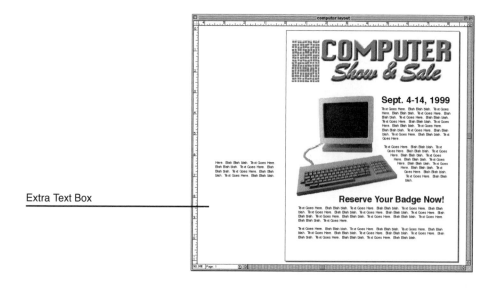

The Modified label indicates that the image has been changed since you placed it in your document.

Fig. 8–1   *The Usage palette shows the images in your layout and which, if any, are problematic.*

Extra Text Box

Fig. 8–2   *The text box that falls outside the canvas can cause problems when you output film.*

Collect All Files: Did You Provide...

◆   All images referenced in your file?

◆   All text documents written in programs other than Quark?

◆   The Quark file itself?

Fonts: Did You Provide...

All the screen and printer fonts that you used? To check on which fonts you've used in your piece, choose View -> Usage and click the tab marked Fonts. You can't print this window, so if you have short-term memory problems, you'll want a piece of paper and a pen handy to jot their names down. Remember, I have no idea how you would actually get the fonts over to the service bureau, considering the copyright laws. I would never tape a rented movie that has that FBI warning in it and I would never drag my fonts onto a Zip disk and hand them over to a service bureau. You're on your own with this one.

Sample Printouts: Did You...

Print out the final version of your work on your desktop printer to provide the service bureau something to refer to?

What If I Forget an Element of My Project?

Eventually, it's going to happen. If you take the route of providing the raw files, you will inevitably get the phone call from your service bureau saying, "we're about to output your files, but you forgot an image." It could be a font, it could be an illustration—it doesn't matter. Eventually, you'll forget something. If that happens, you really don't have much choice: put whatever was missing on another disk and drive back down to service bureau. Seems obvious, but the point is that unless you are under some extreme deadline in which every second counts, there is nothing to panic about.

Providing the Postscript Files

Well, I've already admitted that this is not my favorite chore, and believe me, the idea of writing about your least favorite chore is actually less fun than the chore itself. But in the interest of fairness and providing non-editorialized information, I will do my best to give you direction on how to create a PostScript file for your Service Bureau without using terms like "this sucks," or "don't waste your time with this."

Creating the PostScript file will allow your service bureau to do little more than push a button and wake up periodically to make sure the output device is still running. You will have complete control over your files and how they are output.

 If you plan on providing the PostScript files to your service bureau, make sure you read this section carefully. Once you deliver it, it can't be changed, and you will be financially responsible for re-outputting it should there be a problem.

The information provided below encompasses the standard adjustments you should have to make and should go a long way toward helping you understand the process.

This should allow you to have an intelligent discussion about it. This may be more or less than what you would actually need and I would implore you to discuss the PostScript file creation process with your Service Bureau before attempting to do this on your own.

Checking Your Document Before You Set Up Your PostScript File

Before you actually get too deep into creating your PostScript file, you'll want to make sure that certain things are in place and correct. Much of these are the same things you'd want to check if you were just handing over the raw files, plus a few others. These include:

◆   Is the spelling checked and all the layout in place?

◆   Is any text overflowing beyond the confines of your textboxes?

◆   Do you have all of the fonts that you used and are all of the images that you referenced updated and in the right place?

◆   Have you consulted with your printer as to the proper line screen and other important information that you'll learn more about by the end of this chapter?

Once you have checked to ensure that everything is in place, check it again. It can't be changed once you deliver it, so I'd suggest even printing out a copy and having an unbiased associate who is unfamiliar with the work look it over—they may be more capable of seeing your mistakes that you are.

If you are confident that everything is set, you can begin creating your PostScript file, or what's called *printing to disk*. The procedure you take to do this will depend on which platform you are using.

POSTSCRIPT FILES FROM EITHER MACINTOSH OR WINDOWS

As with anything else, some things you can do on a computer are exactly the same on a Mac as they are on a PC, while other things are radically different. Printing to your desktop printer or creating your PostScript file for your service bureau are no different. To go through the whole process, I'll start off explaining the print dialog box in QuarkXPress first, which is largely the same on both platforms. From there I'll go into a separate explanation of how you'd perform other functions from either Mac or Windows.

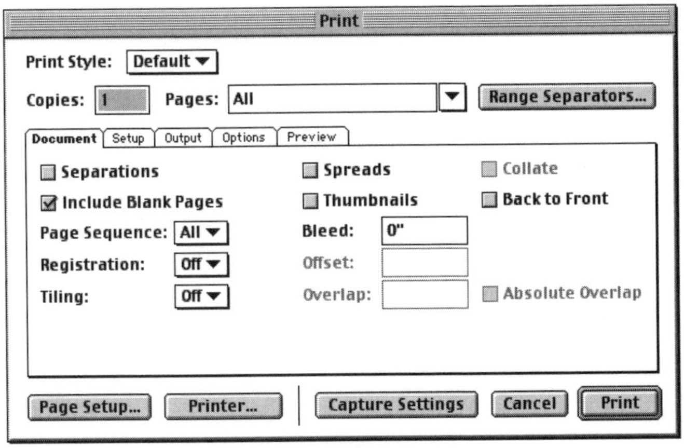

Fig. 8–3   The Print dialog box (Document Tab).

QUARKXPRESS PRINT DIALOG BOX

Back in Quark XPress, choose File -> Print to access the dialog box shown in Figure 8–3. The information underneath each tab is different depending upon which tab you choose, but the information and choices you can make on the top portion of the dialog box stay the same throughout. These are fairly straightforward.

Print Styles

There is a lot for you to do, know, and fill in in the upcoming pages. Enough so that the fewer times you do any of it, the happier you'll be. Print Styles are like memory banks of sorts, remembering the settings that you suffer through so that you don't have to keep going through this over and over again. It's an especially great feature if you are going to be sending the same type of files to the same service bureau or desktop printer, or if you have a lot of different types of files that will be going to a lot of different printers or bureaus.

To set a Print Style, exit the Print dialog box and choose Edit -> Print Styles. In the dialog box, shown in Figure 8–4, choose New (or Edit if you already have a Print Style you want to make changes to). The Print dialog box will appear again, or at least a very close carbon copy of it. Make any of your settings here, as you would if you were going to print something or create a PostScript file. When you're through, click OK. Back in the Print Styles dialog box, push the Save button.

If you're doing this for the first time, read through the following directions before trying it. You'll notice that not all of the fields and information are contained in the Print Styles dialog box, so you should be as familiar as possible with the print features before setting up your files for print. This is especially true if you're setting up PostScript files for film output.

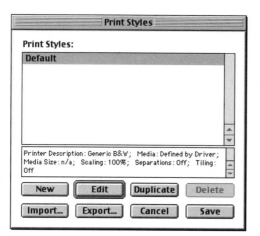

Fig. 8–4   The Print Styles dialog box.

Copies

This is pretty simple, but it's important. Unless you want multiple copies, make sure that this is set to 1. Anything other than that and you could end up paying for more than you want.

Pages and Range Separators

These allow you to print only certain pages of your file. Unlike earlier versions of XPress that only allowed you to print continuous pages, 4.0.4 allows you to print discontinuous pages, such as 2, 4, 6-11, 15. The Range Separator lets you change the character used to separate the pages, instead of the comma or hyphen.

By default, the tab marked Document will be open. I'll explain the rest of the instructions on a per-tab basis.

DOCUMENT TAB

These are the default controls that appear when you open the Print dialog box.

Separations

It's funny how sometimes the most unassuming aspects of anything can hold some of the most important value. If you are going to be printing a color piece or submitting film to a publication for a color advertisement, this is going to be an important button.

If you are working on a one-color piece, then this option will be grayed out.

Clicking this box will activate information and controls in other portions of the print dialog box. We'll look at separations in depth at the appropriate times in this section.

Include Blank Pages

No big deal here one way or the other, unless you're a true environmentalist, Al Gore, or a Brandeis University graduate (synonyms, really). Click this checkbox off to avoid any wasted effort time, or (if you're just printing to your desktop printer, click this off to not waste any paper).

Page Sequence

Of the three choices in the pull-down menu, choose All. If you ever, in your lifetime, need to choose either Even or Odd before you send a PostScript file to the service bureau, please email and enlighten me.

Registration

The printer who receives the film from your service bureau needs to have certain information to follow. When you choose either Centered or Off Center (ask your printer which they prefer—probably centered), your film output will include:

Crop marks

These are small hash marks put at the corners of your page to show the edges and let the printer know where to trim the paper.

Registration marks

It's never easy to get all of the color plates to align correctly—if they're off by a fraction of a point, it could spell doom for your project (see Chapter 9 for more information on this). The registration marks help the printer properly line up the color plates.

Color Bars

The color and grayscale bars help the printer determine whether or not the colors are being created properly. Chapter 9 looks into this with more detail.

Job Info

A brief line will print in the upper-left-hand corner of your page, above the crop line. This info will display the name of the file, the time, date and page number. Besides being useful info, I remember thinking that it looked really cool the first time I saw one.

Figure 8–5 shows a sample of some of these elements.

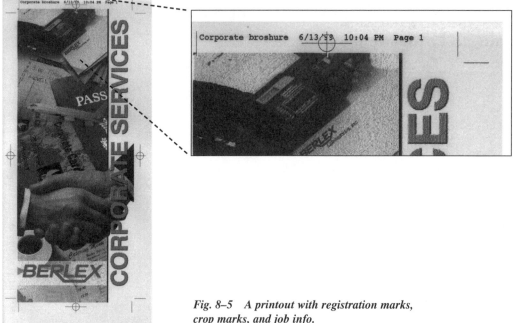

Fig. 8–5   A printout with registration marks, crop marks, and job info.

Tiling

Tiling is for instances when you will be printing oversized documants, say for a billboard or a tradeshow booth. This function will print your image in individual sections, or tiles, for ease of output. By choosing Manual or Automatic from the Tiling pull-down menu, you decide whether you want to specify the dimensions of each tile by using the ruler, or have XPress measure the sections for you. Each separate document will print in at least two overlapping files.

Overlap

When tiling an oversized image, fill in the value in inches (or other measure) where the tickmarks will be placed for ease of reassembly.

Spreads

These are largely for your own personal use if you are checking things on a personal printer. Turning this option on will print multiple pages on one spread, between one set of crop marks and with one registration mark. Unfortunately, it doesn't create printer's spreads for you, and I would, unless you have a unique way of working, keep this option off when preparing Postscript files.

Thumbnails

If you're preparing the PostScript file for your service bureau, make sure this box is unchecked. If you're printing sample files from your desktop printer, I suppose you could find a use for this. Thumbnails will take the pages of your document, shrink them down to just over 10 percent of their original size, line them up vertically and horizontally, and print a page with as many of these icon sized replicas as possible. They're typically to small to be of any use, though, and they don't print any faster than each page would individually.

Bleed

When an image is said to *bleed* off the page, it simply means that the image extends to the edge of the paper. An image that does not bleed will have a certain measure of white space between it and the edge of the paper. A typical question that printers will ask when arranging to quote you a price is "how many bleeds are there?" If the image extends to the paper's edge on all 4 sides, then there are 4 bleeds. If the image extends to the top, left, and bottom paper edge, then there are 3 bleeds (and the right edge will contain white space between the image and the paper edge). The same philosophy exists for 1 and 2 bleeds. Figure 8–6 shows a few different printed pieces and their associated bleeds.

So why are bleeds important? Even in this age of precision and accuracy, you can never count on a printed piece to be cut to the exact dimensions that you desire. In other words, if you don't pay attention to your bleeds, you run the risk of having your project cut incorrectly, or slightly off, leaving unwanted borders around images where they don't belong.

Fig. 8–6   A few samples of pages that bleed. The bleed occurs anywhere the ink extends to the edge of the page.

To ensure that the ink on your printed piece actually does extend to the edge where it's supposed to, commercial printers will print on a larger area of paper than is needed and cut the excess off after printing is finished. This is why the crop marks, discussed earlier in this section, are so important.

Set the bleed value in the Print dialog box for somewhere between .125" and .25". This should give the printer plenty of space to allow for miscalculations when cutting.

Just setting the bleed value in the Print dialog box is not enough. You have to create images and color for the bleed from within the program that the bleed originates—not just the layout program. Figure 8–7 provides an example of an 8.5" x 11" flyer in which the entire background is one large photograph, bleeding to all edges. As you can see, there are text effects that were done in Photoshop that are vital to the flyer's message. In Figure 8–7, the image was set up to bleed correctly, with the original Photoshop image done at 9" x 11.5", leaving .25" per side for bleeds. Figure 8–8 is the same flyer set up incorrectly. The original Photoshop image was set up at the flyer size, 8.5" x 11", not taking bleeds into consideration. The image was stretched to include bleeds in the layout program. Notice how the stretching of the image has caused the Photoshop text effects to wander dangerously close to the edge of the page. Ask your printer how much bleed they like for you to leave.

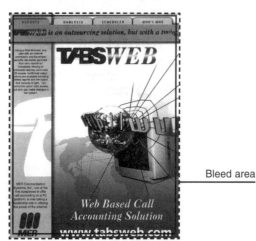

Fig. 8–7   This piece consists of one large graphic, bleeding to all sides. Bleeds were set up properly in Photoshop so the image didn't stretch.

Fig. 8–8   The same image, this time prepared without allowing for bleed. Notice how the type, set in Photoshop, is stretched to the edge when a bleed is created in XPress.

Offset

This will allow you to move your crop marks and registration marks further from the page. Ask your printer how far off they like them and set this value.

Collate

Exactly as it sounds—if you are outputting more than one copy of your pages, checking the Collate box will force them to print out in order—pg. 1 then pg. 2, etc. This is instead of outputting all copies of pg. 1, all copies of pg. 2, leaving you to sort them out yourself. It takes pretty long to print this way, but it could be helpful. Leave it off, though, if you're printing to disk. This option is most useful for those who are just printing comps from a desktop printer.

Back to Front

If you're printing just from your desktop laser printer and the pages come out facing up, click this box to print the last page first. The rest of the pages print in backward order and the first page of your document will be the last page that prints. If you're setting up the PostScript file for your service bureau to output film, you can leave this off—the bureau won't care what order you output in.

QUICK CHECKLIST OF DOCUMENT TAB:

If you're outputting film:

Separations:	Click to output film for color work.
Include Blank Pages:	Click off to count yourself among the environmentally friendly.
Page Sequence:	Choose All.
Registration:	Ask your printer. Most likely choice will be Centered.
Tiling:	Job type specific.
Spreads:	Click off.
Thumbnails:	Click off.
Bleed:	Set bleed amount somewhere between .125" and .25".
Offset:	Ask your printer.
Collate:	Click off.
Back to Front:	Click off.

SETUP TAB

This is the second tab you'll encounter, and is primarily concerned with the output source for your files, and how your files will appear on film or paper. The dialog box is shown in Figure 8–9.

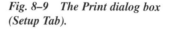

Print
Print Style: Default ▼
Copies: 1   Pages: All   ▼   Range Separators...
Document [Setup] Output [Options [Preview]
Printer Description: Generic B&W ▼
Paper Size: Defined by Driver ▼
Paper Width: ☐   Paper Offset: ☐
Paper Height: ☐   ▼   Page Gap: ☐
Reduce or Enlarge: 100%   ☐ Fit in Print Area
Page Positioning: Left Edge ▼   Orientation: 🖥 🖥
Page Setup...   Printer...   Capture Settings   Cancel   Print

Fig. 8–9   The Print dialog box (Setup Tab).

Printer Description

Choose the printer that will be outputting your work. In order for a printer to appear in the list, your computer has to be armed with its PPD file (PostScript Printer Description). For printers that are preinstalled on your system, the PPD should be a nonissue—it should be there. For any other printers that you purchase, the PPD should be included on the install software that comes with the printer. If you're outputting to film, you need to call you service bureau and get the PPD for the device they're using to output. They may direct you to a manufacturer's web site or just give you a disk. Either way, install the PPD and select this from the Printer Description pul-down menu.

Choosing a printer in this menu does not change the systemwide printer that you have selected in the Chooser (Macintosh) or Printer (Windows). This pull-down menu is only XPress specific, though you should try and make them the same.

Some programs, like Word or PageMaker, reflow the document when you change PPD. Set this up *before* you start work.

Paper Size and its Underlings

Chances are, the default choice here will be Defined by Printer, and all other options (including the Paper Width, Height, Offset, and Gap) will be grayed out. This means that the PPD for the output source that you specified in the Printer Description pull-down menu has already told Quark that the output device only works with a certain size paper or other material.

If the choices are available for you to make adjustments to (not grayed out), you should still leave the defaults alone—as long as the paper size is greater than the page size within your Quark document, you'll be okay. If you're concerned about this, ask your service bureau to confirm the settings for you before you set this up to deliver PostScript file.

What if your paper size is smaller than the page size in your Quark document? What if you are trying to design posters for large-quantity printing that are 48" x 36"? No page size from a desktop printer or film output device will print that large, and the quantity desired may be too high to make economical use of large-format printing (see Chapter 9). If this is the case, read Tiling in the Document Tab portion of this section.

Reduce or Enlarge

If you want to check out a smaller version of a poster you are designing by outputting it on your desktop printer, you can reduce the size to fit a standard 8.5" x 11" page. If you are sending that same poster (let's say 48" x 36") to be output and don't have the RAM to create designs that large in Photoshop, you can create a file half that size and then enlarge it 200 percent before printing. This is fine for taking the poster to a large-format printer. If you are going to mass produce these posters, and are preparing a PostScript file for your service bureau to output film, then use this in conjunction with the Tiling feature discussed in the Document Tab portion of this section.

Page Positioning

Select where on the page you want your image to appear. Of the four choices, Left Edge, Center, Center Horizontal, and Center Vertical, Left Edge is the default. Where on the page they would fall is fairly obvious and if you're outputting to film it really won't make any difference—just leave the Left Edge default selection.

Fit in Print Area

By clicking this, Quark will automatically calculate and set the Reduce or Enlarge percentages for you, so that your Quark page fits as nicely as possible on the printed page. This is great if you're printing to your desktop printer but awful if you're outputting to film for high quantity print—I think it's rather important to know for sure exactly how large each page will be instead of playing guessing games with this option.

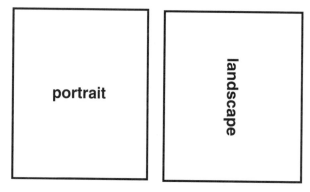

Fig. 8–10   The two page-orientation choices.

Orientation

If you've done any desktop printing at all, you know what this is. Figure 8–10 shows both the Landscape and Portrait options, basically just setting the direction of your XPress pages.

Q<small>UICK</small> C<small>HECKLIST OF</small> S<small>ETUP</small> T<small>AB</small>

If you're outputting to film:

Printer Description:	Use PPD of output device.
Paper Size:	Use Default.
Reduce or Enlarge:	Up to you—most likely 100 percent is fine.
Page Positioning:	Use Default.
Fit In Print Area:	Leave unchecked.
Orientation:	Depends on the direction of your pages.

OUTPUT TAB

This is the scary tab, where we will control all of the color and halftones of your pages. This could also be the tab that makes you want to print in just black and white—maybe shades of gray to add some excitement to your life. But if you're working with color and providing the PostScript file to the service bureau, you've got no choice—and you will get used to it. The tab options are shown in Figure 8–11.

Print Colors/Plates

This first selection will be named differently depending upon whether or not you have the Separations box checked on or off back in the Document tab.

If you have it checked off, XPress will name this pull-down menu Print Colors. Back in the Setup tab, you selected the printer description for the output device. If you're

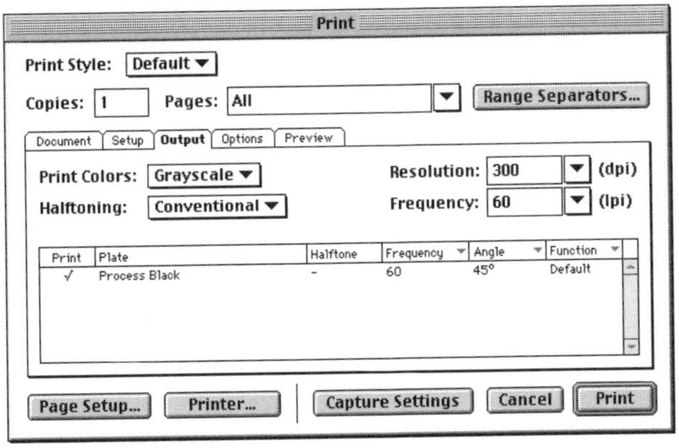

Fig. 8–11   The Print dialog box (Output Tab).

printing from your desktop printer and the PPD tells Quark that your printer is only capable of black and white, your choices in this pull-down menu will be either Black and White or Grayscale. If your printer is capable of printing in color, then Color will also be available.

If the Separations box is checked to the on position for doing color separations with your service bureau, this option will be called Plates. Choose either Process and Spot or Convert to Process (see That Big, Crazy Box at the Bottom further ahead in this section) from the pull-down menu.

Halftoning

You will only have to worry about this if your file is Grayscale and meant for certain desktop printers. Between the two choices, Conventional and Printer, choose Conventional for halftone settings to be sent to the printer with the image. The Printer setting won't send any halftone info—if your printer won't read them, it doesn't matter. What's even better is that if you are preparing files for color separations, the Printer option will be grayed out completely (if you checked the Separations box in the Document tab). If you're interested, you can read more about halftones in Chapter 5.

Resolution

I typically find that it's best to leave this option alone. XPress won't set the default resolution any higher than your output device can handle. This will make the output quicker, as well as output your images at the maximum quality possible.

Frequency

This is where you set the line screen (lpi—lines per inch) that was detailed in Chapter 5. If you're setting up a PostScript file for your service bureau, make sure you find out from your printer what line screen he'll be printing at and fill in that number here.

That Big, Crazy Box at the Bottom

This is it—the fun part. That big, imposing box at the bottom of the Output tab. This is where the color separation information is stored. This will only be interesting if you have the Separations checkbox in the Document tab turned on. (See? I told you before that that was a really important option.)

If Separations is turned off and you're printing to your black-and-white desktop printer, only the black plate shows, since that's all there is to print. If it's turned off and you're printing to a color printer, four plates will show—one for each of the CMYK values (spot colors in this case get turned into their closest process equivalent).

If it's turned on and you're going to be outputting film separations at the service bureau, you'll have chosen either Convert to Process or Process & Spot from the Plates. (For more on process color and spot color, check out Chapter 1). Convert to Process will turn all spot colors to their nearest CMYK equivalent. Process & Spot will maintain your spot colors as well as your CMYK colors.

If you look at the color palette in XPress, you'll see that all the native colors (as well as any colors you may have brought over from your imported Illustrator documents) will show specific names, such as "red," "blue," etc. If you lay text or a border in red, for example, that red will appear as a spot color and cost you extra money. Chances are you don't want to print a fifth or sixth color just for this. If you want everything to print in only mixtures of CMYK, make sure you choose Convert to Process from the Plates pull-down menu.

If you want to print one XPress color as a spot color but convert the others to process colors, you'll have to choose Process and Spot from the Plates pull-down menu. Before doing so, though, back in your Quark document choose Edit -> Colors. Click on any color that you do not want to print as a spot color. Push the Edit button and remove the check mark for Spot Color. This will turn unwanted spot colors into their nearest CMYK equivalent.

Going through each of the options in the Color Plates info box:

◆ **Print:** Leave a check next to each of the colors that you want to print. Remove the check to supress that color and keep it from printing.

◆ **Plate:** Lists each color in your project.

CHAPTER 8 • PREPARING FILES FOR PRINT   **239**

◆ **And the Rest:** The remaining four settings all have to do with the halftone screens. In Chapter 5 we discussed halftoning—what it is, and what the results are of printing halftones at the correct and incorrect angles. The Halftone portion of the Color Plates dialog box gives you the opportunity to set your own angles for each color. If you've chosen the proper PPD for your output device (from the Printer Description pull-down menu in the Setup tab), the default settings should be fine. LEAVE THEM ALONE!! You really shouldn't need to play with these and the less you play, the better off you'll be. But since there might be a rare occasion when you'll need to change something here, I'll explain what each one is.

Halftone

You'll notice that each of the four process colors have a dash mark under the Halftone setting. That's because there is nothing to change—their halftone is their halftone. The halftone of the Cyan plate is going to look like a lighter cyan, no two ways about it. It's the remaining setting for each color that can be manipulated. However, if you're using spot colors, you'll see a single letter in the Halftone setting column. This letter indicates which of the process color settings the spot color will assume. So if the letter Y appears in the Halftone column for your spot color, then it will print at the same Frequency, Angle, etc. that the Yellow plate will print. To change this, click on the spot color of your choice to highlight it and select your desired process color to emulate from the Halftone pull-down menu (notice the small triangle next to the Halftone title to indicate that the title bar is also a pull-down menu).

Frequency

Again, this is the line screen (lpi) we discussed earlier in this section. The values here are obtained by XPress from the PPD for the printer chosen in the Printer Description pull down. To change these, again, click on the color of your choice and select Other from the Frequency pull-down menu. Enter a numeric value and hit OK. Call your service bureau if you're unsure of what values to enter.

Angle

Because developing the ideal halftone pattern is so essential to the printing process, many companies have tried to develop new technologies to help the process. Some of these technologies have gained universal support among service bureaus and will rely on the default XPress angles to help achieve their goal. The default in XPress normally puts the Cyan angle at 75 degrees, the Magenta angle at 105 degrees, the Yellow angle at 90 degrees, and the black angle at 45 degrees. These values could be different depending on your PPD. Before you change any of these (click on a color and choose Other from the Angle pull-down menu), check with your service bureau or printer.

Function

Each halftone dot has a different shape that it can print in. For the most part, as discussed in Chapter 5, you really won't need to change this. They can create some really cool effects if you're so inclined, but otherwise leave this. If you do want to change it, though, click on the color and choose your desired shape from the Function pull-down menu.

QUICK CHECKLIST OF OUTPUT TAB

If you're outputting to film:

Plates:	Either Process & Spot or Convert to Process (depending upon your project).
Halftoning:	Conventional.
Resolution:	Leave default.
Frequency:	Ask your printer.
Color Plate Info:	Ask your service bureau if you're uneasy with these defaults.

OPTIONS TAB

The Options tab, shown in Figure 8–12, is a fairly uncomplicated field of specs that serve a variety of purposes:

PostScript Handling Error

Since it is not uncommon for the printer to receive a PostScript file with an error in it (it is most common when you're in a rush, of course), Quark adds this cool little option. Click it on and a file with an error that the Printer can't get past will print to the point of the error. It then prints out another page with PostScript programming code and

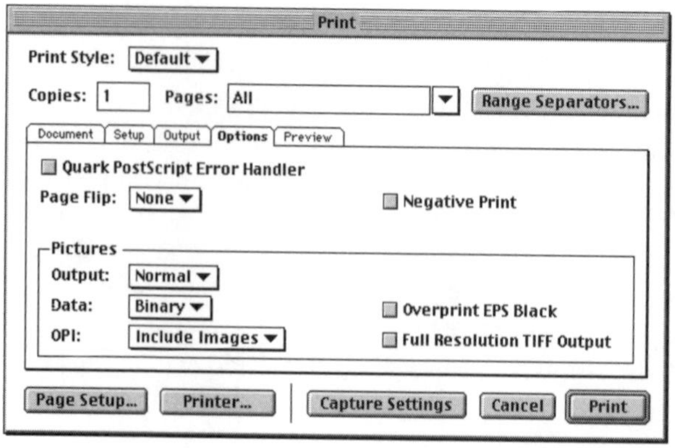

Fig. 8–12 The Print dialog box (Options Tab).

a visual aid to help determine where the problem occurred so you can try and fix it. If you leave this option unchecked, then all you'll get back is a message telling you there is a PostScript error with the file (this is usually relayed to you over the phone when the service bureau calls—believe me, when the service bureau calls, it's almost never good news).

Page Flip

If you plan on submitting an ad to a publication who is expecting you to send them film, the specs from their production department will usually ask for film to be output at *x* lpi (fill that number value into the Frequency setting in the Output tab), right reading, emulsion side down. If so, then this is where you go to set that up.

When the film moves through your service bureau's output device, one side of the film is covered with a chemical (emulsion) that is exposed to a laser. At the default setting of None in the Page Flip pull down, the film comes out of the output device legible from left to right as intended, with the emulsion side facing your direction. This is otherwise referred to as *right reading, emulsion side up.* Choose either Horizontal or Vertical to make your film right reading, with the emulsion side facing away from you, or *right reading, emulsion side down* which is the way most printers and publications want it. Ask your printer or publication which they prefer.

Negative Print

This will universally change the pages in your document into what seems to be a film negative. All the whites turn to black, the blacks turn to white, and skin tones will get that spooky blue color. You can leave this off unless you plan on printing outside the US, where printers typically have a different way of working.

Picture Output

All of the options in the info area control how XPress works with the images in your document and especially in how these images get to the output device.

◆ **Output:** Choose Normal (default) for the best quality in your images. If you're putting together the PostScript file for your service bureau, keep this setting.

Choose either Low-Resolution Output or Rough to reduce the quality and time it takes to download and print pages with images on them. The Low-Resolution Output option will print the low-res image preview that XPress uses to represent pictures. The Rough option will print all images as large X's for even quicker printing. These are good options if you're printing comps in a hurry from your desktop printer.

◆ **Data Format:** Of the three formats to choose from, choose Binary for film output unless otherwise instructed by your service bureau. It creates smaller PostScript files and rarely has problems regardless of the system you are using.

◆ **OPI:** The OPI (Open Preface Interface) gives you a choice in its pull-down menu of Include Images, Omit TIFF, and Omit TIFF and EPS. Contact your service bureau to find out what type of OPI prepress system they are using and which of these options you should choose. In short, depending on the type of prepress system used, the option you choose here will replace either your TIFF or TIFF and EPS images with OPI comments in the file or leave all images in place and insert unavailable hi-res files with their screen previews.

◆ **Overprint EPS Black:** In Chapter 7 we discussed overprinting and trapping at length, so if you haven't done so yet, this would be a good time to review that section. Click this checkbox to On to override any EPS settings and force all black to overprint the rest of the image.

◆ **Full-Resolution TIFF Output:** Quark will reduce the quality of all TIFF images that you've used in your document to print at no greater resolution that what you need given the lpi, image size, and image resolution. Click this option to print your TIFFs at their full size.

QUICK CHECKLIST OF OPTIONS TAB

If you're outputting to film:

PostScript Handling Error:	Turn on.
Page Flip:	Choose Horizontal or Vertical for *right reading, emulsion side down* film.
Negative Print:	Turn off for domestic printing.
Output:	Normal.
Data Format:	Binary.
OPI:	Include Images (ask your Service Bureau).
Overprint EPS Black:	Turn off.
Full-Resolution TIFF Output:	Turn on.

THE PREVIEW TAB

Whew! Finally a tab (Figure 8–13) with no controls in it! Just some information that you'd be wise to review.

Paper Size

Shows the paper size measured in Width and Height, as determined in the Setup tab.

Document Size

Shows, also in Width and Height, the original size for your document. Compare these measurements with the Paper size (which should be the larger measurement) to be certain that the paper is not too small for the document.

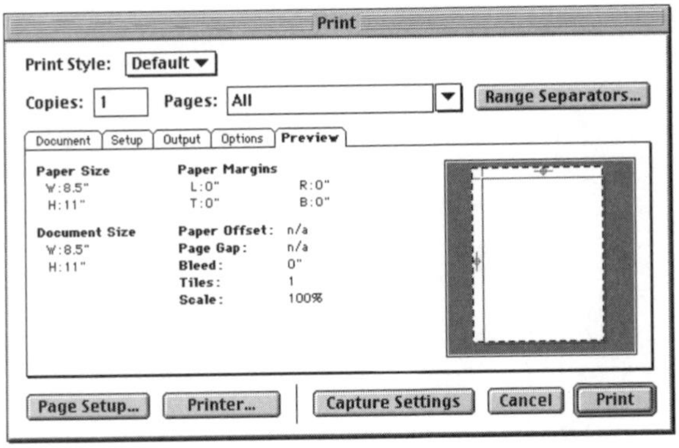

Fig. 8–13   The Print dialog box (Preview Tab).

Paper Margins

Displayed as Left (L), Right (R), Top (T), and Bottom (B), these measurements are more than the guides that show up on your page while you're working. These are actual limitations of the output device as mandated in the PPD. Any portion of your document that falls outside these margins simply won't print.

Print Info

These are a regurgitation of the information you have already entered elsewhere in the Print dialog box, but conveniently assembled together for ease of review.

Preview Graphic

This graphic displays important information that is sometimes easier to take in visually more than numerically. With this, you can see where your crop marks will fall, your registration marks will land, how much bleed is provided, etc.

> **Note** It does not reflect *all* aspects of the specs, leaving out a few important ones, like Page Flip.

TO CREATE A POSTSCRIPT FILE FROM A MACINTOSH

1. Open the Chooser from the Apple pull-down menu (click on the little Apple icon at the top left of your monitor.)

2. From the Chooser, shown in Figure 8–14, select one of the LaserWriter printers as your output source. Don't worry if you don't have a LaserWriter hooked up to your computer or even have any printer hooked up at all—you just need to designate a PostScript device as your source.

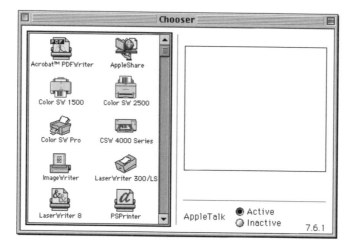

Fig. 8–14 The Chooser in the Macintosh allows you to select your output device.

 Discuss this with your service bureau. They may require you to use a driver other than the LaserWriter, and will, in those cases, provide you with the output device software to install into your machine.

There is no OK button on the Chooser, so just click the small box at the top left of the window to close this when you've made your selection.

3. Back in Quark, choose File –> Print.

4. Set up the print specs as we just reviewed.

5. Click the Page Setup button at the bottom of the Print dialog box to access the dialog box shown in Figure 8–15. You'll recognize many of the options here—you just filled in the exact same ones in the Setup tab. In fact, these are exactly the same, but rather than do things twice, you're better off disregarding the ones here and making sure that you've filled in the options in the Setup tab correctly.

6. Click on the button marked Options to access the Options dialog box shown in Figure 8–16. Since many of these aren't important and I don't want to take too much time getting into them, I'll just go over each one briefly:

♦   **Visual Effects:**

♦   **Flip Horizontal, Flip Vertical, Invert Image:** These are all replicas of things you've already filled in in the Options tab. Leave these unchecked here, regardless of how you filled in the Options tab specifications—those take precedence.

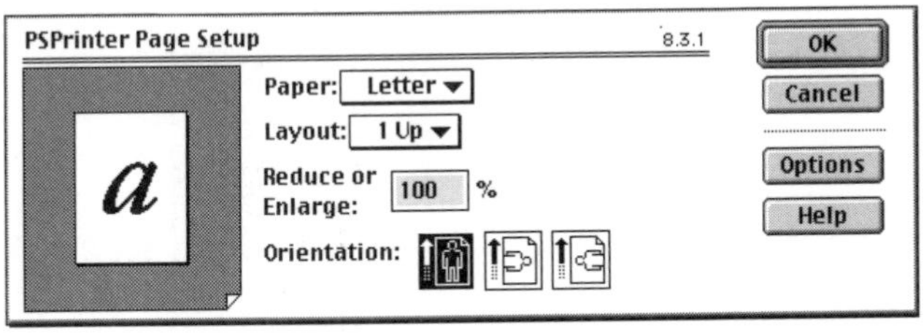

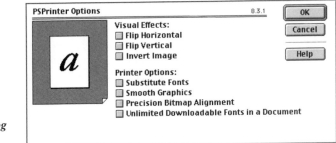

Fig. 8–15 The Print Setup dialog box.

Fig. 8–16 The Print Options dialog box.

♦ **Image & Text:**

♦ **Substitute Fonts:** This gives permission to XPress to exchange Times Roman, Helvetica, and Courier for New York, Geneva, and Monaco, respectively. That's because those three former bitmap fonts (now TrueType fonts) are considered to be somewhat ugly. Leave this off—substituting fonts will almost definitely screw up your spacing and layouts. If you thought these fonts were ugly, you wouldn't have used them in the first place.

♦ **Smooth Text:** If you are using bitmapped fonts and want them to be smoother, click this off. Since you're probably not using bitmapped fonts, leave this off.

♦ **Smooth Graphics:** This has no useful purpose if you're outputting to film and are using medium to hi-res graphics. Even if you're using low-res color graphics it's pointless. But if you're working with very low-res, black-and-white images, go crazy and click this box on! Otherwise leave it off.

♦ **Precision Bitmap Alignment:** More fun with low-res graphics here, using a scale-down method to increase the quality of these images, this option magically also reduces the size of everything else on the page. Leave this one off.

♦ **Unlimited Downloadable Fonts in a Document:** Too many fonts spoil the broth, so they say. If you use so many fonts that the page can't print, click this on. Better yet, don't use that many fonts. Leave this off regardless though—the service bureau that will output the film should have plenty of juice in the computer to output pages with a lot of fonts.

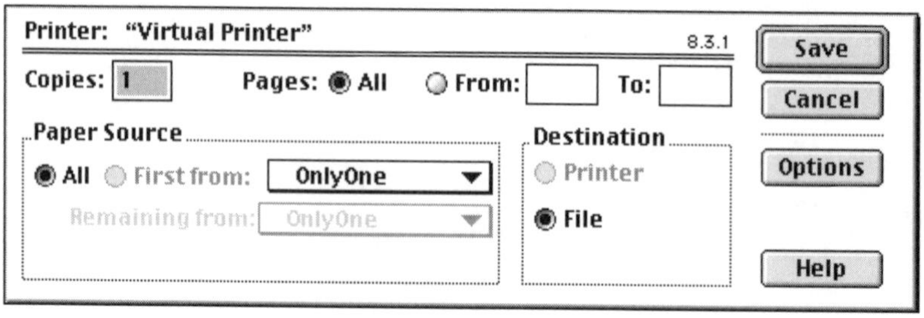

```
┌─────────────────────────────────────────────────────────────┐
│ Printer: "Virtual Printer"                  8.3.1  ┌────────┐ │
│                                                    │  Save  │ │
│ Copies: │1│       Pages: ● All   ○ From: │    │ To: │   │   └────────┘ │
│                                                    ┌────────┐ │
│ ┌Paper Source─────────────────────┐ ┌Destination┐ │ Cancel │ │
│ │ ● All ○ First from: │ OnlyOne ▼│ │ ○ Printer │ └────────┘ │
│ │   Remaining from: │ OnlyOne ▼│   │ ● File    │ ┌────────┐ │
│ │                                │ │           │ │Options │ │
│ └────────────────────────────────┘ └───────────┘ └────────┘ │
│                                                    ┌────────┐ │
│                                                    │  Help  │ │
│                                                    └────────┘ │
└─────────────────────────────────────────────────────────────┘
```

Fig. 8–17   The Printer dialog box.

◆ **Larger Print Area:** If you're outputting to film, you have no need for this. If you're printing to your desktop printer and can't handle that half an inch border around your paper, click this to reduce that border to around a quarter of an inch. But don't bother if you use a lot of fonts—the memory needed to increase the print space is at the expense of the fonts.

If you didn't do your math, the above text should indicate that you leave all checkboxes turned off. Click OK to leave the Options dialog box.

7. Back in the Print Dialog box, click the Printer button to access the dialog box shown in Figure 8–17. You've probably seen this dialog box, or some variation thereof, other times you've tried to print things. Make sure the number of copies is set to one (if that's all you want), and adjust other settings as they apply.

8. Click on File within the Destination control. This will direct XPress to create the PostScript file and save it on the local drive rather than be sent to a desktop printer. Notice that the button that was marked Print changes to Save when you choose File as your destination.

9. Push the Save button and choose the location on your drive to store your file.

TO BEGIN PRINTING AND POSTSCRIPT PREP FROM A WINDOWS MACHINE

Unlike adjusting all the settings through Quark as you would from a Macintosh, you'll adjust some of the settings in Windows from the Printer folder.

1. Make sure that you have a PostScript printer installed and selected. Talk to your service bureau as to which printer to choose. You may need to install their output device software for the proper PPD information.

2. Select your printer by pushing the Windows Start button, and selecting Settings -> Printers. Find the printer you're going to use and click on it.

3. Push the Properties button to access the dialog box.

4. Open the Details tab and choose File from the Print to Following Port list. Click OK when through.

5. Back in XPress, adjust your settings as described earlier in this section. When you're through, click on the Print button. When it prints, XPress will print to your hard drive instead of a printer. Give the file to your service bureau.

DON'T FORGET THE MATCHPRINT

You don't want to go to print without having your client sign off on the project first. That means obtaining an actual signature and date, acknowledging that they have had the final edit and agree that all copy is correct, layout is approved, and fonts are correct, etc. Approval can be gained on all of these elements with a printout from your desktop printer. All of the elements except on important one: color. Do not, under any circumstances, try to save an extra $100 or so by having you client sign off on anything less than a Matchprint. Matchprints are as close to being true to color as you can get without a press proof, which is a sample that comes right off the press and displays exactly how the piece will print. These are, as you may expect, so extremely expensive as to rarely be cost-effective.

Note

Matchprints have a glossy surface to them that make our images really pop off the page. This is okay for projects that are to be printed on coated stock or will have a varnish applied on the press. But for projects that are going to be printed on a stock with a dull finish, like a matte, the glossy Matchprint finish could be deceiving. Ask your service bureau for alternatives in cases like this, like Rainbow proofs that don't have the same gloss.

To give a quick and humbling example, when I first started my agency many, many years ago, I made the mistake of not providing a Matchprint to one of my first clients for a pocket folder and brochure I had designed for them. For my first project I thought the piece was pretty nicely designed—I was excited to send it to print. I had bought the Matchprints for them to sign to their office and had all of them with me except for one—the back of the pocket folder. No big deal—it was just the logo, address, and other standard info. The client signed off on all the pieces I had given to him and said not to worry about the Matchprint for the back. He just wanted me to double-check it myself first. After all, why waste the $3.00 in gas money it would cost me to drive back there just for one more signature?

As you've probably guessed, the $3.00 that I saved by not making the return trip didn't quite cover the $3,000 I spent to reprint the piece when it came off the press with the wrong fax number on the back. Not a great first experience in the world of prepress care and preparation, but an immensely valuable lesson. You can bet that ever since then, the agency I have grown has lived by two simple rules: quadruple check everything, and nothing goes to print without the client's signature.

Period.

MAKING THE HANDOFF

Whether you decide to give your service bureau the raw files or a PostScript file, you have to somehow present it to them. In most cases, your files will be too large to send via the Internet. At the time of this writing, modem speeds are just beginning to creep into the 56.6 bps range on a more widespread scale. That's fast enough to make web sites come up in your browser with less frustration, but not nearly fast enough to transfer a project whose combined size is upwards of 100 Megs or more.

Currently the industry standard is Zip cartridges, which hold approximately 100 Megs of information. Most service bureaus will accept Jaz disks, too, which hold up to 2 Gigs of information, and some will still even work with old SyQuest 44 Meg or 88 Meg disks. SyQuest storage systems were all the rage about 5 years ago, and they politely waited until I had bought six drives before vanishing in relative obscurity. But, no…why should I be bitter about that? Anyway, ask your service bureau how they prefer to receive your files.

GETTING THE FILM BACK

When you get the film back from the service bureau, check it before you just hand it over to the printer. Giving the printer problematic film will result in problematic printing, which will inevitably cost you money—possibly lots of money.

The following are some of the things you should check for on your film before finally going to press:

◆ **Scratches and Ingrained Dust**

If the film is mishandled by the service bureau or the output device hasn't been properly cleaned, it can become damaged. Scratches, ingrained dust, or dirt particles can cause problems at press time.

◆ **Clarity**

Make sure that all your images are clear and all the text looks tight and crisp.

◆ **Over and Underexposure**

Just like the problems you're likely to have after bringing your vacation film to a one-hour developing shop, the service bureau can possibly overexpose or underexpose your file film. Either extreme can have very bad effects on the halftones, type, and other elements in your project.

◆ **Proper Fonts**

Fonts are a tricky subject. Even if you provide the service bureau with all of the fonts rather than trust his copies, it seems like there's always a chance that the fonts can shift, kerning or spacing can change, or some other dilemma can occur. Check carefully that none of the type has fallen off the page or changed in any way.

◆ **Registration**

It'll be tough to see, but hold all four films together and line them up as best as you can. Try to eyeball the results to see if perfect registration occurs.

◆ **Any Other Problems**

It may seem inconceivable, but check to make sure that no object meant to be on the film is unexpectedly dropped out. Also check to make sure that unwanted elements haven't made their way onto your film. Scan for any other discrepancies that could have occurred at this time as well.

Once you are content that there are no problems with the film, check them again. This is the last exit before the toll—your last chance to make any changes before going to print

SUMMARY

The fun part is over. And I've done this long enough that I'm not the one who will try to convince you that preparing files for the service bureau is a picnic. It can be nerve-wracking and filled with potential problems and hazards. But if you follow the directions in this chapter, and go out of your way to establish a relationship with your service bureau, you'll be in much better shape, and not have to worry about wasted time or dollars to fix mistakes.

PRINTING —

FINALLY,

THE LAST STEP

Commercial printing is a complex science. Complex because it's more than just a science—it's an art, and truly talented printers can be hard to find. There's no way you can learn about the entire printing process from a short chapter in a prepress design book—entire publications have been dedicated to the topic. However, this chapter will help you find the right printer for your needs, list for you the right questions to ask, and give you an overview of what you need to know when you bring your project to be printed.

MATCHING YOUR PROJECT TO THE RIGHT PRINTER

The term *printing* can mean different things to different designers. To some, "printing" means little more than running something off on your desktop printer. To others, "printing" means watching large sheets of paper come off a Titanic-sized press for thousands of units. Each type has its place in the world of desktop publishing and print design and each will continue to play a vital role in the development of your projects. The type of printing you choose will largely depend on a number of factors, including the kind of project you're working on, the budget, and the number of pieces you need to print.

DESKTOP PRINTERS

Desktop printers are strictly limited to draft uses in the professional print world. They're an invaluable tool but will almost never be the print mechanism of choice for the final project.

Desktop printers run in a variety of sizes, with the most common ones able to support paper widths up to 8.5" and lengths up to 14". Quality also varies, with the clear distinction falling between ink jet printers and laser printers. Whichever printer you decide to purchase, you will not be able to print full bleeds on them (the printer does not like ink or toner on the rollers). You also should not present desktop printer proofs to you clients as a final representation of what their completed piece will look like. The color will most likely be far off from the final relative to an IRIS or MatchPrint, and you could end up liable for color shifts if the client is unhappy with the final piece. Even if you purchase a color laser printer and add RIP software to your computer for more accurate colors, be aware of potential color shifts off the final press.

Laser Printers

Laser printers can be found in both color and black-and-white versions. Traditionally, these are known to be rather expensive, and, although the prices in recent days have begun to drop sharply, they may still be a bit cost prohibitive for simple throw-away work.

If you want to do a short run of flyers or handouts, especially for inter-office use, but still want good quality output, laser printers might be the way to go. They're not very fast, especially for color output work, which has to run each CMYK color separately, but could do the job if your intent it is to provide a message in a hurry or at a minimum of expense.

Make sure you research what you are getting before you buy it. Most laser printers will print 600 dpi (dots per inch), while some will print 1200 dpi and still a few others up to 2400 dpi. Of course, you'll pay for the higher resolution work and still not be able to run an impressive piece in high quantities with cost or financial efficiency. Make sure you need a very hi-res printer before you buy one.

Ink Jet Printers

Ink jet printers, which "spray" the CMYK colors on the paper in single passes, have improved exponentially in quality and in price over the past couple of years. Again, they are not reliable for final sign-offs on projects and print far too slowly to be useful for even a small run project, but they are great for draft purposes.

Typical ink jet printers, like the popular stylus series by Epson, run between $400 and $800. The real quality difference, though, is in the paper you use. Copy paper will be OK for some things, but for a few dollars more, you can get some pop from your printer and a real-useful proofing device. Look for Hammermill gloss-coated ink jet paper in the computer or supply store and test the results. You'll see that there is a marked difference in the image quality.

DIGITAL PRESSES

Digital presses are a relatively new phenomenon, quickly gaining momentum, popularity, and confidence in the design community. Also referred to as *direct-to-press*, digital printers offer a number of distinct benefits to the designer, although they are not without their limitations.

With a digital press, the plates are not created in the traditional way, by being burned from the film and then placed on the rollers. Instead, they are placed on the press first and then burned. The PostScript image is burned by a dedicated computer and sent to a series of lasers, which burn the image on the plates for each color. The plates are finished with a liquid solution and are soon ready for printing.

Notice that in all of this, the image has gone directly from the computer to the press—there was no intermediary step of outputting film.

What's So Good About Digital Printing

There's a lot for the designer and client to get excited about when it comes to digital publishing:

◆ **Quality:**

The first and most important thing about any press or printing style is the quality of the finished work. Digital presses have improved dramatically over the past few years, to the point where quality is not an issue. Most pieces look as good coming off the digital press as they look coming off the commercial press.

◆ **Run Length:**

Digital printing is ideal for projects that require a short print run. Although it often makes economic sense to use the digital press for anything up to 1,000 units, it is perfectly acceptable to do a print run of 100, 10, or fewer units.

◆ **Customization:**

One of the truly cool features about digital printing is the ability to customize your projects. Let's say that you're designing a full-color direct mail campaign, with a target audience of 500 families. You can, if you have each family's name, incorporate their names onto your printed piece individually, so that you in essence have 500 slightly different pieces from one print run. With this technique, your mail campaign is no longer ambiguous and generic, but a targeted, personalized piece that speaks to each audience member individually.

◆ **Price:**

Digital presses are *direct-to-press*, which means that your project goes from the computer directly to the printer, skipping over the film that a commercial press would use. Because there is no need for film, you save a significant amount of hassle and expense. With film prices ranging anywhere from $15–$35 per color per page, the cost savings in film alone can be significant. In addition, you will save the cost of providing Matchprints (typically $50–$105 per), as the digital printer can provide you with single samples as color proofs of exactly what will come off the press.

◆ **Speed:**

Although this may not always be true, you'll find, more often than not, that getting a project finished off the press will be far quicker than running the same job off a commercial press. This is partly because of the significant timesavings associated with not outputting film or having to make plates.

◆ **No Trapping:**

Because of the power and accuracy of the lasers that burn the plates, there is no concern that there could be any misregistration. Therefore, if you had read the portion of Chapter 1 that dealt with setting traps for problem areas in your work, you can print in the peaceful knowledge that it won't be a problem.

◆ **Far Fewer Headaches:**

Because you can stop the presses at any time during the run, even after the first unit, you can make any emergency changes that may be necessary without a severe cost penalty. Even if the entire print run is completed with an error that proves to be your fault, paying for a rerun of a short-run job off a digital press will be far less of a blow than paying for a rerun of any job off of a commercial press.

What's Not So Good About Digital Printing

For all of the benefits there are to digital printing, there are drawbacks and limitations as well. Digital printing is not for every job you'll do, and you'll have to take the following points into consideration before deciding to go the digital route.

◆ **Quality:**

There is no question that the quality of digital prints has steadily and dramatically improved. But there is one thing that no digital press seems to do well and that's print large fields of color. Areas in your layout that are filled with large areas of a single color, especially lighter colors, will usually print with an unwanted and obvious pattern.

◆ **Paper Type:**

You'll be limited in your choices of paper for your project. Unlike the commercial presses, which can handle a wide array of paper types, thicknesses, and coatings, the digital press has a more limited selection to choose from. Ask your digital pressman for samples of paper types that the press can handle.

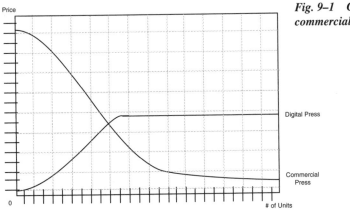

Fig. 9–1   Cost per unit graph for commercial & digital presses.

◆ **Paper Size:**

There will also be a limit to the size of the piece you can print. The size limitations will depend on the actual press, but the largest piece you can get off a typical digital press will usually be a fraction of the size you can get from a commercial press.

◆ **Price:**

At some point, digital printing no longer makes economic sense. You'll have to determine on your own what point that is based on the quote you receive from the digital print shop. I usually find that after the 1,000th unit, it starts making more sense to use the commercial press. That's because the per-unit price tends to go up and then level off the more pieces you print digitally, while the per-=unit price goes down the more pieces you print off the commercial press. Figure 9–1 makes this point graphically.

CHECKLIST FOR USING A DIGITAL PRESS

As you can see, there are many factors to consider when deciding whether or not to use a digital press. The following checklist should provide a quick overview of which projects would be best to print digitally:

___ Need for customization

___ Small print run ordered (usually up to 1,000 units)

___ Limited budget

___ Paper type and size less of an issue

___ Need for quick turn-around time

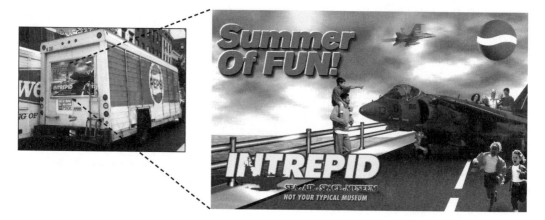

Fig. 9–2   This 4' x 2' image was posted on the back of Pepsi trucks for the Intrepid

LARGE FORMAT PRINTING

Not everything you create in print is going to fit on a nice, neat 8.5" x 11" page, nor will it need to be printed in large quantities. Figure 9–2 shows a project my agency designed for the Intrepid Museum in New York City. The poster campaign was meant for display on the sides of Pepsi trucks throughout the city. Each poster was 4' x 2', and only about 200 of them were needed for the local campaign.

At only 200 units, we can eliminate the commercial press as an option for printing. As for the size requirement, the digital press wasn't going to be much help. The only option left for printing was to use a large-format press. (For very large print runs, screen printing can be an economic option, but a full description is beyond the scope of this book).

For the most part, large-format printers are really just very, very large ink jet printers with a very hefty price tag. Quality printers will have powerful RIPs and interpret PostScript like the other output devices we've described. Ink is placed on the page with a combination of high-quality CMYK inks, much like in a commercial press. However, unlike the commercial press, which uses rolls to place color, large format printers do not use rolls, plates, or film. They apply color much like your desktop ink jet, by making passes across the page and literally "spraying" the ink to the paper.

Large-format printers typically handle widths up to 60". Since the paper comes in a roll, the maximum length is beyond measure—almost definitely beyond normal needs. You can use these presses for posters, banners, practically anything you'd like. However, while most smaller pieces come off the press almost ready to use (expect for cutting, folding, and binding), large-format projects usually need to be mounted and laminated. Discuss these options with your large-format printer—your best choices for mounting and laminating will depend on the purpose of the piece. For example, a piece that will have a one-time use indoors may get away with an inexpensive foam backing.

The foam will eventually warp in the heat, though, so if your piece is intended for extensive outdoor use, you may opt for gator board with a weather-resistant lamination. Your printer will be able to advise you.

Because there is no film, you can print as little as one poster cost-effectively. Budget your time well, though—large-format printing can be a slow process. I typically keep the names of three or four large-format printers handy so in the event of an emergency job, with too many units for one place to handle, I can break up the job among a few of them. (Of course, the colors won't be consistent, but that's the price you pay for rush jobs.)

Like the digital press, watch out for large areas of solid colors. While the digital press will tend to display a dot pattern in these areas, the large-format printer will tend to band up the color, producing large stripes. Combat this by adding just a touch of noise to the solid color areas, or, better yet, create your design with a minimum of solid color.

COMMERCIAL PRINTING (LITHOGRAPHY)

The commercial press is your most expensive printing option but also the one with the highest quality. These are typically used for large print runs, with "large" being a very wide variable: quantities can run from a few thousand to a few hundred thousand (or higher).

In short, as has been explained in bits and pieces throughout this book, the commercial printer takes the film that the service bureau provides (or that he outputs himself). He uses this film to burn an impression onto plates—one plate for each color. These plates get affixed to the press, and presto! your job is ready to print. Well, actually it's a little more involved than that, but the details fall more on the technical side that you don't really need to know and fall outside the scope of this book.

What to Look for (and Not to Look for) in a Commercial Printer

The last thing you'll want after all your hard work in the prepress stages is to see your job ruined due to an unskilled printer.

When I say "printer" in this context, I am referring to the person, not to the machine.

Printing takes far more skill than just flipping a switch and finding a skillful pressman can be difficult. Keep the following in mind when you start your search for a qualified printer:

◆ Check their portfolio

An experienced printer should have plenty of samples to show you of his previous work. Although he'll undoubtedly only show his best pieces, look for signs of mis-registrations, color fades, cracking in the spines of folded pieces, and anything else that makes a piece look bad. (But don't blame the printer for bad design!)

◆ How many colors can the press handle at once?

If you're producing a four-color job, make sure that your printer is running a four-color press. You can probably get a better price from a printer who only has a two-color press, but don't chance it. Two-color presses are great for two-color work—but to produce a four-color piece, the press would first have to lay down two of the four colors, then let the paper dry (probably overnight), and then run the last two colors. The problem is, not only does this take more time, but once the first two colors are set, there is no going back. On a four-color press, last-minute adjustments can always be made when the paper first comes off the press.

◆ Do they run 24 hours a day?

This is not a very major point, but some print shops do run 24 hours a day, which can help when deadlines are critical.

◆ Are they a union shop?

This is not a political book, so I'll keep my opinions about unions to myself. But if you compare the prices of a union print shop and a nonunion shop, nine times out of ten the nonunion shop will be priced lower—and they'll be faster.

◆ How expensive are they?

Obviously, like everything else, price matters. You won't want to sacrifice quality for price, but you will want to make sure you are not paying for extraneous things. Location, for example—New York printers are probably paying far more for rental space than New Jersey printers. This increase will raise their prices. It may be worthwhile to hike out to NJ in that case to save some money. Get a few prices for comparison before making a decision.

◆ Will they allow you to do a print check?

Print checks will be especially important when you are first getting to know a new printer. Basically, a print check involves you, the client, or a representative to phys-ically be on location at the shop when your project is being printed. By being there, you can make last-minute color adjustments (even though the plates have already been burned, you can increase or decrease the intensity of any of the four compo-nent colors) and ensure that you will be happy with the finished result. Or, in the case of an emergency, you can halt production at the very beginning at a minimal cost (compared to what you would spend on the completed job).

◆ Will they directly interact with the service bureau?

Especially important with your first couple of jobs, it may be invaluably useful for your printer to speak directly with your service bureau to provide output direction. Most printers will not have a problem with that, but it's a good question to ask when making your decisions.

◆ Do they provide post-printing services in house?

Post-printing services include cutting, folding, binding, die-cutting, shrink wrapping, etc. This may not be an important factor to you, as it certainly won't reflect on their skills as a printer. But if they farm too much out, you can probably expect higher than necessary prices and longer completion times. Personally, I like for my print shop to do all cutting, folding, and binding in-house. Die-cutting and shrink wrapping, which I only need occasionally, are okay to be farmed out.

◆ Do jobs run individually or get grouped together?

Make sure that your job is run individually. Oftentimes printers will try to reduce costs by running multiple client projects on the same print run, bunching them all on the same sheet of paper, and cutting them apart later. Yes, this may lead to a reduction in cost for you and your client, but believe me, it will only lead to headaches in the long run. Because of different demands by different clients on the same print run, it is unlikely that your colors will match exactly when you need to reprint your pieces in the future. In general, for a color quality standpoint, it's a bad practice and you should stay away from it.

There are plenty of good, quality printers out there. Make sure you ask the right questions, look for the right signs of competency, and just choose a printer you feel comfortable with and you'll have a great shot of producing fantastic printed pieces.

SUMMARY

Like preparing files for the service bureau, working with the printer is a part of the process that will give you ulcers. Will the colors be right? Will the paper be cut correctly? Who will be responsible if there is a mistake? But unlike preparing files for prepress, working with the printer has one huge draw—when it's all over, you get to see all of your work come to fruition. In your hands is perhaps the most exciting thing you can hold—your own imagination.

I hope this chapter, and this book, have helped you to better prepare for your journey into print. Good luck in your printing endeavors!

INDEX

FAX OR MAIL THIS ORDER FORM TO BEGIN YOUR TRAINING!

*Name:*_____

*Address:*_____

*Phone:*_____ *Fax:*_____

*E-Mail:*_____ *Type or Work:*_____

QTY	Title	Price	Total
_____	Photoshop 5.0 Level I	$49.95	_____
_____	Photoshop 5.0 Level II	$49.95	_____
_____	Photoshop 5.0 for the Web	$49.95	_____
_____	Web Site Development	$49.95	_____
_____	Digital Prepress	$54.95	_____
_____	Illustrator 8.0	$44.95	_____
_____	Director 7.0 Level I	$49.95	_____
_____	Director 7.0 Level II	$49.95	_____
_____	Video Production	$59.95	_____
_____	Video Editing	$59.95	_____
_____	Multimedia Magic	$59.95	_____
_____	Authorware 4.0	$59.95	_____
	Sub Total:		_____
_____	Package I: Any Two Videos	7% off Total	_____
_____	Package II: Any Three Videos	10% off Total	_____
_____	Package III: Any Five Videos	15% off Total	_____
	Total:		_____

Payment Type: ___ *Check*   ___ *Money Order*   ___*Visa*   ___*MC*

*Credit Card #:*_____ *Exp. Date:*_____

Signature: _____

Or Order By Phone

pfs NEW MEDIA

1.800.PFS.2080

973.616.2700 • Fax 973.616.7227